CLAYTON ESHLEMAN

Edited by Stuart Kendall

Praise for Clayton Eshleman

Gary Snyder on *Coils*
On a looping ourabouros scale—of patience and practice into poesy—
unwrapping family (kula) flashback inner voices—over and over, Diana
glimpst naked bathing—Clayton Eshleman's tender vibrating personae
mythos keeps winding, (and current passed thru)—the coil—a field
of force.

Diane Wakoski on *The Name Encanyoned River*
In spite of Eshleman's reputation as a brash *enfant terrible* of the avant
garde, he is a rather gentle, sensitive connoisseur of the beautiful, the
fragile, and the unusual... He speaks, like an American in the Whitman
tradition, as a mythic heroic 'I,' a singer who uses the personal voice not
to speak of himself but of all mankind. The intense lyricism which comes
from this personal voice, the search for wholeness, ecstatic fulfillment, and
the constant praising of all that is common to beautiful human life, makes
Eshleman one of the strongest, most unique voices in American poetry
today. ... Eshleman's *The Name Encanyoned River* is a book to savor.

Hayden Carruth on *Altars*
We do not doubt Eshleman's seriousness, integrity, or ability ... He is
producing work of astonishing originality.

Adrienne Rich, from her foreword to *Companion Spider*
[*Companion Spider*] is the accumulated prose-work of a poet and translator who has gone more deeply into his art, its process and demands, than
any modern American poet since Robert Duncan or Muriel Rukeyser. As
a poet, Eshleman has wrestled with his vocation and, in some senses, created himself through poetry. At the same time, he has offered poetry his
inspired and tireless service. ... He has written on the self-making and apprenticeship of the poet and of poet as translator, as no one else in North
America in the later twentieth century.

Adrienne Rich on *Nora's Roar*
I could not wish a truer, more urgent language for Nora Jaffe's life and art than Clayton Eshleman's extraordinary poem. And had I not known Nora and her work, I would still call this poem extraordinary.

Gary Snyder on *Sulfur*
In an era of literary conservatism and sectarianism, the broad commitment of *Sulfur* to both literary excellence and broad, interdisciplinary, unbought humanistic engagement with the art of poetry in America has been invaluable. To my notion its critical articles and notes have been the sharpest going over the last several years.

Hugh Seidman
The poet Robert Duncan once said that he wrote poetry the way other men sought wealth and power, or waged war—to exercise his faculties at large. Certainly, such a description would fit the poet Clayton Eshleman. In fact, Eshleman is probably the most powerful living American exemplar of such a vision of poetry making—a vision that is rooted in the high modernist traditions of Europe and the Americas, but which also seeks bedrock among the oldest remnants of human art.

Gary Snyder on *Juniper Fuse*
Archeologists and artists have written on southwestern European cave art, but none have given us a book like this. Clayton Eshleman has explored and inspected almost all of the great cave art of southwestern Europe including many caves that are not open to the public and require special permission. Now with visionary imagination, informed poetic speculation, deep insight, breath-taking leaps of mind, Eshleman draws out the underground of myth, psychology, prehistory, and the first turn of the human mind toward the modern. *Juniper Fuse* opens us up to our ancient selves: we might be weirder (and also better) than we thought.

Robert Duncan on César Vallejo, *Human Poems*
Clayton Eshleman has brought us not only a translation of César Vallejo, faithful to the Spanish but – what only a poet who is spiritually akin could have done – a translation faithful to the poetic inspiration. This is the rare thing: that this bilingual edition is a bridge between two poetries, and that in Eshleman's vision Vallejo becomes a power in our American conscience. Acknowledging in ourselves what Vallejo suffered, and keeping his life work alive and at work in our lives, we come, through these *Poemas humanos,* to a greater human resource and responsibility.

Gary Snyder on *Novices*
Clayton Eshleman's rich text is a poet's instruction in what the medieval hunter called "excoriation"—the venerable art of opening up the insides, "dressing out"—presenting the anatomy of the interior. It is a physical book on the soul meat of poetics. Cut through the "sensitivity" surface: get to the bowels: begin again. How needed!

Mario Vargas Llosa, from his foreword, César Vallejo, *The Complete Poetry*
Clayton Eshleman discovered Vallejo in 1957, while still in college and not yet fluent in Spanish. As he himself recounts, he has spent a good part of his life reading, studying, and trying to render this poetry in English. He was never satisfied with the results: again and again he revised and polished his versions to achieve an elusive perfection. There is a sort of heroism in his undertaking, like that of those creators in pursuit of a work as beautiful as it is impossible. His case reveals an admirable fidelity to a poet who no doubt changed his life. His tireless loyalty and determination have made possible this edition of the complete poetry of Vallejo in English, perhaps the one that comes closest to the texts of the poet's own hand. Only the dauntless perseverance and the love with which the translator had dedicated so many years of his life to this task can explain why the English version conveys in all its boldness and vigor, the unmistakable voice of César Vallejo.

Forrest Gander on César Vallejo, *The Complete Poetry*
An astonishing accomplishment. Eshleman's translation is writhing with energy.

Ron Padgett on César Vallejo, *The Complete Poetry*
Every great poet should be so lucky as to have a translator as gifted and heroic as Clayton Eshleman, who seems to have gotten inside Vallejo's poems and translated them from inside out. The result is spectacular, or as one poem says, "green and happy and dangerous."

Robert Hass on César Vallejo, *The Complete Poetry*
César Vallejo was one of the essential poets of the twentieth century, a heartbreaking and groundbreaking writer, and this gathering of the many years of imaginative work by Clayton Eshleman is one of Vallejo's essential locations in the English tongue.

CLAYTON ESHLEMAN
THE WHOLE ART

Edited by Stuart Kendall

BLACK
WIDOW
PRESS

www.blackwidowpress.com
Joseph S. Phillips and Susan J. Wood, PhD, Publishers

Text and cover design: Kerrie Kemperman
Cover photograph: From *Mexican Masks* by Donald Cordry © 1980. Used
by permission of the University of Texas.

ISBN-13: 978-0-9856122-5-2

Printed in the United States

10 9 8 7 6 5 4 3 2 1

CONTENTS

For some readers of contemporary American poetry, Clayton Eshleman needs no introduction. His poetry, essays, and translations have been a fixture in leading poetry magazines nationally and internationally for more than five decades. The two magazines he founded and edited – *Caterpillar* and *Sulfur* – were crucial outlets for both emerging and established poets that shaped discussions of poetry, the arts and politics, over these same decades. His writings and translations have been honored with the National Book Award in Translation, a Guggenheim Fellowship in Poetry, two grants from the National Endowment for the Arts, two grants from the National Endowment for the Humanities, a Rockefeller Study Center residency in Bellagio, Italy, and other awards, including the Landon Translation prize from the Academy of American Poets, which he has won twice.

For some readers, though, Eshleman might be known uniquely for his achievements in one area of his literary life – poetry, translation, or editing – but not in one or another of the other two. He might be known as a poet but not as a translator or editor, or vice versa. In the case of his work as an editor, younger readers in particular may not have been exposed to *Caterpillar* or *Sulfur* when those magazines were active. Similarly, readers of modern poetry in translation might not be readers of contemporary American poetry.

That possibility in mind, one purpose of this volume is to shed light on Eshleman's corpus as a whole – his poetry, prose, translations and work as an editor – and more specifically as a corpus created with the whole in mind. Eshleman's second magazine, *Sulfur,* bore the subtitle, *A Literary Tri-Quarterly* [in later issues *Bi-Annual*] *of the Whole Art.* The phrase owes something to Robert Duncan's notion of a "symposium of the whole," from a section of *The H.D. Book* first published in Eshleman's magazine *Caterpillar,* wherein "all the old excluded orders must be included." Jerome and Diane Rothenberg borrowed the phrase for their 1983 anthology, *Symposium of the Whole: A Range of Discourses Toward an Ethnopoetics,* which includes a chapter by Eshleman. Many of the essays included herein touch on these connections so I will leave them aside for now, and say only that, in some ways, Eshleman's entire corpus can be read as an extraordinarily complex, poetic "anatomy" of life, art, and politics in our times, combining poetry, prose, translations, and edited works, original writing and research, subjective and objective forms, all coiled together as multiple perspectives on and reflections of one another and of our world.

With such a territory as its cartographic ambition, this volume gathers together a representative selection of writings about Clayton Eshleman, including both recognized and frequently referenced "classic" essays on his work as well as new pieces commissioned for this volume. Roughly one third of this collection has been previously published in some form. Where significant, dates of previous publication appear at the end of a piece; all undated pieces are recent. The oldest piece is now forty years old. Not all of the compelling critical writing about Eshleman generated over these last forty years could be included in a volume of manageable size. Nor should it need to be. My purpose here has been to gather the best writing on as wide a range of areas within Eshleman's work as possible. Martha Sattler's *Clayton Eshleman: A Descriptive Bibliography* includes citations for a number of additional reviews and critical writings addressing Eshleman's work through 1987. And Paul Christensen's monograph, *Minding the Underworld: Clayton Eshleman and Late Postmodernism* (Black Sparrow Press, 1991), should also be mentioned here as a pioneering full-length study of Eshleman's work, particularly of his original poetry in its cultural context, through the 1980s. Rather than excerpt from Christensen's work, I will suggest that readers seek it out.

Most of the writing gathered here is however new, or substantially revised. Some of these pieces are the work of friends and colleagues of Eshleman's, comrades in arms or co-conspirators of long-standing, like Robert Kelly and Jerome Rothenberg, who have known and collaborated with Eshleman in various ways for more than fifty years. Other pieces are by younger poets and scholars who have been drawn to Eshleman's recent work in particular for its vitality and pressing topicality. A number of the essays in this volume take a comparative approach to Eshleman's work. This is appropriate since Eshleman has devoted himself so frequently to engagement and dialogue with other poets and writers, living and dead, through translations most notably, but in prose and poetry as well.

A premise of this collection is that Eshleman's major work as a poet and intellectual is to be found in his book *Juniper Fuse: Paleolithic Imagination & the Construction of the Underworld*. The culmination and precipitate of a twenty-five year investigation into the imagination embodied in the Paleolithic painted caves, particularly of southwestern France, *Juniper*

Fuse gathers original poetry and prose, fueled by research in the field and by studies in anthropology, depth psychology, and a wide-range of other disciplines of thought. That in mind, a number of essays gathered here grapple with Eshleman's writings on the painted caves from a variety of perspectives. Other essays focus on his ekphrastic writing, his writing about and through images beyond those of the painted caves. Still others examine his politics and politically motivated and informed poetry.

Generally speaking the initial essays in this collection approach Eshleman's work more globally, offering several different approaches toward an overview of the corpus as a whole. This includes my introduction. Thereafter, Eric Mottram's essay "The Poetics of Rebirth and Confidence" examines Eshleman's early work in context. That piece is followed by a group of essays on the Paleolithic imagination, that are in turn followed by other, more topical and comparative pieces. The essays toward the end of the book concern Eshleman's more recent writings.

A certain amount of repetition is to be expected from any group of essays that course through the shared terrain, as these do, as well as within a body of criticism in conversation, wherein pieces fall into dialogue not only with Eshleman's work but with each other. Hopefully, this repetition functions as both reinforcement and redirection, revealing unexpected connections across the oeuvre and carrying thoughts in, one hopes, unexpected directions. The result, I think, resembles one of Eshleman's totemic images, a web. The collection as a whole might have taken the title, borrowed from *Coils*, "webs of entry." Another possible title for this collection might have used the word "variations," following the musical notion of a variation on a common melody, in this case a variation on the life and work of Clayton Eshleman.

Endnotes immediately follow the essays to which they refer. Unless otherwise stated, works cited in the notes are by Clayton Eshleman. For brevity's sake, most references are by title and page number only. Full bibliographic information for works by Eshleman can by found in the bibliography at the end of the book. I have regularized endnotes across this collection only to a limited extent. The pieces gathered here derive from a variety of venues and, to some extent, eras. They include prosaic essays and scholarly works of exegetical and comparative analysis. Most are in fact prose writings by poets. Rather than force the pieces into or through an overly rigid academic mold, I have let their idiosyncrasies stand alongside their diversity of voice and contents.

In closing this preface I would like to acknowledge the unstinting and generous help and support Clayton Eshleman has offered this project since I first mentioned it to him. His help has been particularly vital in preparing the Chronology and the Bibliography included herein. The many contributors whose writings make up the substance of this collection should also be acknowledged for their creative devotion to this work.

—Stuart Kendall

Robert Kelly

Things I Think About When Eshleman Comes To Mind

Years and years ago, Clayton and I were walking across the grassy triangle in front of my house. Out of nowhere, he asked if I thought of him and his work as not spiritual enough. I hardly know what that word means, but I had some feeling for what Clayton was asking me. I assured him as well as I could that spirit hunts in unlikely places. And I was righter than I knew:

Eshleman has been inscribing an Emerald Tablet of his own all these years. A guide to the operations of the breath in this world of flesh.

Where Paul Valéry warned us to go down into the self armed to the teeth, Eshleman's journeys, for half a century, have with a kind of gentle ferocity sought the meaning of the social inside the body, then the meaning of the body deep inside the earth.

Thinking of that makes me remember Eshleman's long dedication to the ideas and therapeutic practices of Wilhelm Reich, who sought in the repressed or degraded body the etiology of political evil—the fascist body of priest and commissar.

Eshleman's adventure began long ago still on the surface of the earth, when Mexico's living clash of ancient and modern, race and language, then Japan's ornate archaic modernity fueled his own youthful assault on the "quietude" of American poetry at mid-century. This is the time we were beginning to be shaken and renewed by the intelligential energies of Olson, the earthly and heavenly passions of Duncan, the exactitudes of Spicer, the "vulgar eloquence" of Williams.

Then Eshleman's work turned literally inward, to his own excavations, his own territory, that fleshly miracle one calls one's own body, its caverns of rapture and surfeit, the muscles of mind.

His probings in Reich and Blake led him to the body of the earth itself—the Upper Paleolithic caves, the bones of imagination. He has gone down and seen and felt and been alone with them. And spoken on behalf of thirty thousand years of silence.

I admire his ability to endure the weight of earth, literally, over and around him as he humped and squatted his way through the caves of the Dordogne. Me, I would be scared to death in such entombments. He though is an enchanted literalist, he had to go there and see it for himself, feel the chill air and secular drip. This seeing-with-his-own eyes is what's so really, keenly, different about him.

How different the images on the wall are, must be, when you see them over and around you, curved in real space, not flattened out as designs on a page. Eshleman got to know the ancient scrawls and gouges as people in his shared space. The shocking discord of imagery in his poems merely and truthfully reflects his decades of conversation with stone men, his passionate embrace of stone women.

He can never escape from the clutch of the body, the fateful awareness that we live in the body, can only live there. For him, the body leads back always into itself, bowels of the earth bowels of the human. Inward, power, more shit than splendor, but a dark exultation of pure sensation. Which the poet can coax into feeling.

For the poets of desire (Rilke, Duncan come to mind), beauty is always in the direction of the other, and the body is a chreode of the soul reaching outward—out towards a glory or a union that at worst might turn out to be, or seem, vacuous or (Shelley's word) inane. But for Clayton, the body, like the earth around us, is centripetal, whirls and torques always inward; his poems drag us down, joyous into the dark, mouth full of words, mind full of images to thrill us on the way down.

He may not meet, or make us meet, Persephone down there. I don't think he is as much interested as I am in the Queen of Hell—but what he finds down there not only fuels the rage of his poetics and his translations (as if Artaud and Césaire and Vallejo were alcaldes he interviewed in those dark

16

caverns). It also enfranchises him to write *Juniper Fuse,* which it seems to me is the greatest book ever written about humans (or whoever we are) in the Palaeolithic, our kinfolk, their arts and mind.

His work gathers and disperses. Lately he seems to want us for the most part to direct us towards the more recent work, the last two decades of his striving. The penetralia of personal experience can best be known, best chanted, in the penetralia of time. A geological poet he, a skeptic Novalis in tune with rock.

When he speaks (whereas so many nowadays vaguely do) of alchemy and alchemists, he does so with the authority of a man who has obeyed the terrifying commandment the ancients called *Vitriol:* By visiting the interior of the earth, thou shalt discover the hidden Stone.

Nobody is like him in his struggle. With ornery stubbornness he has kept visiting the dark occasions, and brought back for us poems unlike anybody else's. His style is impasto, the gouge and splash of images, unrelenting, thingly, their weight always pressing on us.

At times he makes the wildness of most poetry seem effete. Because he has gone down and done so with a language fit for his researches: clotted, angry, surprised, full of grunts as a cartoon, full of magical gleams like sunlight striking through chinks of rock, hard as tourmaline, sheets of mica peeled away.

I know of no poet who has fed so richly from the thingliness of the world beneath his feet, none who so resists the glamour of beliefs. He is a shaman with only one superstition—the flesh we share.

Stuart Kendall

Life Commitment

The most sublime act is to set another before you.
  William Blake

I is an other.
  Arthur Rimbaud

In 1960, Clayton Eshleman – who was then twenty-five years old and a graduate student in English at Indiana University – sent some of his poetry to Cid Corman with a note describing his admiration for *Origin*, the magazine Corman had founded and edited from 1951 to 1957. Corman's response to the young poet was immediate and searing. The poems, he said, were a waste of his and of Eshleman's own time: either get serious about poetry or stop writing it. Eshleman later wrote that the comment "smacked [him] in the face *and* implied that there was a life commitment – indeed a commitment to life – in writing poetry."[1] It is undoubtedly unnecessary to observe that Clayton Eshleman made that commitment.

But exactly what kind of commitment is implied here? What is entailed by a life commitment to poetry when that commitment is indistinguishable from a commitment to life? Eshleman's remark implies a relationship between poetry and life that is not circumscribed by the Romantic notion of living the life of a poet. The Romantic notion of a poet's life has been lampooned in myriad popular images of the poet as an effete, disengaged, sensitive soul, caught up in his or her own musings, cut off from the common stream of life in his or her times. The commitment of the Romantic poet might be a commitment to poetry but that does not necessarily entail a commitment to life, rather the opposite in fact. Poetry in the Romantic model – and in others besides – strives to be autonomous, a thing unto itself, hermetic and sealed, art for art's sake. Such an art implicitly and explicitly avoids questions of justification and responsibility. Written purely for itself, it needs no justification and, isolated from the world, it takes no responsibility. The question concerning literature – asked perhaps most famously in 1919 by André Breton and other then proto-Surrealists: "why write?" – finds no answer.

Eshleman's commitment to poetry is of an entirely different kind. In his commitment, poetry becomes a vehicle for life and life a vehicle for poetry: the two interpenetrate and are entwined. "As a lost soul in the Midwestern 1950's," Eshleman wrote in another context, "I discovered [poetry's] power to change and enable one to stand more self-revealed."[2] The remark recalls – but significantly modifies – an observation from Charles Olson's *Maximus Poems:* "people / don't change. They only stand more / revealed. I, / likewise."[3] Self-revelation here is linked to commitment and to a tradition – a genealogy – in American poetry. But for Eshleman, poetry has the power to change the self, to become a vehicle of self-emancipation.

Olson also speaks to the power of commitment in "The Kingfishers": "I have my kin, if for no other reason than/ (as he said, next of kin) I commit myself, and, / given my freedom, I'd be a cad / if I didn't."[4] Here commitment entails taking a stand, committing oneself to an idea or opinion. Olson's language here alludes to Ezra Pound's famous remark, from the preface to his *Guide to Kulchur:* "Given my freedom, I may be a fool to use it, but I wd. be a cad not to."[5] Freedom is freedom to commit oneself, to take a position, to assume responsibility for some idea, thing, or person. Such commitments are not to be entered into lightly.

Thus while in the autobiographical note to his book *Altars,* Eshleman can write: "my poetics are the oldest and most engaging human adventure: the emancipation of the self"; he can also claim, in *Under World Arrest:* "I […] refuse to release myself from the complexities of an eros that while not cruel in itself is congruent to the news reports of the suffering of others and must make its way into articulation burdened by its awareness."[6] Elsewhere he describes the challenge of the poet's journey in these terms, alluding to Arthur Rimbaud: "If the poet is the thief of fire, he is the one who journeys into the depths of his subconscious in order to bring up the dark treasures that are concealed there. And he may pay a dear price for doing so, as the derangement process may result in addiction, dereliction, or in the kind of being out of it that makes it impossible for an individual to function in society."[7] There are dangers, in other words, all around, within and without, as well as in the very process itself of uncovering and expressing the material that is the life of poetry. Consistent with these views and challenges, in *The Alchemist With One Eye On Fire,* Eshleman offers the following definition of the poetic art: "Poetry is about extending human consciousness, making conscious the unconscious, creating symbolic consciousness that in its fineſt moments overcomes all the dualities in which the human world is cruelly and eternally, it seems, enmeshed."[8] Poetry, it seems, is the drama of consciousness enfolding the world in its embrace, in all of its tragedy and triumph, tenderness and terror.

To date, pursuing these commitments across a career spanning more than fifty years, Clayton Eshleman has published ninety-seven books and chapbooks of original poetry, translations, and nonfiction writings, and edited seventy issues of magazines and journals. The experience of that work is life experience, a record of human experience – passionate, political, poetic – in our times. Some points of orientation – incidents and trajectories – might be helpful before setting out to explore such a territory (here and through the other essays collected in this volume). As may already be clear, I will attempt to let Eshleman speak for himself through quotation as much as possible.

As a contemporary writer, Eshleman's hiſtory is our own: his writing a reflection of our years. But there are hiſtories in this hiſtory that can only be evoked here; introduced, and in the broadeſt frame – politics, social movements – suggeſted only in these words. Eshleman's ſtory is the ſtory of mid-America meeting the world in the 1950s, of the collapse of colonial empires and the rise of the global South; the ſtory of 1960s radicalism and counterculture raising a voice in poetry and in art; of the challenges, fruſtrations and anomie that befell that counterculture and of the continued and indeed on-going drama of empire and overreaching power, from El Salvador in the 1980s to Afghaniſtan and Iraq, to name only specific cases traced in Eshleman's poetry.

From another vantage point, one can observe that Eshleman discovered poetry in the late 1950s at a precipitous moment defined in some ways by the scope and intent of Donald Allen's *The New American Poetry 1945–1960*. This was also the moment of the mimeograph and small press revolution in American culture and counterculture. Eshleman's earlieſt publications were part of that moment and, by the late 1960s, with his *Caterpillar* books and magazine, in significant ways helped to define it. Eshleman published his firſt translations of César Vallejo with Grove Press in 1968 and his firſt major collection of his own work, *Indiana,* with Black Sparrow Press in 1969. Black Sparrow would be the primary publisher of his own writing – and for many of those whose aeſthetic was closest to his own – for the next three decades. But, significantly, when Eshleman published a second version of his work on Vallejo in 1978 that book was published by an university press and when he founded his second magazine, *Sulfur*, in 1981, it too was sponsored, in part, by an academic institution, initially by the California Institute of Technology though ultimately by Eastern Michigan University. By the time Eshleman folded the magazine almost twenty years later, even academic and public forms of funding for contemporary poetry had become tenuous and unreliable. Amid these uncertainties a new culture of poetry dominated by workshops and academic writing programs had become hegemonic. And new forms of digital distribution and publishing – new online journals, new more flexible modes of small press, print-on-demand, and personal publishing – have emerged even as some publishers have reinvested in book design, marketing, and presentation, invigorating or attempting to invigorate the literary marketplace from both the bottom and the top.

These are cultural and social events visible in the work. There are obviously personal ones as well. At this level, one might observe that there are "only a handful of primary incidents in one's life,"[9] while also admitting that there are tides in a life, periods of ebb and flow, in which a life turns upon itself, gathers, looks back with a pause. Life from this perspective can also be both slow and fast, moving in months and years as well as moments. Looking at Clayton Eshleman's life and at his creative life, several periods and turning points become apparent, beginning with his discovery of poetry in 1958. His experiences in the late 1950s and very early 1960s were formative through his repeated trips to Mexico and his encounters with other poets, both established and emerging, but his true apprenticeship in poetry – his experience of "the crisis of becoming a poet"[10] – took shape most decisively in Kyoto, Japan, from 1962 to 1964, where he was teaching English, translating César Vallejo, and struggling with his own writing and life. That apprenticeship continued back in Indiana then in Lima, Peru, and in New York in the mid-to-late 1960s, culminating in the foundation of *Caterpillar* magazine in 1967, his first published translation of Vallejo's *Poemas humanos* 1968, his completion of Reichian analysis with Sidney Handelman in 1969, and, finally, after moving to Los Angeles, with the publication of *Coils*, a book-length poetic self-interrogation, a decade in the making, in 1973. The last issue of *Caterpillar* appeared that same year.

The following year while living in France, Eshleman and his second wife, Caryl, discovered the Paleolithic painted caves of the Dordogne, which beaconed a descent into physical and psychical underworlds that would last twenty-five years and more. The poetic record of that descent can be traced through most of Eshleman's own writing produced in these years but the precipitate is his major work, *Juniper Fuse: Upper Paleolithic Imagination & the Construction of the Underworld.* Alongside this work, Eshleman coiled back into Vallejo, retranslating *Poemas humanos* along with his other posthumous poetry with José Rubia Barcia, and back into Aimé Césaire, whose work he first translated in the 1960s with Denis Kelly, as well as branching out, or digging down, translating Antonin Artaud and other "conductors of the pit," often re-translating them in turn over the years. *César Vallejo, The Complete Posthumous Poetry* won the National Book Award and marked another watershed moment in Eshleman's career. Another magazine, *Sulfur* soon followed.

In 1986, Eshleman become a professor in the English department at Eastern Michigan University, moving to Ypsilanti, where he and Caryl still live. His publications in the second half of the 1980s included a group of retrospective volumes: *The Name Encanyoned River: Selected Poems, Antiphonal Swing: Selected Prose,* and *Conductors of the Pit,* which is effectively a volume of selected translations, as well as *Novices: A Study of Poetic Apprenticeship,* a work whose purpose presumes a sense of accomplishment.

Eshleman concluded *Juniper Fuse* near the turn of the millennium, and published *Companion Spider,* another volume of prose, as well as the final issue of *Sulfur,* in near coincidence. Shortly thereafter he retired from teaching, freeing time and energy for his own work. That work again includes summational volumes, a second edition of *Conductors of the Pit* and *The Grindstone of Rapport: A Clayton Eshleman Reader,* as well as new translations of Vallejo – now including Vallejo's complete poetry – and Aimé Césaire, alongside new writing.

The figure of the coil is significant here, as is that of the labyrinth. One has the image of the poet digging further and further into himself, his work, his times, visiting and revisiting, envisioning and re-visioning his experiences, relationships, processes and strategies of encounter. "I am fully in a labyrinth of, and not of, my own making – I've gained entry, fought my way to the center."[11] The task is endless and unfinished, unfinishable. As Eshleman observes, there is a "bitter" combat in the labyrinth of life in poetry, the realizations of writing remain partial, incomplete: "The Minotaur is at best crippled, never slain, and the poet never strides forth from the labyrinth heroic and intact."[12]

In the introduction to *Fracture*, Eshleman evokes the moment in which he began writing as well as his motives for doing so: "I thought back to when I had begun to write in 1958. Forces were breaking out like diseases, and for years I was beside myself with the mid-western hydra that had been unleashed. The main thing that kept me going was a belief that if I fully worked through the sexism, self-hate, bodilessness, soullessness, and suffocated relationships which encrusted my background, I could excavate a basement. I would have torn down the 'House of Eshleman' and laid out a new foundation in its place."[13] Eshleman's search for emancipation is a search for emancipation from these things.

Eshleman's poem "The Death of Bill Evans" – published in *Fracture* – evokes a similar landscape of childhood trauma in a figure he elsewhere calls an inner leper and equates with the alchemical *vilifigura*, "the reviled face, the shame of your own face"[14]:

> Can't see the wound for the scars,
> a small boy composed of scabs is staring into
> the corner of his anatomy – where walls and floor end
> he figures he ends, so he wears his end
> like glasses before his eyes,
> beckoned into the snow he will be beaten
> by children he thought were his friends,
> the implication of his hurt is so dark
> it will scab over to be rescabbed the next time,
> and he will grow not by an internal urge to mature
> but by scabbings until, grown big, he will be the size of an adult
> and his face will look like a pebbly gourd.
> He will stay inside the little house I have built for him, in which to
>   stand he must stoop.[15]

Elsewhere Eshleman adds some more specific details to this portrait of wounds, scars and scabs: "I was brought up in an anesthetically clean Presbyterian home where smoking, drinking, swearing and gambling were not permitted, where I was an only child who was not allowed to play with Catholics, Jews, Negroes, children younger or older than I was, children whose parents smoked, drank, etc., or whose mothers wore slacks away from home."[16] Eshleman's mother, Gladys, devoted herself to him. His father, Ira Clayton Eshleman senior, worked as an engineer and efficiency expert at a slaughterhouse and meat packing plant in Indianapolis. The poet's fascination with the flayed flesh painted by Chaim Soutine may have its origins in childhood memories: "I carry the slaughterhouse," he wrote, mingling memories and creative imagination, in his portrait of the painter in *The Gull Wall*.[17]

In a poem about another visual artist, Henry Darger, Eshleman reflects on his own childhood: "Darger is the reminder of the huge absence I felt as a child, / 'staring at the corner for hours,' my mother told Caryl, / 'he was such a good boy.'"[18] "Good" here is synonymous with a vacant, empty, all but anonymous, self as cipher.

There are other similar memories, other evocations of vacant, repressed, and wounded youth throughout the work. We need not catalog them here. They are not the end of the story, nor even the "apex of the pain": that apex is found in the poet's experiences as a pledge and initiate in the Phi Delta Theta fraternity at Indiana University in 1953.

> Hell Week, 1953,
> a postcard Hades mailed to me,
> his kids in demon suits tied a string
> about my penis led up through my white shirt
> tied to a "pull me" card dangling
> from my sport-coat pocket. The personal
> is the apex of pain[19]

A portrait can be sketched of the poet as pledge suffering humiliations at the hands of the brothers, paddled bloody each night of Hell Week, running in a pack of young men on the make, screwing the girls who would in the backs of cars. As Eshleman later recognized, the humiliation imposed by the fraternity structure was "devastating for women, for all the guys back then were taking their brutalization out on women. The coeds in those days were icy virgins, or, if they allowed any sexual contact it became a feeding frenzy. The process turned the woman into an unpaid whore."[20] At a low point, he helps a friend examine the remnants of a back-alley abortion by the headlights of his car: "We might as well have been looking into a mirror […] we were searching for pieces of flesh."[21] The story here is one of a socially imposed will and willfully accepted personal humiliation, drawing everyone involved into a vortex of personal and interpersonal objectification, violence, and trauma.

The story of Phi Delta Theta is a story of initiation, but, in this case, the initiate would ultimately turn away from the tribe, reconstruct his personality, and struggle into an entirely different way of life. The poet grappled with these experiences for decades and continues to acknowledge their power in some of his most recent writing.[22] He even returned to spend time in the fraternity house more than a decade later, in 1968, hoping to wrest the memories into poetic life. "Still-Life, With Fraternity" in *What She Means* offers one poignant take on this moment in Eshleman's mid-century, mid-Western, American life, but it is not the only one.

Poetry would be the key to Eshleman's own personal emancipation, his emergence into a psychologically healthy adulthood, capable of caring for himself and for others, but there were other, earlier harbingers of that emancipation in other forms. His first experiences with the arts were not literary at all but visual and later musical. As a child and young adolescent, he enjoyed the "funnies" in the newspaper, collected comic books, and took drawing classes. "I think I might have become a painter had there been a more intense art atmosphere to involve myself with in Indianapolis at the time."[23] As it is, Eshleman would explore Federico Garcia Lorca's remark to Jorge Luis Borges that Mickey Mouse was the symbol of America through numerous pop and post-pop references to comic or cartoon figures, as in "Visions of the Fathers of Lascaux" and "The Tomb of Donald Duck" in *Fracture*.[24]

Jazz music struck, as it were, a deeper chord. "While reading Sunday comics on the living-room floor was my first encounter, as a boy, with imagination, [Bud] Powell was my first encounter, as an adolescent, with the figure of the artist."[25] Eshleman stumbled into jazz music in the early 1950s, while in high school. He had been taking piano lessons in his neighborhood since his early youth, playing classical music, but jazz was something else entirely. "Somehow it got through to me in a very rudimentary way that these guys were not following the melody, but were changing it, improvising on it, which immediately suggested one could change the way one lived. In other words, I had been brought up in a very strict family where I was being programmed to be a Xerox of my father and go into business school. But [Bud] Powell was varying the melody, he was creating his *own* melody line. It translated into: you can vary your life, you can play variations on what you've been given."[26] Even as he was pledging Phi Delta Theta, Eshleman was deeply involved with playing jazz music. During the summer between his freshman and sophomore years he traveled to Los Angeles with a friend to listen to West Coast jazz and study piano with Bud Powell's brother, Richie. During graduate school, he would support himself playing piano in a cocktail lounge. But somehow even jazz was not powerful enough to pull him out of Indiana. Drawing and music were both encouraged by his parents, within limits, and Eshleman recognized the limits of his talents in these areas. Poetry however was an art that he discovered on his own, without parental sanction, and one without similar limitations.[27]

But Eshleman's emergence as a poet would take time, as noted above, he had to pass through a period of prolonged apprenticeship.[28] The notion of apprenticeship is itself odd-sounding to ears tuned to contemporary youth-oriented culture. In its youth, the generation immediately following Eshleman's own – the Baby Boomers – promoted a fascination with youth exemplified by the phrase: "I hope I die before I get old." Since the 1960s, market driven cultural production has become all but entirely centered on the young, channeling consumption for children by parents and later, in other spheres, by the young themselves. The notion that a young person or young people might need to pass through a humbling period of potentially prolonged apprenticeship is all but incomprehensible today, generally speaking.

But apprenticeship is a doubly challenging concept here since in Eshleman's usage the term does not signify a process terminating in mastery, if indeed one can say that it terminates at all. There is always more to learn about oneself and one's craft, indeed the point of poetry as Eshleman conceives of it is to be a means of consistent and repeated engagement with self and world. Internalizing this practice as a reliable means of doing so marks the end of apprenticeship.

The growth traumas of this period and process of apprenticeship were literary, psychological, and social by turns: those of a man discovering his capacities as a writer, but more importantly his self-relation through writing, while at the same time coming to grips with his background and horizon of experience – who he has been and is – as well as with his place in the world, as a citizen, friend, and lover. The scope of this endeavor is a measure of Eshleman's commitment to poetry and to life as well as to his understanding and vision of both.

Eshleman discovered poetry around 1958 and immediately began writing condensed, largely observational verse, some of which would be published in *Mexico & North*. As suggested by the title of that volume, these poems were already engaged with the problem of the self and its limits, with testing the boundaries of the self through personal encounters and experiences with other people and cultures. By 1962, however, living in Kyoto, Eshleman recognized that he had reached something of a stalemate in his writing and in his life. He sat for hours agonizing over single lines on his typewriter. He struggled with nervous disorders affecting his digestion, among other things, and once passed out when reading William Blake. During this period, Eshleman set for himself the challenge that he believed would constitute his personal apprenticeship in poetry: translating César Vallejo's *Poemas humanos*. By setting this goal for himself, Eshleman allowed Vallejo to become something of a spiritual mentor to him, a guide or tutelary spirit, which would show him the way or at least one way to live a life in poetry.

There were other mentors as well. In some senses, Eshleman's struggles with his father and with his fraternity brothers are early forms of his search for a reliable model of adult male behavior. His later friendships with Paul Blackburn and Cid Corman, coincident with his Vallejo-apprenticeship, both testify to a similar yearning for counsel. In "The Gull Wall," Eshleman recounts an incident with Paul Blackburn in which the slightly older poet – Blackburn was nine years older than Eshleman – responded to reading one of Eshleman's early poems by blowing him a kiss: "By doing so at just the right time he confirmed the fact that I had, on my own, at least got up on my feet [… This was] a covenant given by an already-confirmed poet to another nonconfirmed one."[29] Corman served a similar function during their friendship in Kyoto. Eshleman visited Corman once a week for two years at the Muse, a coffee shop in downtown Kyoto that Corman used as an unofficial office. Looking back years later, Eshleman observed: "Corman became the first substantial literary person with whom I had an ongoing, reflective association."[30] Corman was editing the second series of *Origin* at the time as well as translating and writing his own poetry.

He demonstrated a mode of practice in all three of these areas – poetry, translation, editing – as well as a means of combining them or allowing them to play off of one another, that would deeply influence the development of Eshleman's own work. Particularly through his translation of Basho's *Back Roads to Far Towns* (the book itself as well as Corman's co-translation, with Susumu Kamaike, of it), Corman also signaled a means of combining thorough scholarly research with creative imagination that would become a cornerstone of Eshleman's practice.

Alongside his translations of Vallejo, and friendships with Blackburn and Corman, Eshleman was also studying William Blake, Northrop Frye's book on Blake, *Fearful Symmetry*, Joseph Campbell's *The Masks of God*, and the *I Ching*. Hart Crane had become a key reference – a "poet companion" as he says[31] – for him around 1960. In "Eight Fire Sources," an essay on the major influences on his art, Eshleman lists Bud Powell, Hart Crane, William Blake, Corman's *Origin* and his Basho translations, the painter Chaim Soutine, Wilhelm Reich, and Mikhail Bakhtin's book *Rabelais and His World*, which he read in the 1970s when first beginning to explore the painted caves. César Vallejo and Emily Dickinson were omitted from the published list but nevertheless significant. Other major influences or interlocutors are apparent enough from the work: Charles Olson, Robert Duncan, James Hillman, and Norman O. Brown, for example. Antonin Artaud and Aimé Césaire are poets whose works have occupied much of Eshleman's creative life as a translator and essayist, but they should not necessarily be understood as having influenced his formation, since his concerns, methods, and orientation had largely been established before he began substantial work on them.

This is not the place to attempt a thorough analysis of the poetry born of this web of influences. The point I am pursuing here is one essential aspect or quality of the work, the fact that it was self-consciously born of influences, influences it bears in its language, strategies and structures; it is a work of imagination imbedded or grounded in a context defined by influence and experience, literary, political, and personal. This notion is encapsulated nicely in the title of Eshleman's volume of selected poetry, *The Name Encanyoned River*. The title itself derives from a line cast off by César Vallejo in his worksheets. But Eshleman's "name encanyoned river" is also Heraclitus' river, refracted through Charles Olson's observation, from "The Kingfishers": "What does not change / is the will to change."[32] All the names of history echo off the canyon walls.

The purpose of Eshleman's poetry, as noted above, is the "emancipation of the self," but the pursuit of emancipation reveals the extent to which the self is entwined with others, with its origins in the material context of the earth, its location in culture(s), its unfolding through history, personal and transpersonal. Ultimately, as Eshleman admits, "the attempt to get rid of the 'I' is as crippling as the attempt to get rid of the 'other.' Both are valid points of dynamic interchange and it is only when one is fixed and made central that the flux of contrariety is halted and opposites appear."[33] Here it is significant to note that Eshleman's writing is deeply rooted and personal – occasionally almost embarrassingly so, in its revelation of the details of intimate life – but it is not confessional in the manner of mid-century "confessional" verse culture exemplified by Robert Lowell, among others. Eshleman writes to reveal proximities and distances, relationships of rapport, rather than to revel in his ego.

Here the dynamic, open quality of the verse is also significant. The poems are cast in the form of an inquiry, a search for a relationship that is still unfolding, in process, rather than static, closed or cut off. His writing is by turns observational and searching, sometimes appearing as a series of questions about or notes on a topic. Eshleman writes specifically to break through expected, inherited, static, or stabilized forms and figures, linguistic, moral, psychological or otherwise. Words and phrases coalesce in figures that form or fall into symbols, images, language games, details of fact, stories, myths, dreams, and visions. These figures serve Eshleman in something of the same manner images did for Willem de Kooning, some of whose *Woman* paintings Eshleman worked through in *From Scratch:* the figure or image is a focal point around which intensities of meaning and imagination gather and through which they pass. The poem is a place of encounter. As a focal point, the image is a wall against which the poet pushes his poetic consciousness, seeking points of entry, cracks and fractures, possibilities of recognition, rejection, assimilation, or transformation. "Is not all art which genuinely moves us done in the 'dark' against a 'wall'?"[34] The notion of a wall is crucial throughout Eshleman's corpus as a metaphor and as a literal fact, as in the walls of Paleolithic painted caves that present what Eshleman calls the "back wall of imagination."[35]

The content here is personal, cultural, and trans-cultural by turns, spurred by observations from everyday life, reading and other research, aesthetic objects and images – including Paleolithic painting, objects, and modern art –, and pulled up from the unconscious revealed in dreams and visionary states of waking dream. Eshleman's purpose here, his push against these walls, is a will to encounter resistances, not to dominate them but to meet, engage, provoke, to reveal contradictions and seek connections between them. For Eshlemam, "poetry's perpetual direction is its way of ensouling events, of seeking the doubleness in events, the event's hidden or contradictory meaning."[36]

This is an agenda that he shares with César Vallejo, undoubtedly both through mutual interest and influence. Evoking his readings of Vallejo, he writes: "The most important things [Vallejo] faced me with were contradictions, contradictions to be looked at. The point at which I determined the contradictions were more valuable than the continuities, let alone the formulas, and it would be a mistake in my case to attempt to transcend or repress my Indiana background, I made a commitment that went like this: I must look back into Indiana and try to go through in poetry what it was to be from Indiana so that I could harrow, or hollow out, that Hell. I was convinced that if I did not do so, I would be permanently injured, less than a man, incapable of full manhood, and forever haunted by various paralyzing background attitudes that would continue to manifest themselves and undermine my projects."[37] The agenda here is intellectual, social or cultural, by terms, but it is also deeply personal. Poetry or poetic consciousness is not an idle pastime; it is a necessity for a healthy life.

In *Love's Body*, Norman O. Brown outlined a similar visionary agenda, a search for lost unity through symbolical consciousness: "To make in ourselves a new consciousness, an erotic sense of reality, is to become conscious of symbolism. Symbolism is mind making connections (correspondences) rather than distinctions (separations). Symbolism makes conscious interconnections and unions that were unconscious and repressed. Freud says, symbolism is on the track of a former identity, a lost unity: the lost continent, Atlantis, underneath the sea of life in which we live enisled; or perhaps even our union with the sea (Thalassa); oceanic consciousness; the unity of the whole cosmos as one living creature, as Plato said in the *Timaeus*."[38] Norman O. Brown's understanding of symbolical consciousness derives from Freud and the psychoanalytic tradition but also from Blake, and, like Eshleman, from Northrop Frye's reading of Blake. In *Milton*, Blake claims, in the visionary symbolic terms that are his own: "There is a place where Contraries are equally True / This place is called Beulah, It is a pleasant lovely Shadow / Where no dispute can come. Because of those who Sleep."[39] Beulah, then, is a place of myths, dreams and visions, where all contraries are equally true and all things appear as they are, infinite. This is the place that must be reached.

Already in Kyoto, if not before, Eshleman had begun to write with and through images, real and imagined, as points of focus and vehicles of resistance for his poetic imagination and critical consciousness. Following Blake's model, he invented symbolic Spectres from elements of his imagined self, Yorunomado ("Night Window" in Japanese) named for the coffee shop where he translated Vallejo, and Niemonjima, named for an island near Futomi, mentioned by Basho, that Eshleman and his first wife Barbara viewed from a nearby shore in 1962. The Sons of the Sepik Delta were given a name echoing both that of Eshleman's fraternity, Phi Delta Theta, and that of an area of New Guinea, the Sepik Delta, inhabited by a group of headhunters pictured in an image Eshleman cut from a *National Geographic* in the early 1960s. He imagined Yorunomado as one of them.[40] As noted, images act as simultaneous points of resistance and spurs to imagination.

A decade later, after concluding *Caterpillar* and completing *Coils*, and thereby ending the most concerted moment in his apprenticeship and the excavation of his youth and its legacies, Eshleman developed this strategy in his poetry in several directions simultaneously. Most dramatically, as noted, he undertook the "saturation job" on the Paleolithic imagination that would culminate, twenty-five years later, in *Juniper Fuse*. Alongside this project he also began moving his poetry – and imaginative engagement – out into the world, at first by writing a new kind of critical prose on friends and contemporaries like Paul Blackburn and Gary Snyder and also by writing "portraits" of key progenitors and influences: Vincent Van Gogh, Charlie Parker, Chaim Soutine, Hart Crane, Francis Bacon, Antonin Artaud, and others.[41] Eshleman explained: "If translating is a way of bringing other poetries into focus, then the kind of 'portraits' I have been doing are a bringing of such focuses over into poetry. That is, it is one thing to translate an Artaud poem and another thing, or another kind of translation – a more difficult kind of translation – to do a portrait of Artaud in which all I know of Artaud is material I am shaping to say how I see him, not as a face or bust as is often done in painting, but as an image, as the body of his imagination, which will be a critique, a cutting out of that which I do not see as essential to Artaud, and a manner in which my life material can be set aside to concentrate on his. An *enact-ment* of Artaud, in other words."[42]

During these same years he also experimented with writing in other voices, adopting the perspectives of more fully imagined personae, akin to Fernando Pessoa's heteronyms, from the inside. Works written in this vein include "The 9 Poems of Metro Vavin" in *The Gull Wall, The Gospel of Celine Arnaud,* and *Homuncula* by Horrah Pornoff, this last written and published in magazines in the 1970s but collected in *Under World Arrest.*

Significantly, and as I've suggested, Eshleman's will to include the world in his work, extends beyond mere language to thought, in the sense of both ideas and information. In "Eight Fire Sources", the essay mentioned above on the major influences on his work, Eshleman quotes Wallace Stevens' remark from *Adagia:* "Poetry is the scholars' art," and interprets Stevens to mean that "poetry is the literary art that should hold the greatest appeal to scholars. [And that] poets can also be scholars without lessening the intuitive drive it takes to write substantial poetry."[43] Poetry should appeal to scholars because its combination of carefully wrought, loaded language and formal invention gives scholars – and in fact all readers – ample fuel for the furnaces of imagination, fodder for the work of psyche.

The second half of Eshleman's interpretation of Stevens approaches the relationship between poetry and scholarship from the other side, the poet's side, suggesting that poets too can and indeed should be scholars. Eshleman offers the Japanese haiku master, Basho, as a "sterling example of the spiritual poet / scholar" because, in his travel journal *Back Roads to Far Towns,* Basho not only produced brilliant haiku but also "did his homework on the lore and history concerning the sites and temples he planned to visit."[44] The work alternates between expository or descriptive prose, called haibun, which is alternately personal, historical, and cultural, and poetic expression, in this case, in the form of haiku.

In the preface to *Antiphonal Swing,* Eshleman explains the derivation of the book's title – taken from the last line of Hart Crane's *The Bridge:* "Whispers antiphonal in azure swing" – "Antiphony, or the singing of anthems, involves one side of the choir, or congregation, answering the other side. For me, the swing is between the erotic and the artistic, as well as between prose and poetry."[45] The erotic here is the bodily energy that swings into artistic imagination. Prose here includes a range of writing styles and strategies, as well as modes of inquiry, which are each distinct from but related to poetic imagination. Here again Eshleman recalls what he learned from reading Basho's hike journals: "it was through studying translations of these journals in the early 1960s that I became aware of the extent to which something about a poet's prose itches to transform itself into poetry and, in a less obvious way, something about the poetry seeks an argumentative or explanative base in prose… prose wanting to intensify its gait, poetry wanting to stop and survey the field it performs in."[46]

Along similar lines, Eshleman is also fond of Northrop Frye's use of the term "anatomy" to describe William Blake's *The Marriage of Heaven and Hell.* An anatomy in this description is a "composite work that includes as its 'members' various forms and strategies of the art of writing." Eshleman also mentions Antonin Artaud's later writing with its "fusion of genres incorporating letters, poetry, prose, and glossolalia" as participating in this hybrid approach to literary production.[47] The literary anatomy is a hybrid form or a form of hybridity, a means of fusion rather than fission. It brings together and assimilates discourses while preserving the differences between them. The fusion or assimilation it proposes is not one of complete synthesis. Rather than eliminating the differences between discourses, this approach in some ways marks or illustrates them. The description is significant to Eshleman not only in reference to the antiphonal relationship of poetry and prose across his corpus as a whole but also, and perhaps more interestingly, within individual works: in this way, his poem "Notes on a Visit to Le Tuc d'Audoubert" provides the "nuclear form" of *Juniper Fuse.*[48]

In the introduction to *Juniper Fuse,* Eshleman situates his book in line with Charles Olson's notion of a "saturation job" in which, in Olson's words, one digs into "one thing or place or man until you yourself know more abt that than is possible to any other man… [E]xhaust it. Saturate it."[49] Eshleman takes his distance from the notion of knowing more about a thing than "any other man" but Olson's larger point remains relevant. In *Juniper Fuse* this means to "make use of a pluralistic approach that may result in a fuller 'reading' of Upper Paleolithic imagination than archeological or literary approaches alone might yield."[50] Eshleman's pluralistic approach distinguishes *Juniper Fuse* radically from other works in the study of prehistory but this investigative and pluralistic approach also characterizes and distinguishes Eshleman's corpus as a whole within contemporary writing, contemporary poetry in particular. Early poetry collections, like *Altars* and *Coils,* included sections of prose commentary; later collections included in their fabric occasional essays, introductions and notes; and the corpus as a whole includes poetry, translations, essays, journals, and edited volumes.

My point here is that Eshleman practices poetry as something rather more than a scholar's art, marshalling many means of investigation, many modes and styles of inquiry. This is rather more than a scholar's art because contemporary scholarship has largely locked itself in cages barred by discipline and specialty. Olson's influence is again relevant here through his oft-quoted interpretation of the title of Herodotus' work, *'istoria* – inquiry, in Greek – which Olson takes to mean "find out for yourself." In *The Maximus Poems*, he writes: "I would be an historian as Herodotus was, looking / for oneself for the evidence of / what is said"[51] and again "Herodotus's [concept of history] / which was a verb, to find out for yourself: / 'istorian, which makes any one's acts a finding out for him or her / self, in other words, restores the traum: that we act somewhere …"[52] In thinking about history, about *poiesis* and making history, Eshleman puts the stress on *out* – to find *out* for yourself, "an exit for the self," a mode of self-transformation through inquiry.[53] Inquiry here includes inquiry into the self as well as into the things of the world and their histories, but, as in Olson, the inquiry is always rooted, the self is always situated within and in relation to the world: the inquiry reveals relationship.

The point of research here is less the specific content of the research – all points of entry are in some senses equal – but rather the back-file of language, strategy, and information that derives from research both in form and in content. Eshleman observes: "I think that the main benefit from research for a poet […] is that it builds up a file of materials that cling to the underside of consciousness, and can be brought into play when, in composition, one needs a hoist to move the poem along into another dimension or sounding."[54] Here knowledge is put in play, part of a process, rather than congealed and set apart as a static collection of dusty facts.

As an embodiment of commitment, the poetic process is one of developing an informed consciousness that should ideally always be both symbolical, and hence imaginative, as well as critical. As he puts it: "I believe that I am responsible for every word that I write, and if I am beside myself at times, if the words appear to come from nowhere, this is a gift that I must honor but also evaluate as it arrives in the process of composition."[55] The second half of this statement alludes to the critical function of evaluation, the capacity to stand back from the work, to situate it reflectively, even as it unfolds.

This may seem profoundly anti-poetic but it is a crucial part of Eshleman's understanding of poetry. Some poets, particularly young poets, may be resistant to any form of critical commentary or informed critique, however gentle. For such writers, poetry is self-expression and all criticism is irrelevant. Poetry may even be appealing to these writers precisely because they conceive of it as free of constraints, internal or external, personal or cultural. Eshleman's poetry, on the other hand, is nothing less than a confrontation with constraints, a willful engagement with their source, nature, meaning, and extent.

In *Novices*, Eshleman takes up the question of critical self-consciousness in relation to the use of psychoanalysis in the poetic process. He writes: "The poet's resistance to psychoanalysis is a resistance to discovering his unconscious motives for writing poetry – as if discovering a severing – a witch with a long nose intruding into the play-house window, discovering what the children are 'really' doing there. The fear that more information is the end of information is Blake's enemy, 'doubt which is self-contradiction,' and it hamstrings the novice through developing a reluctance to investigate Psyche – to investigate *anything*."[56] Unfortunately, this reluctance to investigate, to do research of any kind, even research into the history of poetry, has taken root in the culture of creative writing in America today. I'll return to this topic below. For now, my point is simply that Eshleman has pursued the contrary course; his poetry is a scholar's art. And on the subject of research, he is even occasionally prescriptive: "Ideally, every poet should undertake at least one big investigative project that brings into poetry materials that have previously not been a part of it. This is one way that we keep our art fresh, and not diluted with variations played on tried and true themes. The investigative project also makes one responsible for a huge range of materials, the assimilation of which goes way beyond the concerns of the personal lyric."[57] In *Juniper Fuse*, the range of materials assimilated by the poet is indeed huge. It begins with personal visits to the sites themselves, not once or in passing, but repeated and persistent visits, over two and a half decades of research. It also includes readings in archeology and anthropology as well as materials outside of those fields, narrowly defined: C.G. Jung, Sandor Ferenczi, Geza Róheim, Mikhail Bakhtin, Weston La Barre, Charles Olson, Norman O. Brown, Kenneth Grant, James Hillman, Hans Peter Duerr, Maxine Sheets-Johnstone, among others.[58] At the end of *Novices: A Study of Poetic Apprenticeship*, Eshleman appends two reading lists that might be of use to novices. The lists include poetry but also books "that taught [him] something about life and poetry and [...] that bear upon poetry as I understand it."[59] These books include works of anthropology, psychology, philosophy, comparative religious studies, and women's studies, among other fields. All of this is to say that Eshleman's poetry – and his writing in general – is both formed and informed; it is poetry with content: personal, particular, psychological, political.

The broad question of research and investigation, of the relation between creative consciousness and critical consciousness, finds a precedent in Blake, who wrote, in the preface to *Milton:* "The Daughters of Memory shall become the Daughters of Inspiration." The facts of history, which is to say the content of memory, personal and cultural, must not be avoided, as burdens, but rather integrated or at least indicated, noted in marks of relation. This is also a comment on Eshleman's approach to the anxiety of influence, which cannot be avoided and therefore must be faced, assimilated or rejected in one manner or another.

The tendency toward investigation is also evidenced throughout Eshleman's prose, and he has published four extended collections of prose writings in addition to *Juniper Fuse,* which, like several other works, includes both poetry and prose. Additional uncollected prose pieces – reviews and remarks, letters and other writings – can be found in *Caterpillar* and elsewhere. The four published volumes gather the poet's prose according to various schemas, both logical and chronological, giving each volume autonomous sense without disrupting the continuities of form, strategy or concern that link them. Across the volumes, the pieces fall into several more or less distinct but also overlapping and related formal categories: journals, interviews, memoirs, essays and reviews on poetry, poetics and the arts, and, more broadly, writings in what might best be termed the history of consciousness. Each of these types of writing can be found in each prose volume. A different organizational schema might have gathered all of the journals together, all of the interviews, or all of the essays on poetry and poetics. As it is, readers can see the types of prose writing coiled around each other, breaking the boundaries of each collection.

In keeping with their form, the poet's journals stand close to the events they describe, even though he has often revised – even substantially rewritten – them for publication. They serve as workshops for thought and experience that are at once notational and ruminative, observational and speculative. Many of Eshleman's poems share this same rangy, searching, speculative, and notational form: the difference is thus only one of degree, wherein the poems – if that is ultimately the right word for writings in these hybrid forms – demonstrate a higher degree of metaphoric invention, transformation, and intensity than do the journals. Here I have in mind the difference between works like "Notes on a Visit to Le Tuc d'Audoubert" and journals like "Our Journey Around the Drowned City of Is."[60] The condensation of the material in the shorter work is only partly responsible for this heightened level of intensity.[61]

The majority of Eshleman's prose writings are memoirs and essays on poets, poetry, poetics, and the arts. These include moments of memoir and analysis as well as introductions to the works of key contemporaries: Cid Corman, Paul Blackburn, Gary Snyder, Allen Ginsberg, Robin Blaser, Jack Spicer, Ron Padgett, and others. Frequently his essays consider some of the poets who have influenced him most, his key progenitors, like Hart Crane and Charles Olson, as well as the writers whose work he has spent his life working with and through as a translator: César Vallejo, Antonin Artaud, Aimé Césaire, most often. A third group of essays is focused on visual artists whose works (and lives in some cases) have been proximate to Eshleman's experience and concerns: Leon Golub, Artaud again, Michel Nedjar, Francis Bacon, and others. When these works are structured as memoirs – as in Eshleman's memoirs of his relationship with Cid Corman or of his life-project translating César Vallejo, both collected in *Archaic Design* – they are proximate to journals as records of life lived, though also refracted through the essay form of condensed reflection. Other pieces demonstrate Eshleman's patient and informed acumen as a reader and critic as well as his knowledge of poetry.

In her forward to *Companion Spider,* Adrienne Rich observed that Eshleman has "gone more deeply into his art, its process and demands, than any modern American poet since Robert Duncan or Muriel Rukeyser."[62] Her comment is relevant to Eshleman's practice as a poet, but also to his knowledge of poetry. As a young man, Ezra Pound set himself the task of learning more about poetry – its history, art, and craft – than any of his contemporaries. As his essays demonstrate, Eshleman seems to have set for himself a similar task. For him, the practice of poetry entails not only developing a personal idiom but also an understanding of what came before and lies beyond that idiom, what other styles and purposes there might be. As a body of writings, and speaking in terms of intellectual practice, Eshleman's essays offer pointed explorations and incursions into poetics, moments of measurement through which the poet tests his own views on and practices of poetry and poetics against those of his contemporaries, the most relevant great dead of the tradition, and practitioners of other arts. Eshleman has not written a formal poetics, but something like one can be extracted from these writings and the interviews that explore a similar terrain, generally through the prism of questions concerning his own writings.

Another mode of investigative engagement appears in the poet's sustained, and clearly sustaining, practice of translation. Significantly, when Eshleman discovered poetry in the late 1950s, he discovered not just modern or American poetry but world poetry.[63] At its inception, in other words, his understanding of poetry included poets from around the world: Rilke, Lorca, Mayakofsky, St.-John Perse, as well as, and with even more meaning to Eshleman, Pablo Neruda and César Vallejo, along with the other poets included in the anthology of contemporary Latin American poetry Dudley Fitts' published through New Directions in 1947. The Fitts anthology was bilingual, inviting a comparative reading of the translations with their originals. Other translations of the same poems by Neruda in particular were also readily available for comparison. In a memoir of his encounter with Neruda's work, Eshleman wrote: "I had the experience that I suppose many translators have at the beginning of their careers: one of shock, at the astonishing discrepancies and outright errors (which even I could spot!) in these different versions. To some extent I became a translator reactively, disgruntled with what others had done, and with some unbased confidence that I could do a better job!"[64] Eshleman's confidence was without basis at that moment primarily because he did not know Spanish. His fascination with Neruda and Vallejo lead him to hitchhike to Mexico for the next two summers, to learn Spanish specifically in order to translate their works. Two years later, when living in Kyoto and having completed and published his translations of Neruda's *Residence on Earth*, Eshleman undertook the more demanding task of attempting to translate César Vallejo's *Poemas humanos* – while continuing to work on his own writing and continuing to read deeply in the history of poetry, myth, and thought – to work through William Blake in particular – as part of his apprenticeship in poetry.

As noted above, Cid Corman offered Eshleman a model and mentor of the poet as writer, translator, editor and scholar wrapped in one. In his memoir of Corman, Eshleman recalled this influence: Corman's "meticulousness as a writer brought home to me, in the realm of translation, the necessity to do absolutely accurate versions as well as versions that attempted to rise to the performance level of the originals."[65] Translation in this model is an exercise in scholarship requiring dogged and detailed research alongside creative imagination. In practice, as a translator, Eshleman learned to keep a notebook alongside his on-going translations to contain those irruptions of imagination and reflection that accompany the translation process rather than attempting to ignore or repress them. Translation, pursued in this manner, is an act of devotion, founded upon fidelity to the words and thought of another, requiring the translator to put his or her ego in suspense, to resist too quick an understanding of the source text, wherein imagination or unconscious motives might lead one to impose a meaning or interpretation that is not present in the original text. In this way the act of translation recalls the phrase from Blake that resonates through so much of Eshleman's work: "The most sublime act is to set another before you."

Aside from the direct pleasure of being able to read the translated work in English, the rewards of translation for the translator are complex. Eshleman observed: "I have thought more about poetry while translating Vallejo than while reading anyone else."[66] And elsewhere: "Since translation is such slow work, requiring multiple rereadings, it can require a more prolonged reading-in-depth than when we read poetry written in our own language."[67] Or again, more emphatically: "I have spent much more time with my 2nd Edition *Webster's International Dictionary* as a translator than as a poet. Translation has constantly over the years swept me away from myself, locking me to the minds of those poets I have translated and, by doing so, has challenged and deepened my own base."[68] All of this is to say that translation, like other forms of research, expands the poet's range, his knowledge of the potentialities of the poet's craft, but, like formal exercises, it also expands his reach, his capacities.

Translation has provided Eshleman with another means of engaging with others as well: co-translation. His earliest translations – of Neruda – where done with the help of a native informant, the wife of the man from whom he was renting rooms in Mexico at the time. Later, in Kyoto, he collaborated with Cid Corman on a variety of translations. Returning to the United States, he and Denis Kelly collaborated on a selection of poems by Aimé Césaire. The following year, in Lima, Peru, he worked with Maureen Ahern on Vallejo. In the 1970s, he would work on Vallejo with José Rubia Barcia, on Artaud with A. James Arnold and Norman Glass, and, more extensively, on Césaire with Annette Smith. He continued to collaborate with Annette Smith for the next two decades, while also working with Julio Ortega and Américo Ferrari on Vallejo, and Bernard Bador on Artaud. More recently he and Lucas Klein translated a volume of poems by Bei Dao and he and A. James Arnold have been re-translating all of Aimé Césaire's works in definitive bilingual editions. The community involved in the translation process, for Eshleman, includes the author of the original text as well as, ideally, a native informant.

The story recounted above of Eshleman's discovery of poetry in translation and of the practice of translation also includes, though less directly, reference to another significant practice in his life commitment to poetry: editing. As noted, Eshleman discovered Pablo Neruda and César Vallejo in an anthology of Latin American poetry edited by Dudley Fitts. Shortly after making that discovery, he would find himself editing the Indiana University English Department literary journal. Looking back, he observed: "As a student at Indiana University in the late 1950s, I was simultaneously involved in working on poems, starting to translate Neruda and Vallejo, and editing the English Department literary journal, *Folio*. I have practiced that triadic discipline every since."[69] Significantly, these were also the practices that Eshleman witnessed Cid Corman pursuing in Kyoto a few years later.

Three issues of *Folio* appeared under Eshleman's editorship before conservative tempers in the English Department at Indiana University withdrew its funding. By editing those three issues however, Eshleman was able to reach out to a number of poets, foreign and domestic, of preceding generations as well as compelling contemporaries. The list of contributors is surprising, indeed almost shocking, in range and significance, given that *Folio* was a student run journal. They included William Carlos Williams, Pablo Neruda, Cid Corman, Allen Ginsberg, Robert Creeley, Louis Zukofsky, Robert Duncan and contemporaries like Robert Kelly, Jerome Rothenberg, and David Antin, among others.

Eshleman's next editorial venture came about while he was living in Peru in 1965–66. There he was hired by the North American Peruvian Institute to start a bilingual literary magazine, which he called *Quena*, referring to the traditional one-hole Quechuan flute. Drawing on his international connections, Eshleman produced a 300-page first issue including work by Charles Olson, Cid Corman, and Javier Heraud, translated by Paul Blackburn, among many other pieces. As with *Folio*, five years previously, *Quena* was suppressed by its sponsors. In this case the suppression occurred prior to the publication of the first issue. Whereas the contents of *Folio* had been deemed unacceptable on primarily literary grounds, in the case of *Quena* the contents were deemed unacceptable on political grounds.[70] This would only add fuel to the fires of Eshleman's budding political consciousness.

Back in Bloomington, then continuing later that year in New York City, Eshleman began to publish a series of chapbooks under the *Caterpillar* imprint. The name derived from several familiar sources: a short poem by William Blake, a diagram of the movement of life-energy by Wilhelm Reich, and images of Vietnamese war victims that looked like a "black caterpillar." The first Caterpillar Book was a volume of poems by Aimé Césaire co-translated by Eshleman and Denis Kelly entitled *State of the Union*. Over the next year, nine more titles followed including works by Cid Corman, Paul Blackburn, Frank Samperi, David Antin, D. Alexander, Robert Van Dias, and Jackson MacLow, as well as two books by Eshleman. For Antin and MacLow, these publications were their first books. Eshleman found the chapbooks difficult to distribute and shifted his strategy, founding *Caterpillar Magazine* as a quarterly in October 1967. The following year, *Brother Stones,* a limited edition illustrated edition collaboration with printmaker William Paden was published in Kyoto as "A Caterpillar Book," but no other books appeared under the imprint. The magazine however was a success.

Eshleman explained the origin of *Caterpillar Magazine* succinctly: "The main reason I began *Caterpillar* in the fall of 1967 is because I did not feel that poets like Robert Duncan, Diane Wakoski, Jerome Rothenberg, Frank Samperi, Cid Corman, Louis Zukofsky, and Paul Blackburn had a dependable and generous magazine outlet for their writing."[71] Eshleman's editorial practice was based on the practice he had seen Cid Corman deploy in editing *Origin* in Kyoto, but with key revisions. Where *Origin* had been tightly focused by its 64-page format and Corman's interest in lyric poetry, *Caterpillar* was to be larger in scope and inclusivity. He "wanted to bring things that were not poetry per se to bear on poetry."[72] The first issue included essays by Norman O. Brown and Robert Duncan, from *The H.D. Book*. Other issues featured writings by Wilhelm Reich and Stan Brakhage, a lecture on Scientology, and writings and music by Philip Corner and James Tenney. *Caterpillar* also included examples of visual art, not only on its cover, but in its pages as well, works by Leon Golub, Nancy Spero, Jess, Robert LaVigne, and Carolee Schneemann among them. To some extent the contents of each issue were set by the submissions that came in, though Eshleman deliberately solicited material as well. As he explained, "with *Caterpillar*, I wanted a magazine that was open-ended, where the contributions that expectedly or unexpectedly came in determined the nature of a given issue."[73] The exploratory sense of the endeavor represented an attempt to "do a magazine with a single point of view *and* a magazine that was also eclectic."[74] The tension here is that of an inclusive consciousness, straining against and reaching beyond its limits. After four issues, Robert Kelly joined the masthead as a contributing editor. After twelve issues, Eshleman released *A Caterpillar Anthology*. In June 1973, with issue 20, just prior to leaving for a year to live in France, Eshleman felt he had accomplished what he had set out to do and folded the magazine.

Published from 1967 to 1973, *Caterpillar* appeared at the tail end of a cultural, countercultural and literary period defined in many ways by mimeographed broadsheets and journals, little magazines and anthologies of contemporary poetry. In the 1950s, these magazines included *Origin, Black Mountain Review, Evergreen Review* and others. In the 1960s, Robert Kelly and George Economou's *Trobar* and Rothenberg's *Poems for the Floating World* were proximate to Eshleman's formation and early concerns. But there were many other magazines of the moment: *Big Table, Coyote's Journal, El Corno Emplumado, Yugen, Floating Bear,* and *Kulchur,* to name only these few.[75] More significant, perhaps, were the anthologies that shaped this generation of readers: Robert Motherwell's early *Dada Painters and Poets,* Donald Allen's *The New American Poetry* and, later, *Poetics of the New American Poetry.* In this context as well, Jerome Rothenberg's series of collections *Ritual, Shaking the Pumpkin, Technicians of the Sacred, America, a Prophecy,* and, with Diane Rothenberg, *Symposium of the Whole,* gave lasting shape to a wide range of concerns in postmodern American poetry.

In 1981, eight years after folding *Caterpillar,* Eshleman returned to editing by founding a new magazine, *Sulfur.* The name refers to a species of butterfly with black-bordered orange and yellow wings – and hence an evolutionary stage of *Caterpillar* – as well as to processes of alchemical initiation and combustion.[76] Founded while Eshleman was a Dreyfuss Poet in Residence at California Institute of Technology, and in ongoing dialogue with Robert Kelly, Jerome Rothenberg, and others, "*Sulfur*'s primary ambition [was] to keep the field open and complex, with archival and contemporary writing, along with commentary, generating a multi-generational interplay."[77] Areas of intentional focus included translations of contemporary foreign-language poets and new translations of untranslated poetry, significant archival materials, writing by unknown and young poets, commentary including poetics, notes and reviews, and finally "resource materials," meaning "previously excluded (and repressed) materials and experience," that might be useful toward the "renewal and deepening of content" in the art of poetry.[78] As in *Caterpillar,* the point was to push against and open up the limits of the art, to reach beyond borders, linguistic and national.

Cal Tech provided some support for the first five years, after which point, Clayton and Caryl published a few issues on their own, before finding a new home – for issues 10 to 15 – through the Extension Program of UCLA. In 1986, that funding came to an end in near coincidence with Eshleman accepting a position in the English Department at Eastern Michigan University, which sponsored the magazine from issues 17 to 46, the final issue. From 1981 to 1987, the magazine appeared three times a year, thereafter twice a year; a total of 46 issues over nineteen years; some 11,000 pages featuring roughly 800 contributors. Robert Kelly served as contributing editor on the first issue: Michael Palmer, Jerome Rothenberg, and Eliot Weinberger joined as contributing editors as of the third. Over the years other collaborators joined the masthead as contributing editors, reviews editors, arts editors, or corresponding editors: Rachel Blau DuPlessis, Charles Bernstein, James Clifford, Clark Coolidge, Jayne Cortez, Marjorie Perloff, Dennis Phillips, Jed Rasula, Marjorie Walsh, Roberto Tejada, Keith Tuma, Allen S. Weiss, Pamela Wye, John Yau. The magazine was funded in part by sales and subscriptions, in part (though not always financially) by its various institutional homes, and in part by a series of grants from the National Endowment for the Arts. In the late 1990s, those grants dried up. After struggling on for a few years on a reduced budget, Eshleman recognized that the magazine had achieved its goals and that the turn of the millennium marked an appropriate occasion to stop.

Glancing at the pages of *Caterpillar* and *Sulfur*, one recognizes the extent to which – even more so than translation – editing is a collaborative art. Editors activate voices, bring them together, set them into relation, help them stand revealed; they draw speakers into conversation and let them speak. The work of the editor is like that of a conductor, to borrow one shade of the meaning of Eshleman's phrase, "conductors of the pit." They assemble and conduct, direct and convey, an orchestra of voices, from near and far, present and absent, living and dead.[79] On this topic, Eshleman recently observed: "Editing *Caterpillar* and *Sulfur* enabled me to construct an ongoing active mosaic of poetry and translation, and how the contemporary might mesh with archival materials, artwork, and commentary."[80] Eshleman's achievement as an editor – and its value to contemporary American letters – alongside his contributions as a translator and poet in his own right – has yet, I think, to be fully recognized, let alone digested.

The interpretation I have been developing here is one of a poetic consciousness seeking an ever-wider range of materials and inspirations, resistances and encounters, for consideration, assimilation, and the experience of relation and rapport. Thus far we have observed Eshleman at work as a poet and poet-scholar, as an essayist, translator and editor. Before concluding I would like to point to the limits – the limit-experiences – of his work: the test cases of political writing, the problems of the whole, the abyss, and the Paleolithic imagination, as well as the embracing notion of love.

Eshleman's political consciousness was born in the slums of Lima, Peru, in 1965: experiences he recounts in *Walks* and *On Mules Sent From Chavin*. Though he had traveled to parts of Mexico for two summers at the end of the 1950s, and to Korea and Japan in the early 1960s, in Lima he witnessed first-hand the connection between poverty, politics, military power, and neo-colonialist strategies of international aid. (Ernesto "Che" Guevara had been radicalized by similar encounters a little more than a decade earlier.) These experiences would inform and lend bitter fuel to Eshleman's participation in the anti-war movement in the United States when he returned there the following year. Indeed much of his energy in the late 1960s would be devoted to anti-war protests, primarily participation in the Angry Arts movement in New York and other nation-wide protest activities.

The importance of this aspect of Eshleman's work cannot be overestimated. His purpose is to write a poetry that is responsible for all that he knows about his world, good and bad, beautiful and terrible. But his vision and experience is deeply bifurcated. "As a middle-class American, I am overexposed to the front side of our avuncular top-hatted Uncle Sam. Much of the world has a different view of Sam than I do. Iraqis, Serbs, Laotians, Vietnamese, Cambodians, and Panamanians, for example, see a skeletal backside wired with DU, cluster bombs, dioxin, sarin, napalm (most recently used in Fallujah), and hydrogen cyanide. I know what I see and I keep both sides of Sam's body in mind as I continue to work on myself, to learn, and to love."[81] Or again, put differently, this acknowledgement: "We know that North American abundance is to a great and, ultimately, terrifying extent dependent upon the continuing poverty and torture of others in countries we have no direct contact with, but to whom our eyes are pressed via TV news reports, so that the starving mother in Biafra, seated on the side of a cot, with a starving infant too weak to even try to suckle her mother's utterly empty breast, poses a complicated set of questions to North American poets: by responding in our writing to such a scene, to what extent do we fulfill our human responsibility to it? To what extent is our response a mere appropriation of materials that mirrors imperialistic ideologies?"[82]

Here Eshleman's moral outrage joins a stream of similar reflections at the limits of political vision. In a passage from Northrop Frye's *Fearful Symmetry* that Eshleman quotes in *Altars,* Frye observes: "All pleasure is at least partly a dream under anesthetic. Something is always suffering horribly somewhere, and we can only find pleasure by ignoring that fact. We must ignore it up to a point, or go mad; but in the abyss of consciousness, to which Enion [in Blake's *Four Zoas*] has been banished, there lurks the feeling that joy is based on exclusion, that the Yule log can blaze cheerfully only when the freezing beggars in the streets are, for the moment, left to freeze."[83] For me, this sentiment has been most powerfully stated by Salmen Lewental, a *sonderkommando* at Auschwitz who buried fragmentary notes about his experience near crematoria III in Birkenau. Unearthed years later, this chilling recognition of social reality in extremis appears among those notes: "There was a time in this camp, in the years 1941–42, when each man, really each one who lived longer than two weeks, lived at the cost of lives of other people or on what they had taken from them."[84] Part of the staggering power of Lewental's statement derives from his status as a participant, implicated in the experience to which he is witness: life in the camp was life lived at the expense of life.

These notions serve as first premises for an ethics and thereby also a politics. Eshleman endeavors to hold himself to them and to measure his work by them. Thus he claims: "While I am open to the invention of 'new worlds,' I insist on inventing them while addressing the cruelty of the present one."[85] Or, as measure, he asks rhetorically: "the depth of your life? / Nothing if severed from the life of a man in rags / going off into the dark of Siberian cold."[86] This is a problem and a challenge for all American poets. "As a citizen of a country that has supported such terrorists as the Nicaraguan Contras, UNITA in Angola, the Moujahedeen in Afghanistan, Cuban CIA agents in Miami, the governments of El Salvador, Guatemala, and Chile, the American poet reaps and suffers the rewards of American terrorism, which are part of his spectre, his anti-imaginative blockage, whether he acknowledges such or not. All of us are connected to the rubble of Fallujah by a poisoned umbilicus."[87] This statement invalidates or at a minimum profoundly diminishes a great deal of the poetry written in America today.

Unsurprisingly, given his importance to Eshleman, César Vallejo provided a poignant model of political poetry that would become Eshleman's own. As Eshleman explains: "*Human Poems* redefines the 'political' poem. With one or two exceptions, the poems in this collection have no political position or agenda in the traditional sense. Yet they are directly sympathetic, in a way that does not remind us of other poetries, with the human situation [...] They are so permeated with Vallejo's own suffering as it is wedded to that of other people, that it is as if the dualisms of colonial / colonized, rich and poor, become fused at a level where the human animal, aware of his fate, is embraced in all his absurd fallibility."[88] The model here is one of recognition and identification grounded in a fundamental position of mutual mortal fragility.

The political poet in Eshleman is witness to suffering caused by atrocity; his testimony transcends the merely ethical through the pointedness of its barely contained fury. In the 1960s, that fury was haunted by events in Peru and Vietnam; in the 1970s, by Hiroshima and the Holocaust – place-names like Dachau, Mauthausen, and Auschwitz; in the 1980s, El Salvador; more recently by the atrocities of the Bush era, the invasions of Afghanistan and Iraq.

But there are limits to ethical consciousness and political opportunities in those limits. Self and other are separated by a biological abyss that can be bridged only in part by imagination. In the end, we are each profoundly alone before the uniqueness of our experiences and the fact of our death. Suffering is always radically specific. While the witness can and must testify to the violence that occurs before his or her gaze, comprehension, even in imagination, has distinct and meaningful limits or boundaries. Eshleman admits this with another rhetorical question: "Faced with so much story, I release my grip / from Whitman's hand, 'agonies are one of my changes of / garments' – in the face of Auschwitz?"[89] Walt Whitman imagined that, via imagination, his cosmos was fully comprehensible to him. For Eshleman, such an admission is impossible. It is also perhaps inadvisable, even unethical. However inspiring it may be in some moments, Whitman's synthetic vision is inadmissible in extremis: there are events and experiences that one simply cannot share, cannot comprehend from a distance. In such cases, Eshleman writes with a different purpose, rather than to merely acknowledge and accept incomprehensible horror, he writes to render it, to convey it to his reader in its horror, as horror, which is to say as a wound. "Let me set terror back into the grass, inject it / deeply into the planet's skin / get *chasm* back into *abyss*."[90]

At the limits of consciousness, even symbolical consciousness, there is an abyss of understanding. To reach that place, one must go through hell, perhaps literally, certainly metaphorically and symbolically. Like everything else in Eshleman's cosmology, hell is manifold. It is both Dante's Hell and the Greek underworld, Hades, where Odysseus went in search of visions of the way home. It is also Blake's Hell – the poet's domain, where energy is eternal delight and imagination and reason are one. But, as in Rimbaud's season in hell, hell is also personal, for Eshleman, the hells of Phi Delta Theta Hell Week and of childhood traumas. And following James Hillman's Jungian thought, Hell is the underworld: the unconscious, accessed through dream and poetic imagination. Despite all of these layers of cultural meaning, but recognizing that psychoanalysis is ultimately a materialism, that the unconscious is a manifestation of the body, hell is, in the end, physical, material, a concept derived from our separation from our fellow creatures and from the earth itself. The upsurge of consciousness is indistinct from our exile from Eden, our fall into psychological, biological separation.

Like Odysseus, like Rimbaud, Eshleman has gone to Hades, to hell, in search of vision. His journey has been a journey into himself, crawling through the layers of shame bequeathed by Christian civilization, beyond the gods of the Greeks – and the archetypes they represent, beneath the foundation stones of the West, into the painted caves, toward the origins of consciousness and autonomous imagination. This journey has been a journey through culture but it has also been personal, interrogating the wounds of childhood and modern American life, measuring the self against the legacies that course through and shape it. "Thank god hell is not dead within me," Eshleman wrote in *Indiana*.[91]

In the journal published as *On Mules Sent From Chavin*, we glimpse Eshleman in the mid-1960s working through the psychological ramifications of these concepts as they were reflected in his mythopoetic spectre, Yorunomado:

> Why must I give up hell to live within love? Does Yorunomado mean that my sense of love is narrow and thus will not include hell? Now if I think of hell as a place, symbolic as well as terrestrial, I can understand that – but Blake has so redefined hell as a positive force in creation that I have to take that meaning into consideration too. Must I kill my own energy – my furnaces – to be able to have love? ... I think Blake locates the stomach as 'hell' and Lawrence the solar plexus as the 'power center' the 'sun center' and they seem right in the sense that both appear to be redirecting the 'center' away from the heart & head. That is, center in head makes body top-heavy – how could you dance if you took head as center? You'd fall over, or end up in some grotesque pose – but it seems to me that taking center down to the stomach is not taking it down far enough, that genital center is truer, more accurate to life-energy.[92]

In his early poetry, Eshleman dug down into himself, through the wounds and scars of his psyche, into and through his personal Hell, toward the source of his psychic conflict and, beyond that, his animal, genital life-energy. Working through his psyche, Eshleman traveled through realms of image and imagination, down the name-encanyoned river, to the point where he could say: "I feel the extent to which I am storied, / but the stories are under [...] / pebble histories, midden chapters, / 'Payroll of Bones' indeed!"[93] (Payroll of Bones is a reference to Vallejo.) His vision of the self here is psychoanalytic but also ecological, a vision of a self situated in the context of an immanent, earthly environmental continuum. Having worked through his wounds, *Coils* closes with a prescient phrase:

> Yorunomado closed the left half of my book.
> From this point on, he said,
> your work leads on into the earth.[94]

Thereafter, vision itself appears as originating in the earth: "The earth so fully referential / it appears to press out nothing but / aspects of itself."[95] The garden of delights is a garden of *earthly* delights. Eshleman's vision here is visionary, symbolical consciousness, wherein contraries appear united as one: "Knowledge of the place of origin means: dissolution of the separation of things from each other."[96] And yet, at its furthest reaches, Eshleman's vision is a Blakean vision of paradox: where presence and absence, continuity and discontinuity, unity and disunity, self and self-loss are experienced as one. "My vertical stands on my zero," he writes, echoing Olson's figure for the basis of the ego.[97] "We begin with ZERO – are O," Olson wrote to a young Cid Corman, in a letter Eshleman quotes in *Novices*.[98] Put differently, in Eshleman's terms: "through you, / a tunnel that winds back into total discontinuity."[99] Here absence is the key to presence, to the source of consciousness: "Basis of the 'hidden wealth' of Hades: the fullness of the void experienced not as absence but as hidden presence to be drawn forth as the animal matrix one is exiting."[100] In *Juniper Fuse*, Eshleman calls this exit from animality the separation continuum: it is an endless fall into separated consciousness, out of unity with the earth. The origin of consciousness is the birth of autonomous imagination: a breakthrough born of fracture, separation, from absence, presence. This is the culminating vision – and argument – of *Juniper Fuse*, undoubtedly Eshleman's single most important work, the vision of an absence that gives birth to presence, of a hole that grows. He explicates: "The hole that grows – in a way that is simultaneously transitive and intransitive – may be one of the most fundamental versions of the logos, or story, of the soul which, according to Heraclitus, grows according to its needs – as does, according to the shamans, the World Tree. [...] It is a hole grounded in both absence and appearance, a convexcavatious abyss."[101] The convexcavatious abyss: a vision of primary duality, wherein opposition dissolves into unity. To be at home in symbolical consciousness, in poetic imagination, is to accept the abyss as the substance of the self, to accept loss as the condition of identity. As Eshleman writes in *Juniper Fuse:* "Pure loss pours through. I'm home."[102]

The purpose of Eshleman's mature poetry has been to plunge into this abyss, to explore it, again and again, to confront and conduct the zero. As he puts it: "the prophet's task is / to conduct the savagery of the grass, / to register the zeros rising from circuits of the dead."[103] The abyss of imagination is distinct from its apotheosis in rational knowledge. Though knowledge may be derived from it, the flat and stable register of rational discursive knowledge stands apart, *after* poetic imagination. "To look without understanding. E.M. Cioran writes that this is paradise. / To be penetrated by the observed which enters one and goes through one – without one."[104] For the poet in the abyss, I is an other, a passage through which life travels. This is fundamental to the human condition: "The human is indeterminate, initially unclosed," Eshleman observes.[105] And again: "you are closed and open / in the multiple ambivalence of your fracture / and no resolution is sincere."[106] No resolution is sincere in part because all resolution is provisional. All poetry is provisional as well, it is the work of consciousness in process, part of the separation continuum.

If there must be clarity,
let it be opaque, let the word be
convexcavatious, deep
with distance, a clear
and dense mosaic, desiring
undermining.[107]

A compelling pun emerges from the convexcavatious abyss: Eshleman's art of the hole is also an art of the whole, an art participating in what Robert Duncan called the symposium of the whole in "Rites of Participation," one section of *The H.D. Book* that he published in *Caterpillar.*[108] Eshleman offers this explanation: "Over the years, initially stimulated by Vallejo, I

50

had developed an affinity for a poetry that went for the whole, a poetry that attempted to become responsible for all the poet knows about himself and his world. I saw Vallejo, Arthur Rimbaud, Antonin Artaud, Aimé Césaire, and Vladimir Holan as examples of these poetics. All inducted and ordered materials from the subconscious as well as from those untoward regions of human experience that defy rational explanation. Instead of conducting the orchestra of the living, they were conducting the orchestra's pit."[109] And again, with a more political inflection: "The key lesson Vallejo holds today may be that of a poet learning how to become imprisoned, as it were, in global life as a whole, and in each moment in particular."[110] Poetry in this description is an attempt to embrace and acknowledge – to take responsibility for – the whole of the world, its terrors and its delights. This kind of poetry conceives of emancipation as indistinct from a kind of imprisonment, from an acknowledgement that the self can never be entirely free of the other, understanding the word other in the widest possible sense, as in the symposium of the whole.

Eshleman does not pretend to be alone in his pursuit of this kind of poetry. He is explicit on this point: "I am sure that I am not alone in believing during the late 1960s that an American poetry based in international modernism, and signaled by Don Allen's 'the new American poetry' but not restricted to his perimeter, might become the dominant poetry of the 1970s – in other words that a world-aware, responsible avant-garde might overcome and peripheralize decades of dominant official verse culture."[111] This belief was developed in the poetries Eshleman translated and central to the communities constellated around *Caterpillar* and *Sulfur*. It was common to a major trend in international letters, whose practitioners sought to renew and revivify the role of the poet in society. "Through the efforts of such multiply-based writers as Ezra Pound, Antonin Artaud, and Charles Olson, the image of the poet has been densified and removed from the academic-literary niche that has come to mean that the poet was merely a clever manipulator of his own sensitivity rather than a man or woman of knowledge."[112] Nevertheless, as familiar as this image of the poet may have been in the modern and late modern eras, it has not become dominant or even common in our own.

A poetry like this – world-aware, responsible, dense – is difficult. It requires a life commitment. And this life commitment is a commitment of life to something more than poetry. It is a commitment to life itself. "The poet must always believe that there are a few things a hell of a lot more important than poetry. If he does not, he makes literature and serves what Jack Spicer called 'The English Department of the Spirit.' The most important thing in the world for a man to do is to alleviate suffering and the most important thing for him to be, ecologically speaking, is a grape in the cluster of his species."[113] The push here, Eshleman's push, is through poetry and poetic consciousness but ultimately beyond it. The terms are those of the avant-garde tradition in aesthetic activism. As Eshleman put it in *The Sanjo Bridge:* "Art wants to change the world. Art wants to destroy what all men feel are the limits of this world."[114] Thirty years later, in *My Devotion,* he affirmed a similarly ambitious goal: "I dream of poems that could change something essential / about the way a few people view creation…"[115] It is undoubtedly obvious that not all poets share this same dream, nor is every poet cut out for or fortunate enough to pursue it. Eshleman sees two primary alternatives to the kind of poetry envisioned in his dream: writing intended as easy entertainment, on the one hand, and what he derisively calls "creative writing," on the other.

In conversation with James Hillman, Eshleman describes what he believes is their shared purpose: "We both seek to lift the essential up through the consumer film and work with it in imagination without vatic inflation."[116] "Vatic inflation" is a vacuous – as well as undoubtedly self-important and inaccurate – oracular approach to imagination. "Consumer film" is popular art that aspires to nothing more than mere entertainment and, as Eshleman says somewhat flatly in the same conversation, "The serious poet is not entertaining."[117] The statement might be regarded as an over-generalized remark – after all, Eshleman's own poetry can often be very funny – but the purport of the remark rings true.

Eshleman's condemnation of creative writing programs is perhaps less easily accessible. Put bluntly, in his view, creative writing programs diffuse and deaden the art. "The degree writing programs," he writes, "are in the process of turning the art of poetry into creative writing."[118] More broadly, taking stock, he observes: "The democratization of poetry must be evaluated in light of some three hundred undergraduate and graduate university degree programs offering majors in writing poetry and fiction. This system is now producing thousands of talented but unoriginal writers, most of whom would not be writing at all if it were not for jobs."[119] And elsewhere: "By creating a 'poet-professor' middle class, the writing programs have played into the hands of poetry's traditional enemies: education and entertainment."[120] Entertainment is the enemy of imagination because, however clever it may be, it is the equivalent of junk food for the soul. Education is the enemy of imagination because education is too often replication: the teacher replicating him or herself through his or her students. Education rarely breeches the boundaries of the known; rather it aims to reinforce them. This is not the place to fully detail Eshleman's critique of the curricula of creative writing programs in our times. One quick point of distinction might however be drawn. As I hope I have shown, Eshleman's life in letters has exemplified a commitment to ceaseless, wide-ranging exploration and encounter: with other places, other people, other poetries – foreign and familiar –, other modes of thought and image. By contrast, rather than reaching beyond the barriers of the known, contemporary creative writing programs typically find their focus in student writing produced for a given class and work-shopped in it. Sharing Eshleman's dim view, poet and critic Jed Rasula neatly summed up the results: conformism, careerism, anti-intellectualism.[121] If Eshleman is a deeply informed, *historical* poet, a poet writing in a tradition that *includes* history, creative writing programs evidence something like the end of history. Indeed, in our time, following the research of Eshleman and others, we have recovered the roots of imagination in the Paleolithic painted caves and carved objects but we are also perhaps witness to the all but final strangulation of poetic imagination in academic writing programs. As Eshleman says, "our distinction may become that of being the first generation to have lived at a time in which the origins and the end of poetry become discernable."[122] Looking hopefully ahead, however, Eshleman provides detailed advice to young poets in *Novices* but he also observes elsewhere, if poetry and poetic consciousness is to continue to thrive, let alone to deepen and advance, poets will have to avail themselves of resources beyond the bounds of poetry. He writes: "Poetry, as a psychological art, is still in its infancy, and young writers who seek to create great poems […] would be better off with texts by Bakhtin, Ferenczi, and Hillman, or camped along the Amazon as their workshop, rather than sitting around Argus-eyed, sharpening their defenses in creative writing wards."[123]

But it would be to betray our subject to end on this note. Another passage from Northrop Frye that Eshleman quotes in *Juniper Fuse* is relevant here: "Poetic thinking, being mythical, does not distinguish or create antithesis: it goes on and on, linking analogy to analogy, identity to identity, and containing, without trying to refute, all oppositions and objections. This means, not that it is merely facile or liquid thinking without form, but that it is the dialectic of love: it treats whatever it encounters as an-other form of itself."[124] The dialectic of love here is psychoanalytical, born of the unity of opposites – eros and thanatos – life and death – creation and destruction. Love here is what Norman O. Brown described in his book *Love's Body* as symbolical consciousness, and as poetry. "The antimo-ny between mind and body, word and deed, speech and silence, overcome. Everything is only a metaphor, there is only poetry."[125] In Eshleman's terms, from *Indiana*: "If love means anything/ it means everything"[126] Or again, more recently, from *My Devotion,* an endless promise: "In spite of everything, I love you, and I love the earth."[127] That is Eshleman's life commitment, his commitment to life.

Notes

1   *Archaic Design* 2.
2   *Conductors of the Pit* (2005) 238.
3   Charles Olson, "Letter 2," *The Maximus Poems* (Berkeley: University of California Press, 1983) 9.
4   Charles Olson, "The Kingfishers" *The Collected Poems of Charles Olson* (Berkeley: University of California Press, 1987) 92.
5   Ezra Pound, *Guide to Kulchur* (New York: New Directions, 1970) 7.
6   *Under World Arrest* 11.
7   *Archaic Design* 48.
8   *An Alchemist With One Eye On Fire* 1.
9   *Fracture* 9.
10 *On Mules Sent From Chavin* 8.
11 *Antiphonal Swing* 33.
12 *Juniper Fuse* 81.
13 *Fracture* 10-11; revised version in *Juniper Fuse* 45.
14 "Novices" in *Companion Spider* 8; quoted in *Juniper Fuse* 49.
15 *Juniper Fuse* 44.
16 *On Mules Sent From Chavin* 11.
17 *The Gull Wall* 64.
18 *Reciprocal Distillations* 25.
19 *Juniper Fuse* 13.
20 *Companion Spider* 286.
21 *What She Means* 63.
22 See *The Jointure* 27.
23 *Reciprocal Distillations* 69.

24 See "Visions of the Fathers of Lascaux" *Juniper Fuse* 58. For Lorca's remark in context, see Richard Burgin, *Conversations with Jorge Luis Borges* (New York: Holt, Rhinehart, & Winston, 1968) 93.

25 *Archaic Design* 31.

26 *Companion Spider* 284.

27 *Reciprocal Distillations* 70.

28 On poetic apprenticeship see *Novices* in *Companion Spider*.

29 *Companion Spider* 79.

30 *Archaic Design* 3.

31 *Archaic Design* 32.

32 Charles Olson, "The Kingfishers," *The Collected Poems of Charles Olson* 86.

33 *What She Means* 9.

34 *Juniper Fuse* 16.

35 *Juniper Fuse* 143.

36 *An Alchemist With One Eye On Fire* 6.

37 *Antiphonal Swing* 192.

38 Norman O. Brown, *Love's Body* (New York: Random House, 1966) 81-82.

39 William Blake, *Milton*, plate 30, lines 1–3.

40 The image is reproduced on the cover of *The Jointure* and discussed therein on page 9.

41 See *The Gull Wall*.

42 *Antiphonal Swing* 31.

43 *Archaic Design* 37.

44 *Archaic Design* 37.   ,

45 *Antiphonal Swing* xi.

46 *Antiphonal Swing* xi.

47 *Juniper Fuse* 253-54; see also *Antiphonal Swing* xii.

48 *Juniper Fuse* 254.

49 *Juniper Fuse* xii; See Charles Olson, "A Bibliography on America for Ed Dorn," in *Collected Prose* (Berkeley: University of California Press, 1997) 306-7.

50 *Juniper Fuse* xii.

51 Charles Olson, *The Maximus Poems* 104-5.

52 Charles Olson, *The Maximus Poems* 249.

53 *Juniper Fuse* xxiii.

54 *The Price of Experience* 315.

55 This quotation appears in the notes for Eshleman's forthcoming volume of collected poems, currently in draft form.

56 *Companion Spider* 58.

57 *Archaic Design* 72.

58 See *Juniper Fuse* xv-xvi.

59 *Companion Spider* 74.

60 For "Notes on a Visit to Le Tuc d'Audoubert" see *Juniper Fuse* 68–73; for "Our Journey Around the Drowned City of Is" see *The Price of Experience* 87–121.

[61] The writings I have in mind as "journals" include: *The Book of Eternal Death* (written in Korea, 1962, revised in Bloomington, 1964, published in *Double Room #7* (2007) [online]), *On Mules Sent From Chavin* (written in Peru, 1965, revised and published in 1976), *Our Journey Around the Drowned City of Is* (written in France, 1985, published in *The Price of Experience*), and *Leningrad Journal* (written in Russia, 1989, published in *Archaic Design*). A few long poems written under the influence of LSD might also qualify as "journals": "The Moistinsplendor" (written in 1967, published in *The Price of Experience*), "The Yellow River Record" (written in 1969, published as *The Yellow River Record*).

[62] Adrienne Rich, "Forward" to *Companion Spider* ix.

[63] See *The Price of Experience* 324.

[64] *Conductors of the Pit* (2005) 229.

[65] *Archaic Design* 4.

[66] *Archaic Design* 29.

[67] *Antiphonal Swing* 230.

[68] *The Price of Experience* 349.

[69] *The Price of Experience* 349.

[70] See *On Mules Sent From Chavin* 12, 18.

[71] *Antiphonal Swing* 59.

[72] *Antiphonal Swing* 60.

[73] *Antiphonal Swing* 61.

[74] *Antiphonal Swing* 68.

[75] For two documentary histories of this moment see Elliot Anderson and Mary Kinzie, ed. *The Little Magazine in American* (Yonkers: The Pushcart Press, 1978) and Steven Clay and Rodney Phillips, ed. *A Secret Location on the Lower East Side* (New York: Granary Books, 1998).

[76] See *Sulfur* #24 (1989) 4-6; and *Companion Spider* 270.

[77] *Companion Spider* 277.

[78] *Companion Spider* 274.

[79] See *Conductors of the Pit* (2005) xv.

[80] *The Price of Experience* 349.

[81] *An Alchemist With One Eye On Fire* 6.

[82] *Fracture* 16.

[83] Northrop Frye quoted on *Altars* 109-10. See Northrop Frye, *Fearful Symmetry: A Study of William Blake* (Princeton: Princeton University Press, 1969) 279.

[84] Salmen Lewental. See *Amidst a Nightmare of Crime: Manuscripts of Members of Sonderkommandos,* ed. Jadwiga Bezwinska and Danuta Czech (New York: H. Fertig, 1992) 147.

[85] *Under World Arrest* 11.

[86] "The Loaded Sleeve of Hades" *Fracture* 35.

[87] *An Alchemist With One Eye on Fire* 5.

[88] *Archaic Design* 27.

[89] *Juniper Fuse* 93.

[90] *Juniper Fuse* 91.

[91] *Indiana* 36.

[92] *On Mules Sent From Chavin* 48–49. Written in October-November 1965, the journal from which this statement comes was revised in April-May 1976 and this passage in particular includes language and ideas that reflect formulations of ideas Eshleman encountered after 1965 – Reichian thought and therapy, Bakhtin's interpretation of the grotesque, etc.

[93] *Juniper Fuse* 92.

[94] *Coils* 147.

[95] *Juniper Fuse* 76.

[96] *Juniper Fuse* 82.

[97] *Juniper Fuse* 26.

[98] See *Companion Spider* 5; for the Olson quote in context, see Charles Olson, *Letters for Origin* (New York: Paragon House, 1970) 119-120.

[99] *Juniper Fuse* 50.

[100] *The Jointure* 23.

[101] *Juniper Fuse* 236.

[102] *Juniper Fuse* 100.

[103] *Juniper Fuse* 67.

[104] *The Jointure* 23

[105] *Juniper Fuse* 167.

[106] *Juniper Fuse* 52.

[107] *Juniper Fuse* 19.

[108] See Robert Duncan, *The H.D. Book* (Berkeley: University of California Press, 2011) 154.

[109] *Archaic Design* 23.

[110] *Archaic Design* 28.

[111] *Companion Spider* 275.

[112] *Companion Spider* 4.

[113] *Antiphonal Swing* 10.

[114] *The Sanjo Bridge* n.p.

[115] *My Devotion* 49.

[116] *Antiphonal Swing* 213.

[117] *Antiphonal Swing* 213.

[118] "Wound Interrogation" in *Penetralia*, forthcoming.

[119] *An Alchemist With One Eye On Fire* 3.

[120] *Companion Spider* 276.

[121] Jed Rasula, *Syncopations: The Stress of Innovation in Contemporary American Poetry* (Tuscaloosa, Alabama: University of Alabama Press, 2004) 9.

[122] *An Alchemist With One Eye On Fire* 7.

[123] "Response to Mary Kinzie," *Sulfur* 13 (1985); reprinted in *Antiphonal Swing* 203.

124   Northrop Frye quoted in *Juniper Fuse* xxi-xxii. See Northrop Frye, *A Study of English Romanticism* (Chicago: University of Chicago Press, 1968) 121-122.

125   Norman O. Brown, *Love's Body* 266.

126   *Indiana* 102.

127   *My Devotion* 50.

1935
Born in Indianapolis, Indiana, on June 1, 10:50 AM, son of Ira Clayton Eshleman (1895–1971) and Gladys Maine (Spenser) Eshleman (1898–1970). Ira Eshleman is employed at Kingan and Company, a slaughterhouse and meat-packer, as a time-and-motion study efficiency engineer. On her deathbed, Gladys Eshleman will tell her son: "the most important thing in my life has been to be your mother." The family lives in the 1800 block of North Delaware Street.

As a child the poet is forbidden from playing with children of different races or religions, with children whose parents drink alcohol, or whose mothers wear pants outside of the home.

1941
Family moves to 4705 Boulevard Place in Indianapolis. Begins taking piano lessons from a neighborhood piano teacher. Discovers comic strips and books. Begins drawing comic strips.

1945
Takes weekly lessons in drawing cartoons from a student at the Herron School of Art.

1949
Enters Shortridge High School. Runs track, wrestles, plays right end on the football team. Works as a lifeguard at The Rivera Club in the summer.

1951
Discovers jazz. Attends "Jazz at the Philharmonic" concerts. Buys records by Bud Powell and Lennie Tristano through the mail. Begins hanging out in jazz clubs and other bars. Invited to "sit in" with Wes Montgomery at The Surf Club one Saturday afternoon. He later writes that Montgomery was "the first great artist with whom I had personal contact." Continues to play classical music.

1952

Sells vacuum cleaners as a summer job. (See "The Answer Man" in *The Price of Experience*.)

1953

Graduates from Shortridge High School. Enters Indiana University as a music major in the fall. Studies with Ozan Marsh but does not devote himself to his studies. Pledges to the Phi Delta Theta fraternity.

1954

Spring. Eshleman's music professor, Ozan Marsh, encourages him to "do something else with [his] life."

Summer. Drawn by the West Coast jazz scene, travels to Los Angeles with a friend, John Fish. Parks cars at Systems Auto Park, studies jazz piano with Marty Paitch and Richie Powell (Bud Powell's younger brother).

Fall. Returns to Indiana University. Following his father's suggestion, he changes his major from music to business. Initiated into fraternity, causing enduring psychological trauma.

1956

Academic probation for low grades. Expelled from school for having too many parking tickets. Moves out of fraternity house. Works as clerk in Block's department store in Bloomington.

1957

Re-enters Indiana University as philosophy major. Discovers poetry through classes in creative writing and 20th century American poetry with Samuel Yellin and Josephine Piercy. Friendship with Jack and Ruth Hirschman who introduce him to world poetry in translation: Federico Garcia Lorca, Vladimir Mayakofsky, Rainer Maria Rilke, and St.-John Perse. Mary Ellen Solt provides introductions to Louis Zukofksy, Robert Creeley, and Cid Corman, and puts him in touch with Paul Blackburn, Robert Kelly, Jerome Rothenberg, Jackson Mac Low, and David Antin. Travels by car to New York City.

1958
Graduates Indiana University, B.A. (philosophy). Re-enrolls as graduate student in English literature. Numerous car trips to New York City.
Bill Paden gives Eshleman a copy of Dudley Fitts, ed. *Anthology of
Contemporary Latin American Poetry* (New Directions, 1947), which includes poems by Pablo Neruda and César Vallejo. Neruda's *Residencias*
of particular interest. Publishes his first poem in student magazine *Folio*.

1959
Edits three issues of *Folio* (1959–1960). Gives first poetry reading in
Hirschman organized Babel series, reading a translation of St. John
Perse. Through Paul Blackburn meets William Carlos Williams, Allen
Ginsberg, and Denise Levertov. Earns living as a pianist in the bar at
the Dandale Steakhouse on weekends. Hitchhikes to Mexico City in the
summer where he begins to teach himself Spanish in order to read Neruda
and Vallejo. Works as assistant bartender in Acapulco hotel.

1960
First reading of his own poetry organized by Paul Blackburn in New York
City at Metro Café. Begins reading Hart Crane in earnest. Second summer trip to Mexico, in Etzatlán and Chapala. Rents room from American
ex-butcher named Jimmy George. Translates Neruda's *Residencias* with
help from Jimmy's young mestizo wife. Gets hepatitis and returns to
United States on third class bus.

1961
Student teaching at Shortridge High School. Graduates Indiana University
with Master of Arts in Teaching (creative writing). Correspondence with
William Carlos Williams and Robert Creeley.

June 17 Marries Barbara Novak.

Takes job teaching English for the University of Maryland, College
Park, Far-Eastern Division (Japan, Taiwan, Korea). Over the next year,
teaches literature and composition to military personnel for two months
in Tainan, Taiwan, four months at Tachikawa Air Force Base, outside of

Tokyo, and two months at the Strategic Air Command (SAC) Base in Seoul, Korea. Journal of the two months in Seoul published as *The Book of Eternal Death* in *Double Room* #7 (online).

Meets Cid Corman in San Francisco while on route to Asia. Hosts Gary Snyder and Joanne Kyger at home in Musashu-Koganei, outside Tokyo, when they are en route to India.

1962
Spring. Following a suggestion from Gary Snyder, moves to Kyoto to teach English as a second language at Matsushita Electric Corporation in Kobe, where he and Barbara will remain until 1964.

Begins self-described apprenticeship to poetry by translating César Vallejo's *Poemas humanos*. Forms close friendships with lithographer Will Petersen, Gary Snyder, and Cid Corman, with whom he discusses translation and watches edit much of *Origin* series 2. Correspondence with Paul Blackburn, Thomas Merton, W.S. Merwin, Jerome Rothenberg, and Robert Kelly. Begins "The Tsuruginomiya Regeneration" (a 350 page sequence of poems ultimately reworked as *Coils*).

In October, begins working outside under a persimmon tree inhabited by a large red, green and yellow spider. Several weeks later the spider disappears. Shortly thereafter Eshleman has a visionary experience involving a spider that he interprets as a confirming totemic gift.

Publishes *Mexico and North* and his translation of Pablo Neruda, *Residence on Earth*.

1963
Continues translating Vallejo daily at the Yorunomado ("Night window") coffee shop. Studies William Blake, Northrop Frye's book on Blake, *Fearful Symmetry*, the *I Ching*, and world mythology, through Joseph Campbell's *The Masks of God*.

Sees Chaim Soutine's painting *Hanging Duck* in Ohara Museum of Art, Kurashiki, Japan, which has a profound affect.

1964

Returns to Bloomington, via Los Angeles. Translates an anthology of Latin American poetry on a grant from the Organization of American States in Washington D.C. (unpublished). Barbara works in the university bookstore. Completes third draft of translation of *Poemas Humanos*.

1965

Spring. Takes LSD for the first time with Daphne Marlatt. Discovers French wine and cheese through Denis Kelly.

August. With Barbara several months pregnant, the Eshlemans move to the Miraflores section of Lima, Peru, hoping to see César Vallejo's draft manuscripts for the *Poemas humanos*, possessed by his widow, Georgette.

Hired by the North American Peruvian Institute to start a bilingual literary magazine, which he calls *Quena* (referring to the traditional one hole Quechuan flute). Intellectuals in Lima assume he is a spy working for the United States government.

Political conscience awakened for the first time by wandering through the slum areas of Lima. Visits the Andes on two occasions.

Publishes *The Chavin Illumination* in Lima.

Georgette Vallejo denies Eshleman access to César Vallejo's manuscripts.

1966

February. Matthew Craig Eshleman born in Peru. Due to complications, Barbara nearly bleeds to death several days later. Completes eighth draft of Vallejo translation with the help of Maureen Ahern.

300 page first issue of *Quena* is suppressed by the North American Peruvian Institute, citing the political nature of its contents. Eshleman quits.

The Eshlemans return to Bloomington. While in Bloomington, Eshleman and Denis Kelly publish their co-translation of Aimé Césaire, *State of the Union* as Caterpillar book 1.

The Eshlemans move New York City where they spend the summer in Paul Blackburn's apartment and then decide to separate. Clayton moves into a condemned basement room at 10 Bank Street. Barbara and Matthew move into an apartment at 18th Street and 2nd Avenue.

Meets Pablo Neruda, has several dinners and reads with him at the 92nd Street Y. Friendships with Frank Samperi and Diane Wakoski and romance with Adrienne Winograd.

Begins teaching at the American Language Institute at New York University. Barbara also teaches there.

Begins publishing Caterpillar Books, through fall 1967. Publishes books by Cid Corman, Paul Blackburn, Frank Sampari, David Antin, D. Alexander, Robert Vas Dias, Jackson Mac Low, and himself.

Publishes *Lachrymae Mateo: Three Poems for Christmas, 1966*.

1967
Moves into Joanne Kyger's old loft at 36 Greene Street. Friendships with Nora Jaffe, Leon Golub, Nancy Spero. Through Nora Jaffe meets Adrienne Rich.

Founds and edits *Caterpillar* magazine, published quarterly through 1970, periodically thereafter, through 1973. 20 issues. Fales Library, NYU, begins to purchase the magazine archive.

Consultant to board of directors, Coordinating Council of Literary Magazines, through 1970.

Receives National Translation Center award for translation of *Poemas Humanos*.

Publishes *Walks*, *The Crocus Bud*, and César Vallejo, *Seven Poems*.

Relationship with Marie Benoit, an actress indoctrinated in Scientology, from fall 1967 through July 1968.

Begins Reichian therapy with Dr. Sidney Handelman.

1968
Organizer and weekly participant in "Angry Arts" protesting the American invasion of Vietnam. Arrested and jailed for demonstration at St. Patrick's Cathedral.

Friendships with Carolee Schneeman, James Tenney, Michael Heller, Hugh Seidman.

Introduced to John Martin, editor of Black Sparrow Press, by Diane Wakoski.

Readings with Robert Bly, Robert Duncan, Allen Ginsberg, Ed Sanders and others in Milwaukee and Seattle to raise money for draft resisters.

Organizes "Three Penny Poetry Reading" with Andrei Voznesensky in New York City.

Wins *Poetry* magazine award for "Five Poems" (see *Poetry* 3:2 (November 1967) 76–81).

Receives coordinating Council of Literary Magazines grant for *Caterpillar* (renewed in 1969 and 1970).

National Translation Center grant for *Caterpillar*.

Publishes *Brother Stones* (a special, limited-edition Caterpillar book, with woodcuts by William Paden), *Cantaloups and Splendour* (his first book with Black Sparrow Press), César Vallejo, *Human Poems* (Grove Press), and *Caterpillar* nos. 2–5.

Meets Caryl Reiter on New Year's Eve 1968 and begins to live with her the following summer.

1969
Quits teaching at NYU. Lives on readings, royalties, grants, and the sale of correspondence to Fales Library, NYU.

Completes Reichian therapy.

Visits John Martin in Los Angeles while raising funds for *Caterpillar*.

Participates in the Poets in the Schools Program in New York.

National Translation Center grant for *Caterpillar*.

Publishes *The House of Okumura, T'ai, A Pitch-blende, The House of Ibuki, The Yellow River Record, Indiana*, his first full–length major collection with Black Sparrow Press, and *Caterpillar* nos. 6–9.

1970
Death of Gladys Eshleman, the poet's mother.

Moves with Caryl to Sherman Oaks, California, in the San Fernando Valley.

Joins founding faculty of the School of Critical Studies at the California Institute of the Arts in Valencia.

Friendships with Stan Brakhage, Robin Blaser, John and Barbara Martin.

Publishes *Caterpillar* nos. 10–13.

1971
Teaches seminars on William Blake, Wilhelm Reich, T.S. Eliot, and Hart Crane at Cal Arts. Directs reading series, inviting Theodore Enslin, Kenneth Rexroth, and Cid Corman, among others.

Close friendship with Robert Kelly, who was then teaching at California Institute of Technology.

Death of Ira Clayton Eshleman, the poet's father.

Publishes *Altars, Bearings, The Wand, A Caterpillar Anthology*, and *Caterpillar* nos. 14–17.

1972

Teaches privately in Sherman Oaks. Participates in the Poets in the Schools Program in Los Angeles, where he meets Joyce Vinje.

Friendships with Oreste Pucciani, José Rubia and Eva Barcia.

Begins translating Vallejo's *España, aparta de mí este cáliz* with José Rubia Barcia, which leads to a re-translation of *Human Poems*.

Begins translating Antonin Artaud.

Denis Kelly gives Eshleman Mikhail Bakhtin's *Rabelais and His World*, which has a formative impact. Bakhtin's influence helps Eshleman re-shape "The Tsuruginomiya Regeneration" manuscript into *Coils*.

Publishes *The Sanjo Bridge* and *Caterpillar* nos. 18 and 19.

1973

Publishes *Coils, Human Wedding, The Last Judgment: For Caryl Her Thirty-first Birthday, for the End of Her Pain*, and *Caterpillar* 20, the last issue of the magazine.

Biographical note on *Coils* states Eshleman is writing a prose journal work called *Heaven-Bands* (1968–1973). This 300 page manuscript remains unpublished.

Summer. Moves to France for one year. Teaches American poetry at the American College in Paris. Sublets an apartment in Montmartre from Alberto Cavalcanti.

Meets Peter Blegvad, Jacques Roubaud, Jean Daive, and Claude Royet Journaud.

Continues to co-translate Vallejo with José Rubia Barcia via correspondence.

Caryl begins to work with Clayton in the editing of his poetry.

1974

Spring. Convinced by translator Helen Lane to visit the Dordogne region before returning to the United States, the Eshlemans rent a furnished apartment in the Bouyssou farm complex near Tursac, where Lane also lives. Eshleman makes repeated visits to the painted and engraved caves of that area. Visits Lascaux for the first time. Decides to undertake an extended investigation of what he will ultimately call the "Upper Paleolithic Imagination and the Construction of the Underworld."

Visitors while in France include Matthew Eshleman, Jayne Reiter, George Herms, Margaret Nielsen, and Peter Blegvad.

Fall. Returns to Los Angeles. Lives with John and Barbara Martin in west Los Angeles for several months before renting a duplex at 852 South Bedford St. where he and Caryl will live until summer 1986.

Works as a "reader" for the University of California Press.

Begins teaching in the extension program of the University of California at Los Angeles.

Publishes *Aux Morts, Realignment* (illustrated by Nora Jaffe), Antonin Artaud, *Letter to André Breton*, César Vallejo, *Spain, Take This Cup from Me* (co-translated with José Rubia Barcia).

1975

Teaches privately in Los Angeles.

Publishes *Portrait of Francis Bacon* and, with Black Sparrow, *The Gull Wall* and Antonin Artaud, *To Have Done with the Judgment of God*, co-translated with Norman Glass.

Wins Fels nonfiction award.

1976

Lectures on American Literature at "The Summer Seminar" in Frenstat, Czechoslovakia, by invitation of the State Department. Meets Jan Benda who helps him find the reclusive poet Vladimir Holan in Prague.

Returns to the Bouyssou farm in the Dordogne for one month. Revisits Lascaux and other caves including Font-de-Gaume, Combarelles, and Niaux. With the support of rock art expert Jean Clottes, is given permission to visit the privately owned caves of Garges, Marsoulas, Le Portel, Le Tuc d'Audoubert, and Les Trois Frères.

Reads James Hillman's *The Dream and the Underworld*, which has a formative effect on his cave investigation.

Teaches part time at University of California Los Angeles.

Publishes *The Woman Who Saw through Paradise*, *Cogollo*, and Antonin Artaud, *Artaud the Momo*.

Begins correspondence with Eliot Weinberger.

1977
"Artist in the Community" teaching fellowship through California Arts Council at Manual Arts High School in Los Angeles.

Begins translating Aimé Césaire with Annette Smith.

Translates Milan Exner with Jan Benda via correspondence.

Wins PEN Translation Prize and a Carnegie Author's Fund award.

Publishes *The Name Encanyoned River*, *Grotesca*, *On Mules Sent from Chavin: A Journal and Poems*, *The Gospel of Celine Arnauld* and *Core Meander*.

1978
Guggenheim Fellowship in poetry for research on Upper Paleolithic cave art permits the Eshlemans to spend several months in southwestern France.

Spends one month in Germany under auspices of Visiting Author Program administered by the American Embassy in Bonn, Germany.

First of three meetings with Aimé Césaire in Paris.

Friendships with Michel Deguy, Herbert and Margarit Graf, Karl and Gabrielle Möckl, Marwan and Karin Kassabachi.

Publishes *What She Means*, César Vallejo, *Battles in Spain: Five Unpublished Poems*, and César Vallejo, *The Complete Posthumous Poetry*, the last two co-translated with José Rubia Barcia.

1979
Shares National Book Award in Translation with José Rubia Barcia for César Vallejo, *The Complete Posthumous Poetry*.

National Endowment for the Arts Poetry Fellowship funds another trip to France and Spain.

Visits the Prado Museum in Madrid, fascinated in particular by Hieronymus Bosch's *Garden of Earthly Delights*.

Appointed Dreyfuss Poet-in-Residence and lecturer in creative writing at California Institute of Technology, Pasadena, through 1984.

Teaches part-time as visiting lecturer in creative writing at various branches of University of California, including San Diego, Riverside, Los Angeles, and Santa Barbara, through 1986.

Begins writing book reviews for *Los Angeles Times*. Over the next five years publishes over 50 book reviews therein.

Publishes *A Note on Apprenticeship*.

1980
Receives National Endowment for the Humanities Summer Stipend for research on Upper Paleolithic cave painting.

Hospitalized for one week following car accident outside of Les Eyzies in the Dordogne (see *Fracture*).

Spends a second month in Germany through the Visiting Author Program administered by the American Embassy in Bonn.

Visiting lecturer in Creative Writing at University of California San Diego and University of California-Riverside.

Publishes *Nights We Put the Rock Together*, *The Lich Gate*, and *Our Lady of the Three-Pronged Devil*.

1981
Organizes and with Caryl leads small tour of Ice Age-decorated caves in southwestern France. Interviews several chefs during the tour for an article commissioned by *Frequent Flyer* magazine, which ultimately does not publish the piece. The chefs include Maximin at Hotel Negresco in Nice, Louiseau at the Côte d'Or in Saulieu, Gardillou at the Moulin du Roc near Champagnac-de-Belair, Chabran at the Pont de l'Isère, and Mazère at Hotel Centenaire.

Friendships with Leland Hickman, Bob Peters, Bernard Bador, and Koki Iwamoto.

Receives National Endowment for the Humanities Translation Fellowship for work on Aimé Césaire.

Wins Witter Bynner award from the Poetry Society of America for work on Césaire, with Annette Smith.

Founds and edits *Sulfur* magazine at Cal-Tech; 46 issues – 11,000 pages of material – through spring 2000.

Publishes *Foetus Graffiti*, *Hades in Manganese*, and Aimé Césaire, *Some African Poems in English*.

Hades in Manganese is finalist for *Los Angeles Times* Book Award.

1982
Visits the Dordogne. Develops friendship over the next several years with Jacques and Christiane Leyssales, owners of the Hotel Cro-Magnon in Les Eyzies, Dordogne.

Begins publishing travel writing co-written with Caryl Eshleman in magazines and newspapers. Over the next few years publishes travel writing in *Destinations, Diversions, The Chicago Tribune, Frequent Flyer,* and *Pan Am Clipper.*

Publishes Antonin Artaud, *Four Texts,* co-translated with Norman Glass, and *Sulfur* nos. 2–5.

1983
Organizes and leads another tour of Ice Age-decorated caves in southwestern France.

Friendships with Arthur Secunda, Antonet O'Toole, Joanne Leedom and Peter Ackerman.

Serves as member of the National Endowment for the Art's Literary Magazine Panel and Policy. Co-edits monthly poetry column for *Los Angeles Weekly,* "Ill Fate and Abundant Wine," through 1984.

Sulfur receives partial funding by the National Endowment for the Arts, which continues through 1996.

Publishes *Visions of the Fathers of Lascaux, Fracture,* Aimé Césaire, *The Collected Poetry,* co-translated with Annette Smith, and *Sulfur* nos. 6–8.

1984
Third visit to Lascaux.

Co-translates Vladimir Holan's "A Night with Hamlet" with Frantisek Galan and Michael Heim.

Member of the California Arts Council literature panel.

Director of Poets-in-Residence Program at UCLA. Lectures on poets who are invited to campus to read, followed by dinner and discussion with the class and the poet at the home of MacDonald Carey in Benedict Canyon. Among the invited poets are August Kleinzahler, Theodore Enslin, Lauren Shakely, and C.K. Williams.

Sulfur sponsored by UCLA Extension Writers Program.

Publishes Michel Deguy, *Given Giving: Selected Poems* and *Sulfur* nos. 9–11.

1985
Spends three weeks touring megaliths near Carnac in Brittany.

Correspondence with James Hillman, Clark Coolidge, Michael Palmer, Rachel Blau DuPlessis.

Attends seminar on psychology and alchemy by James Hillman. Notes taken during this weekend seminar form the basis of *Novices: A Study in Poetic Apprenticeship* (1989).

Interview with Hungarian poet and translator Gyula Kodolanyi.

Visiting Lecturer in Creative Writing at University of California – Santa Barbara.

University of California – Santa Barbara Archive for New Poetry acquires Eshleman's personal archive (1970–1985) and the archive for *Sulfur* (1–12).

Publishes Antonin Artaud, *Chanson*, co-tranlsated by A. James Arnold, with drawings by Nancy Spero, and *Sulfur* nos. 12–14.

1986
Soros Foundation travel grant funds one-month trip to Hungary. While staying with Gyula and Maria Kodolanyi in Budapest, translates a small anthology of contemporary Hungarian poetry with Gyula Kodolanyi, published in *Sulfur* 22.

Moves to Ypsilanti, Michigan to become professor in the English Department at Eastern Michigan University. Teaching Introduction of Literature: Poetry and poetry workshops.

Directs dramatic readings of Artaud's *To Have Done With the Judgment of God* in Kerrytown Concert House, Ann Arbor, Michigan.

Writes *Novices* (published in 1989).

Publishes *The Name Encanyoned River: Selected Poems 1960–1985*, Bernard Bador, *Sea Urchin Harakiri*, Aimé Césaire, *Lost Body*, co-translated with Annette Smith, and *Sulfur* nos. 15–17.

1987
Visits the Dordogne during the summer, again staying at the Hotel Cro-Magnon.

Returns to Brittany, France, touring Neolithic stones, dolmens, and menhirs.

Cooper Fellow, Swarthmore College.

Poet-in-residence, Cranbrook Institute Writers Conference.

Board member of CLMP.

Temblor magazine publishes special section "Six Writers on Eshleman" with contributions by Paul Christensen, Rachel Blau DuPlessis, Jed Rasula, James Hillman, Gerald Burns, and Karen Lessing.

Publishes Paul Blackburn, *The Parallel Voyages*, co-edited with Edith Jarolim, and *Sulfur* nos. 18–20.

1988
Shares National Endowment for the Arts Translation Fellowship with Annette Smith for Aimé Césaire.

Organizes and participates in *Sulfur Live: A National Symposium on Poetry and Poetics* at Eastern Michigan University.

Meets Susan Howe and Arkadii Dragomoshchenko.

Arkadii Dragomoshchenko invites Eshleman to international conference in Leningrad (see "Leningrad Journal" in *Archaic Design*).

Michigan Arts Council, Summer Writer's Grant.

Participates in International Poetry Festival, Barcelona, Spain. Visits the architecture of Antonio Gaudi.

Publishes *Conductors of the Pit: Major Works by Rimbaud, Vallejo, Césaire, Artaud, Holan* and *Sulfur* nos. 21–22.

1989
Visits the Dordogne during the summer, again staying at the Hotel Cro-Magnon.

Fall. Visiting scholar in Hispanic studies at Brown University. Co-translates a draft of César Vallejo's *Trilce* with Julio Ortega.

Publishes *Mistress Spirit*, *Hotel Cro-Magnon*, *Antiphonal Swing: Selected Prose, 1962–1987* (edited by Caryl Eshleman, introduction by Paul Christensen), *Novices: A Study of Poetic Apprenticeship*, and *Sulfur* nos. 23–25.

Receives Distinguished Faculty Research/Creativity Award, Eastern Michigan University.

1990
Publishes Aimé Césaire, *Lyric & Narrative Poetry, 1946–1982*, co-translated with Annette Smith, and *Sulfur* nos. 26–27.

1992
Academic Specialist grant from USIA Mexican Translation Project. Travels to Mexico for ten days, giving four lectures.

Receives Michigan Artists award from Arts Foundation of Michigan.

Editorial fellowship, Council of Literary Magazines and Presses, for *Sulfur*.

Summer faculty member at Naropa Institute.

Poet-in-residence at University of Arizona's Poetry Center.

Five-day residence at Simon Fraser University's Institute for the Humanities.

Fall. During sabbatical leave from Eastern Michigan University, rents a house in Les Eyzies to begin organizing the outline of what will become *Juniper Fuse*.

Publishes César Vallejo, *Trilce*, and *Sulfur* nos. 28–30.

1993
Participates in Aimé Césaire tribute reading at Florida State University.

Conducts seminar on Upper Paleolithic cave art for Shaman Drum Bookstore in Ann Arbor, MI.

Publishes *Sulfur* nos. 31 and 32. (Eliot Weinberger guest edited *Sulfur* 33.)

1994
Readings at Rochester University, University of Notre Dame, Indiana University, SUNY-Albany, and University of Oklahoma.

Five-day residence at Poets & Writers, Rochester, NY.

Publishes *Under World Arrest* and *Sulfur* nos. 34–36.

1995
Readings at SUNY-Buffalo, Butler University, Indianapolis, and at the Recovery of the Public World conference, Simon Fraser University, Vancouver.

Publishes Antonin Artaud, *Watchfiends and Rack Screams: Works from the Final Period*, co-translated with Bernard Bador, and *Sulfur* nos. 37–38.

1996

Sponsored by the Eastern Michigan University School of Continuing Education, organizes and leads another tour of Ice Age-decorated caves in southwestern France. Gary Snyder accompanies the tour as a guest lecturer.

Three-day residencies at Naropa Institute and Wichita State University.

Lectures on and readings of Artaud at University of Colorado, Boulder, the Poets House, NYC, the Drawing Center, NYC, and at MOMA, where Artaud's drawings were exhibited as part of a centenary conference. (See "Spectator, Spectre, Sitter" in *Archaic Design*.)

Bilingual presentation of poetry at Maison des Ecrivans, Paris, France.

Publishes *Nora's Roar* and *Sulfur* no. 39.

1997

Visits Lascaux, spends a half hour studying the scene in the Shaft. Realizes that his 23 year investigation of the painted caves in complete.

Participates in the Festival Franco-anglais de poésie, Paris.

Receives Eastern Michigan University Graduate School research grant.

Publishes *Sulfur* nos. 40–41.

1998

Publishes *The Aranea Constellation*, *From Scratch*, *Hades en manganese*, translated intro French by Jean-Paul Auxemery, and *Sulfur* nos. 42–43.

1999

Writer-in-residence, Tennessee State University.

Receives Eastern Michigan University Graduate School research grant.

Participates in Ecrivains présent conference, University of Poitiers, Poitiers, France.

Fall. Visits Céret, France, where Chaim Soutine painted his early break-through work.

2000
Receives honorary Doctorate in Literature from the State University of New York Oneonta.

Summer. Leads tour of Ice Age-decorated caves in France sponsored by Continuing Studies and Special Programs at The Ringling School of Art and Design in Sarasota, Florida.

Featured performer, Bumbershoot Arts Festival, Seattle.

Participates in the Associated Writing Program Conference in New Orleans, LA.

Summer faculty member at the Naropa Institute.

Publishes a revised second edition of César Vallejo, *Trilce*; two chapbooks, *Erratics* and *A Cosmogonic Collage: Sections I, II, & V;* and the final issue of *Sulfur* magazine.

Wins Landon Translation Prize, Academy of American Poets, for *Trilce*.

2001
Continuing Studies and Special Programs at The Ringling School of Art and Design in Sarasota, Florida, sponsors another tour of Ice Age-decorated caves in France.

Publishes a revised second edition of Aimé Césaire, *Notebook of a Return to the Native Land*, co-translated with Annette Smith.

Writer-in-residence at Dalhousie University, in Halifax, Nova Scotia, and at State University of New York-Oneonta.

Seminar lecturer on translation and writing ekphrastic poetry for the Poetry Society of America.

2002

Continuing Studies and Special Programs at The Ringling School of Art and Design in Sarasota, Florida, sponsors another tour of Ice Age-decorated caves in France.

Publishes chapbook, *Sweetheart, Bands of Blackness*, a boxed limited edition collection, in English, French and Japanese, and, major new collection of selected prose, *Companion Spider*.

Receives Eastern Michigan University Graduate School research grant to visit Valleta, Malta, to study Caravaggio's "The Beheading of St. John the Baptist."

Wins Alfonse X. Sabio Award for Excellent in Literary Translation, San Diego State University

Residencies, readings, and presentations at Macalester College, Wichita State University; the University of Maine-Orono, Lakewood (Ohio) Public Library, San Diego State University, University of Louisiana-Monroe; Writers and Books Literary Center, Rochester, NY; SUNY-Albany; and a poetry conference at the Bibliothèque Nationale de France.

2003

Publishes *Juniper Fuse: Upper Paleolithic Imagination & the Construction of the Underworld*, the precipitate of twenty-five years of research and writing. Also publishes a chapbook, *Everwhat*.

Becomes Emeritus Professor of English at Eastern Michigan University.

Residencies at the Poets House, Donegal, Ireland, and the University of Georgia, Athens.

Presents programs on *Juniper Fuse* at Poets House, NYC; University of Texas, Austin, TX; the Kelsey Archeology Museum, University of Michigan, Ann Arbor; the University of New Mexico, Las Cruces; the University of Idaho, Boise; Emory University, Atlanta; UC-Santa Cruz, San Francisco State University, Cody's Bookstore, Berkeley, CA., and California State University at Sacramento.

Programs on César Vallejo at New York University; the University of Texas, Austin; and El Paso Community College, El Paso, Texas.

Interview with Michael Silverblatt, The Bookworm, Santa Monica, CA.

2004
January. Visits Chauvet cave with Jean-Marie Chauvet and James O'Hern.

Spring. Poet-in-Residence, Columbia College, Chicago.

Continuing Studies and Special Programs at The Ringling School of Art and Design in Sarasota, Florida, sponsors another tour of Ice Age-decorated caves in France. Robert Creeley accompanies tour as guest lecturer.

Presents programs on *Juniper Fuse* at UC-Santa Barbara; Bard College; Middlebury College, VT; Wesleyan University, Middletown, CT; Columbia College, Chicago; University of Illinois, Chicago, and the Chicago Art Institute.

Programs and translation workshops on Aimé Césaire at Beyond Baroque, Venice, CA, and Columbia College, Chicago.

Additional readings at the Latin American House, Paris, and a poetry conference at the Bibliothèque Nationale de France.

October 22. By invitation of Robert Creeley, presents lecture "Notes on Charles Olson and the Archaic" for the Special Collection Library at SUNY-Buffalo. (See *Archaic Design*.)

November. One-month residency at the Rockefeller Study Center at Bellagio, Italy, studying Hieronymus Bosch's *Garden of Earthly Delights*. Begins "Tavern of the Scarlet Bagpipe" (see *Anticline*).

Publishes *My Devotion*.

2005

Publishes *Conductors of the Pit: Poetry Written in Extremis in Translation*, a substantially revised second edition of selected translations originally published in 1988.

Conducts a translation workshop and a program on the life and work of Cid Corman at the Poets House, NYC.

Participates in the Memorial Program for Leon Golub, at Cooper Union, NYC.

Poetry reading at The Poetry Project, NYC.

Program on César Vallejo, Rutgers University, NJ.

Lecture and reading at Pennsylvania University, Philadelphia.

Lecture programs on *Conductors of the Pit* and Cesar Vallejo at Wichita State University, Kansas.

2006

Continuing Studies and Special Programs at The Ringling School of Art and Design in Sarasota, Florida, sponsors another tour of Ice Age-decorated caves in France. Dale Pendell accompanies the tour as guest lecturer.

Publishes *An Alchemist with One Eye on Fire*.

Programs on César Vallejo and Eshleman's own poetry at Texas A&M.

Participates on translation panel, SUNY-Albany.

Weekend seminar on *Juniper Fuse*, Vallejo and Eshleman's own poetry, SUNY-Oneonta.

Program on *Juniper Fuse* at Nantucket Atheneum.

Readings of Eshleman's own poetry at Commonwealth Books, Brandeis University, Lame Duck Books, in Boston.

Lecture on Vallejo at Boston University.

Program on *Juniper Fuse* at MIT.

Vallejo programs at Princeton University, Johns Hopkins University, and Woodland Pattern, Milwaukee.

Program on *Juniper Fuse* at the University of Wisconsin, Milwaukee.

2007
Continuing Studies and Special Programs at The Ringling School of Art and Design in Sarasota, Florida, sponsors another tour of Ice Age-decorated caves in France. Wade Davis accompanies the tour as a guest lecturer.

Publishes *Reciprocal Distillations*, a collection of poetry, *Archaic Design*, a collection of prose, and two limited edition collaborations with artists, *Deep Thermal*, with Mary Heebner, and *A Shade of Paden*, with Bill Paden.

Publishes César Vallejo, *The Complete Poetry: A Bilingual Edition*, the culmination of forty-five years of translation and research.

Lectures and readings on César Vallejo at The University of Chicago, Michigan University, the Library of Congress, Boise State University, Washington University (Seattle), Reed College, Oregon University (Eugene), UC-Berkeley, San Francisco University, Mills College (Oakland), UC-Santa Barbara, Notre Dame University, Minnesota University, Macalester College (St. Paul), Carleton College (Northfield MN), University College London (England), the Cervantes Institute (London), the Borough of Manhattan Community College, NYC, Poetry Project, NYC.

Readings of Eshleman's own poetry at Eastern Michigan University, Open Books (Seattle), Powells Bookstore (Portland), Tsunami Books (Eugene), Diesel Bookstore (Malibu).

Lecture and reading of translations of Antonin Artaud at California College of the Arts.

An international symposium on the poetry of César Vallejo, based on the Eshleman's translations, is convened at UCLA where Eshleman is Regents Lecturer in the Spanish Department.

2008
January – March. Visiting Professor in the Spanish Department, UCLA, teaching a seminar on the translation of poetry.

Continuing Studies and Special Programs at The Ringling School of Art and Design in Sarasota, Florida, sponsors another tour of Ice Age-decorated caves in France.

Lectures on and readings of his own poetry, cave painting, César Vallejo, and Aimé Césaire at Turtle Bay Exploration Park, Redding CA; the Hammer Museum, Los Angeles; University of California, Irvine; Stanford University, and San Francisco State University.

Friendships with Mark Polizzotti, John Olson, Andrew Joron, John Wronoski, Joe Phillips, Sarah Fox, and Jose Antonio Mazzotti.

Wins Landon Translation Prize, Academy of American Poets, for *The Complete Poetry of César Vallejo*; the book was also on the International Short-List for The Griffin Poetry Prize.

Publishes *The Grindstone of Rapport: A Clayton Eshleman Reader*.

2009
Reading at the Poetry Project, NYC.

June 28–July 5 Residency at Naropa.

July 2 Reading for Counterpath Press in Denver.

July 12 Reading on radio program hosted by Joe Milford.

2010
October 19 Reading at Tufts University.

October 20 Reading at Pierre Menard Gallery in Cambridge.

Publishes *Anticline*, an extended collection of original poetry, two bilingual, limited edition illustrated books, *Hashigakari* and *Eternity at Domme / The French Notebooks*, a revised edition of his translations of Bernard Bador's poetry, *Curdled Skulls: Selected Poems*, and a chapbook of poems by Bei Dao, *Daydream,* co-translated with Lucas Klein.

2011
Publishes a small collection of poetry and prose, *An Anatomy of the Night*, and two translations, Bei Dao, *Endure*, co-translated with Lucas Klein, and Aimé Césaire, *Solar Throat Slashed: The Unexpurgated 1948 Edition*, co-translated with A. James Arnold.

Readings and programs of his own poetry and Aimé Césaire at America's Society (NYC), the Poetry Project (NYC), Wesleyan University, UC Berkeley, St. Mary's College, California College of the Arts, San Francisco State University, St. Luis Obispo Poetry Festival, UC Santa Barbara, Beyond Baroque Books (Venice, CA), Loyola Marymount, UC San Diego, and Cal State-San Marcos.

2012
April 26–27 Conference on Latin American Poetry at Texas A&M. Reads Vallejo and his own poetry.

September 20 Program on *Juniper Fuse* at Carnegie-Mellon University in Pittsburgh.

October 4 Césaire program on *Solar Throat Slashed* at Tufts University.

October 25 Césaire program on *Solar Throat Slashed* at University of Michigan.

November 23 Radio interview with Joe Milford.

Publishes *The Jointure.*

2013

Publishes an extended collection of prose, *The Price of Experience,* and Aimé Césaire, *The Original 1939 Notebook of a Return to a Native Land: Bilingual edition,* co-translated with A. James Arnold.

January 24 Reading from *The Price of Experience* at Nicola's Books in Ann Arbor, MI.

April 4–6 Participates in Aimé Césaire conference at Wesleyan University, reading a paper on *Lost Body* and doing a program with co-translator A. James Arnold on the original 1939 *Notebook of a Return to the Native Land.*

May 30 Program on Césaire, *The Original 1939 Notebook of a Return to the Native Land* at Nicola's Books in Ann Arbor, MI.

Clayton Eshleman lives in Ypsilanti, Michigan with his wife Caryl.

Eliot Weinberger

The Spider and the Caterpillar

In a recent survey, 90% of American high school students stated that they do not believe in the existence of the future. What was once a philosophical proposition, an aesthetic obsession, has filtered down to become, for the children of the millennium, a reigning truth. Nothing is certain; the sun may not rise tomorrow.

At the moment of doubt, worlds open up, and each fresh report from those strange worlds leads to further doubt. This has been the century of the invention of the unconscious (personal and collective), of anthropology, paleontology, of science fiction and scientific cosmological speculation: the creation of thousands of other worlds, terrestrial and extraterrestrial, apparent to the eye of a traveler or beyond the reach of the telescope, buried in the earth, hidden within an unsuspecting mind. It has been the century where physical science and mathematics are built on fundamental contradiction, where the increasingly precise observation and description of the natural sciences leads only to essential inexplicability.

At the moment of doubt, possibilities become limitless – all of them equally impossible. For poetry, the end of certainty has meant, first, that the poem can no longer be a discrete object, the "poem itself," for behind every poem there is another poem (written or unwritten) that contradicts it, and behind that, another poem. The poem is a becoming, not a being; and the poem, breaking out of its isolation, can no longer be contained by the traditional forms. There is no closure: the poem is only a passage leading to another.

Second, it has meant that the poem must be open to everything, and moreover, that everything must come into the poem. Most of the best American poets of the century have demanded the admission of that which was previously excluded: history, economics, found objects, colloquial speech, the works of the Machine Age, the unbeautiful, scientific vocabulary, frank autobiography, the whole body, non-human species, idiosyncratic prosodies, icons of mass culture, pictographs, glossolalia, the life of the ghetto.

Third, there has been an impatience with isolated subject matter, the Grecian urn or its homely complement, the red wheelbarrow. For in the century of uncertainty, of mass man and the bombardment of images, one can see the world in a grain of sand only if one simultaneously sees the thousands of undressed oiled bodies baking on the beach, the web of their social interactions, the raw sewage pumped into the sea and the contaminated lives of marine animals, the kiosks with their pink bunnies and rubber ducks, the thumping transistors and careening frisbies, the bumper-to-bumper traffic snaking along the coast. A macrocosm without microcosm: in the poem all ages are contemporaneous, all events synchronous, each thing is itself and the metaphor of something else. (Metaphor: to move from one place to another. In Greece the moving vans are labeled METAPHORA.)

Fourth, it has meant a criticism of (and despair over) the inadequacy of language: a sense that the poem has lost the language that speaks it, that the poet must either wrestle the language back to (a temporary) meaning or surrender to meaninglessness, perhaps even revel in meaninglessness.

And yet, despite the hopelessness of existing words and forms, the infinity of pressing subject matter and structural possibilities, the poem has retained its ancient identity as an image of wholeness – or more exactly, an image toward wholeness. The 20th century poet is a maker of intricate and beautiful shards who dreams of the golden bowl: not the poem that is, or was, but the poem that should be.

It is a dream that has provoked, among the best poets, a journey. A journey whose path – as there may be no future ahead – can lead only in one direction: back, toward the origins. An uncovering of the past as it lies within, not a nostalgic return. A psychoanalysis of the self and of the species, that the mouth of the snake will finally finds its tail, the poem end, and this cycle of history close.

It is of course a mythic and impossible quest. Tragically, it has often led to easy answers: the submission to higher orders (the Church, Eastern or Western; the state religions of Communism and Fascism) or lesser orders (elites, literary movements, reversions to a perceived "tradition"). Often it has led to disorder: the little neuroses, the madnesses and suicides.

An extraordinary poet on this track – and one who has managed to remain resolutely himself – is Clayton Eshleman. No other American poet has gone deeper into human history, personal history, and the body itself. Few have invented, as Eshleman has done, the language to carry him.

A few biographical facts cue the poems:

Ira Clayton Eshleman, Jr., born in Indianapolis, Indiana in 1935, the only child of Gladys and Ira Clayton Eshleman. It was a Middle American childhood as imagined by a West German filmmaker: his father, deacon of the church and efficiency expert at a slaughterhouse; his mother, the meticulous housewife who forbade her son to play with children who were not Protestant and white, whose parents smoked or drank, whose mothers wore slacks. The boy himself is described by the man as "Charlie McCarthy": a well-scrubbed, well-groomed wooden dummy.

The piano became his first window onto a world outside of Indiana. The boy started playing at age seven, gave it up in adolescence to be a jock, then, at 16, discovered bebop: it was the making of a 1950s "White Negro." He entered Indiana University in 1953 as a music major, but switched to business as he became immersed in the world of the Phi Delta Theta fraternity, with its torturers and victims (Actives and Pledges), its Caligulan rites of Hell Week, its saturation bombing of the opposite sex.

In 1957, having bounced in and out of school, he stumbled into poetry, and within a year much of the rest of his life had fallen into place. He edited the university literary magazine, *Folio*, and was in touch with Zukofsky, Creeley, Corman, Duncan, Olson; in New York he met many of the best poets of his generation, all still in their twenties: Rothenberg, Antin, Kelly, Wakoski, Schwerner, Economou, and, of particular importance, the slightly older Paul Blackburn. He hitchhiked to Mexico – his first experience of the rest of the world – and, in the course of bumming around, happened upon a book of César Vallejo's poetry. A year later he was in Mexico again, translating Neruda's *Residence on Earth*. These aspects of the life – Blackburn and Vallejo, magazine editorship, translation, literary friendship, travel to the other worlds – would continue to be central to the work.

He married Barbara Novak in 1961, spent a year in Taiwan, Korea, and Tokyo, and two years in Kyoto, teaching English. He returned to Indiana for one last year, and then in 1965 he and Barbara moved to Lima, Peru, where he continued his work on Vallejo and edited an ill-fated bilingual magazine, *Quena*, which was officially sponsored and suppressed for political reasons before the first issue was published. In 1966, his only son Matthew was born, and they returned to the U.S. to live in New York.

The couple soon separated, and Eshleman was deep into the 1960s: the antiwar movement, Reichian therapy, hallucinogens. Affairs with

89

two women, Marie and Adrienne, enter the poetry. In 1967, he founded *Caterpillar*, the major American poetry magazine of the time, which
gathered together most of the then-living masters, the young poets of
Eshleman's generation, a range of translation from Akutagawa to Artaud,
and kindred spirits like Norman O. Brown, Leon Golub and Stan
Brakhage.

In 1969 he met Caryl Reiter, his second wife, and in 1970 they moved
to Los Angeles, where they lived until the mid-1980s. Both his parents
died the same year. *Caterpillar* ended in 1973, to be reborn eight years later
– the fourth incarnation of the Magazine – as *Sulfur*. In 1974, Eshleman
began his continuing study of the Paleolithic caves of France and Spain.
In 1978, after nearly 20 years of work, his translations of Vallejo's *Complete
Posthumous Poetry* was published. Translations of Artaud, Vladimir Holan,
Michel Deguy, and the complete poetry of Aimé Césaire have followed
since.

An outline of the life is helpful, for the poetry is full of autobiographical
specifics, and the progression of Eshleman's major books has closely followed the course of the life: from the first book, *Mexico & North* (1962)
and its early views of the Third World; to *Indiana* (1964), the poet's childhood and early manhood; *Altars* (1971), an artifact of the 1960's; *Coils*
(1973), the synthesis of the earlier books and Eshleman's final coming-
to-terms with Indiana; *The Gull Wall* (1975) which breaks out of autobiography to center on Paul Blackburn and a series of personae "portraits";
What She Means (1978), an exploration of woman, as incarnated by Caryl
Eshleman; and most recently to *Hades in Manganese* (1981) and, his best
book, *Fracture* (1983), the poet's descent into the Paleolithic.

It is a poetry that sees the life of the mind, and the meandering path of
the work, as a series of imaginative confrontations with the "other" – other
humans, other species, the historical other, the geographical other, the
personal other. Encounters without resolution: each an act of a continually revised self-definition, as the Indiana Eshleman – the mid-century
Middle American, middle class, white Protestant heterosexual male – sets
out to wander in a world that denies every Indiana assumption.

The other humans along this path form a quaternity: the Parents (Ira
Clayton & Gladys Eshleman), the Woman/Wife (Caryl Eshleman), the
Master (César Vallejo), and the Friend (Paul Blackburn). These are at-
tended by hosts of angels and demons: spirits of creation – Artaud, Van

Gogh, Frida Kahlo, Bill Evans, Max Beckmann, Bud Powell, Francis Bacon, among others – and forces of destruction – murderers, torturers, psychopaths. (And typical of Eshleman's work – where each thing flips to its other side – the creative spirits are often victims of self-destruction, the destroyers inadvertent makers of the poem.) Without these others, the I would be the soundless tree falling in the forest; each is a figure of struggle and love, each a mask to be assumed in the stations of the poet's simultaneous dismantling and invention of the ego.

(Here a word should be said of Eshleman's two other primary activities, magazine editing and translation. The magazine: not only a service to the republic and a personal map of the literary landscape, but also a small, selfless participation in the sympathetic work one has not written. As for translation: the dissolution of the translator's ego is essential if the foreign poet is to enter the language – a bad translation is the insistent voice of the translator. Eshleman, in such poems as "The Book of Yorunomado" and "The Name Encanyoned River" presents his long apprenticeship to Vallejo in terms of the lives of the Tibetan saints or of the Castaneda-Don Juan legends: the master Vallejo must break down the disciple Eshleman to come into English; the disciple's ego resists; and ultimately the disciple learns from the struggle of his own strengths, the strengths that will aid both the translation and the creation of his own poems.)

The other species are a rain forest of insects and animals, real and imagined; the poems *teem*. Yeats, in *A Vision*, writes of a man who, "seeking an image of the Absolute," fixes on the slug, for the highest and the lowest are "beyond human comprehension." Eshleman, however, in "The Death of Bill Evans," rejects interspecies apartheid to enter into slugness itself, transforming other into brother, finding an animal helpmate as guide to his meditation on the life of the jazz musician. And where many recent poets have resurrected Coyote and other indigenous trickster figures, Eshleman introduces into the poem, in a way that cannot be misconstrued as "pop," the contemporary American trickster, Donald Duck: the final image of the animal at the death of nature.

The geographical other is, in one instance, Czechoslovakia (the suffering of imagination repressed) but mainly it is the Third World: Peru, Southeast Asia, El Salvador, South Africa (the sufferings of poverty and the imperial wars). It is the Morlock-Eloi vision of Wells's *The Time Machine:* Eshleman is one of the few poets to explore, beyond facile polemic, how "Indiana" – the comfort of the American middle class – is

dependent on global misery. He has taken a classic American image –
Hawthorne's or Parkman's or Cooper's terrifying "savages" in the dark
forest, just beyond the settlement clearing; Poe's or Lovecraft's "unspeak-
able horror" in the basement of the house – and shown its obverse: we are
the cannibals who feed on *them*; our house is *built* on horror.

The invention of the historical other has become almost programmatic
in 20th century American poetry: for Pound, ancient China; for H.D.,
classical Greece; for Olson, Mesopotamia; for Snyder, the Neolithic.
Eshleman has pushed the historical back about as far as it can go: to the
Upper Paleolithic, and the earliest surviving images made by humans.
As a result of his literal and imaginative explorations of the painted and
gouged caves, Eshleman has constructed a myth, perhaps the first compelling post-Darwinian myth: that the Paleolithic represents the "crisis"
of the human "separating out" of the animal, the original birth and the
original fall of man. From that moment, human history spins out: from
the repression of the animal within to the current extinction of animals
without; the inversion from matriarchy to patriarchy, and the denial of the
feminine; the transformation of the fecund underworld into the Hell of
suffering; and the rising of Hell, in the 20th century, to the surface of the
earth: Dachau, Hiroshima. The poet's journey is the archetypal scenario of
descent and rebirth: he has travelled to the origin of humanness to reach
the millennium, end and beginning. In an early poem he had written:
"God why has it taken me 31,000 years / to stand at the threshold? / Why
has it taken 31,000 years to leave home?"

It is Eshleman's confrontation with the personal other that has proved
the most controversial. He is, surprisingly, probably the first poet even to
deal, in the poem, with the realities of infancy: not an allegorical "infant
joy," but the drooling, babbling selves that are our private Lascaux. More
noticeably to his detractors, he has admitted what he calls the "lower
body" into the poem: excrement, semen, menstrual blood. This has led the
New York Times Book Review to sniff, "He will not cooperate with taste,
judgment, aesthetic standards…" (an essay could be written on that word,
cooperate!) and an otherwise sympathetic critic to conclude that "Eshleman
is not a happy man."

Such response is a bizarre reduction of the poetry to obsessive scatol-
ogy. One of the main drifts of the century has been the literal re-embodi-
ment of the poem. Thus Williams, in "How to Write" (1936): poetry is
"the middle brain, the nerves, the glands, the very muscles and bones of

the body itself speaking." Or Olson's "Proprioception" (1962): "... that one's life is informed from and by one's own literal body"; "Violence / knives: anything to get the body in." While it is quite true that the facts of the lower body are prominent in certain Eshleman poems, it is always in context: an implied or apparent yoking with the upper body. It is the "amplitude of contradiction": face and ass, art and shit, menstrual blood and the blood of violence, each turning around and into the other in the poet's "yearning for oneness," the "challenge of wholeness."

Eshleman is the primary American practitioner of what Mikhail Bakhtin called "grotesque realism." It is an immersion in the body; not the body of the individual, the "bourgeois ego," but the body of all: the "brimming over abundance" of decay, fertility, birth, growth, death. Like the collective body, it is unfinished, exaggerated; protuberances and apertures are prominent; animals, plants, objects, the world blend into its undifferentiated and essentially joyous swirl. The mask is its primary device: not as concealer of identity, but as image of each thing becoming something else.

Grotesque realism is "contrary to the classic images of the finished, completed man" (and to the finished, completed poem), "cleansed, as it were, of all the scoriae of birth and development." And it is contrary to what Bakhtin categorizes as "Romantic grotesque": the reaction against classicism which sought to restore the grotesque not in its original celebratory function, but as the malevolent underside of sunny classicism: the opening of the Pandora box of aristocratic gloom, fear, repressed desire and longing for death, where the ordinary "suddenly becomes meaningless, dubious, and hostile."

Eshleman's critics tend to read him in terms of the Romantic grotesque, when his intent has been clearly the opposite. His grotesque is ecstatic and comic; through a systematic shedding of the oppressive weight of national identity and personal biography, he has taken the grotesque beyond Bakhtin's Medieval carnival back to its source: the grotto, the cave. And there he has sought, and partially found, what Bakhtin calls "the complete freedom that is possible only in a completely fearless world."

It is precisely Eshleman's utter fearlessness that scares people off. ("He will not cooperate...") No other American poet has laid so much of his life literally on the line. It is illuminating, for example, to read Eshleman's 1970 poem on his father, "The Bridge at the Mayan Pass" alongside such celebrated, nearly contemporary poems as Robert Lowell's "Commander Lowell," Sylvia Plath's "Daddy," Allen Ginsberg's "Kaddish." In the case of Lowell and Plath, it is difficult today to imagine what all the fuss what about. Lowell's poem on his father depends on a safe titillation – the eccentric side of a well-known family – much like his "confessional" poems, which carefully reveal a few autobiographical details shocking to polite society (Mr. Lowell takes tranquillizers, Mr. Lowell was in the bughouse) without saying much at all. Plath has a cloying "more neurotic than thou" machismo; its scandal is a "nice girl" calling her Dad a vampire and a Nazi. Ginsberg's frank autobiography, still startling to read, serves a similar, elitist "band of loonies" function: this is what has made me crazy, this is my admission ticket to the "hipsterheaded angels." Eshleman, however, never wears the proud badge of neurosis. His violent, extremely disturbing rant is intended as a sign of health: the dismantling of the father (and the father in the son) as Indiana, that which denies life. It is an act of making love on the father's freshly-dug grave.

Fearless too is Eshleman's language: dense, glucy, wildly veering from the oracular to the burlesque, strewn with neologisms and weird bits of American speech (*cruddy, weenie, chum, goo; tampax* as a verb). An Eshleman poem is unmistakable from the first glance. Image jams against image, not impressionistically, but in the service of a passionately argued line of reason, a line where an idea, before completion, turns into another idea, and then another, much like the walls of the Paleolithic caves. ("Image is cross-breeding / or the refusal to respect / the single individuated body.") The poems are nearly impossible to excerpt.

It is surprising that no published critic seems to have noticed that Eshleman is, at times, extremely funny. Where else would one find, in the same poem, Apollo, Persephone, Ariadne, and "Silk Booties & Anklets Knit Soaker & Safety Pins/ Hug-me-tight a Floating Soap Dish with Soap Rubber Doggie"? With minor (usually stoned-cute) exceptions, the idea of the comic poem has become so alien to American poetry – who today thinks of Pound as he described himself: "a minor satirist"? – that the poet runs the serious risk of appearing foolish.

It is a foolishness measured by the last vestiges of the distinction between "poetic" and "unpoetic." Wordsworth, despite his championing of the life in common things, went to elaborate lengths in one passage of *The Prelude* to avoid writing the words "tic-tac-toe" (or "naughts and crosses"). To a certain extent that reticence still holds. To bring Rubber Doggies – weird artifacts of the popular grotesque – into the poem's art aerie, to place France Bacon and Little Lulu in the same phrase, remains, in poetry at least, an act subversive to "taste, judgment, aesthetic standards." For Eshleman, Little Lulu is the lower half of Francis Bacon's body; to incorporate the two is the work of a comic wisdom.

It is a poetry and a life conceived as a "name encanyoned river" (Eshleman's turn on a Vallejo phrase): a river that springs up in the arid wilderness of Indiana and flows toward a Utopic vision of personal and global wholeness; a river that was nearly all rapids and is flanked by canyon walls. Along the way one writes, paints, leaves one's mark on the walls: both an act of testimony for the community (this is where we are) and an imaginative leap to the other side.

Eshleman's totems for the journey have been two insect spinners: the spider and the caterpillar. Both draw their art entirely from their own bodies. For one, the web: constructed with astonishing mobility, slung from branch to branch, a net almost all air, through which the world is visible beyond, in which the stuff of the world is randomly trapped. For the other, the cocoon: immobile, opaque, the prison where, in utter solitude, one effects transformation. What better allies could a poet have?

[May 1985]

This essay was first published as an introduction to Eshleman's The Name Encanyoned River: Selected *Poems, 1960–1985* (Black Sparrow Press, 1986). *It was subsequently reprinted in Eliot Weinberger,* Works on Paper *(New Directions, 1986).*

James Hillman

Behind the Iron Grillwork

How does a person outside the playground go in there without getting beaten up? You guys behind the iron grillwork are so tough and always fighting, and you push the swings and turn the merry-go-round. I can't even get on. You know all about poetry and I don't even know what I like. (I feel ashamed when I like a piece, feeling it must have been too easy.) But I do know some poets, and whom I like.

What I get from Clayton is the sincerity of power or the power of sincerity. A virtue, sincerity, that I have come to value after sitting through hours and hours of analysis. Not the confession, not the oppression in personal agony makes the 'good patient'; but the sincerity of the engagement with the material: life, dreams, symptoms, desires. Not shying away even in the midst of shyness: sincerity.

Intelligence too. But then all poets seem to me intelligent. Clayton's is the kind that takes in and sorts out. It pursues: maybe this is psychoanalytic intelligence. He is in pursuit of uncovering; ambitious, relentless tracking. And it's *him*: not the work as independent icon, or his line or rhythm and the accounts in terms of terms, language. I don't get just language from Clayton, poems about writing about poems. I get pursuit; words at work trying thought, tearing thought out of obdurate stuff. Psychoanalytic.

I suppose it is psychoanalytic in another way: the recovery of the repressed, flesh as equivalent of the repressed, flesh in its interiority always at the edge, lapsing into, emerging from, offal. What could be more Incarnational?

When he pursues depth and origins, I don't take him literally, that is, deep into literal pre-history or into literal inseminating and birthing bodies. Maybe he does, at one level. But Clayton isn't writing at one level, though it feels strongly so. (That's a special talent that his metaphors don't seem such.) I read depth and origins as the rejected and abhorred, the organic coil as an alchemical *putrefactio*, matters releasing spirits under torture, his torturing words and his being tortured by them, matters that confident bourgeois like myself throw over the shoulder without a backward glance. Clayton takes "The backward look behind the assurance / Of recorded history, the backward half-look / Over the shoulder, towards the primitive terror." (Eliot, *The Dry Salvages*, II)

Beside all this, he has invited me into the playground and come visited mine, and never beaten me up.

[22 February 1987]

This essay first appeared in Temblor 6 (1987).

Jerome Rothenberg

Three Notes

1. From *Poems for the Millennium*

Today I have set my crowbar against all I know
In a shower of soot & blood
Breaking the backbone of my mother.
        Clayton Eshleman, *Indiana*

When Clayton Eshleman came to us first there was already a force in him, a hardcore probing that would close in, later, on lost levels of our body-mind entanglements — both in each of us as individuals & in all of us as a species. That thrust in his work (his *project* as such) is summed up in the idea of a *grotesque realism*, drawn from the Russian writer Mikhail Bakhtin (in his study of Rabelais) & transformed by Eshleman into a proposal for an *American grotesque*. Of Eshleman's own practice, Eliot Weinberger has written: "It is an immersion in the [lower] body; not the body of the individual, the 'bourgeois ego,' but the body of all: the 'brimming over abundance' of decay, fertility, birth, growth, death ... unfinished, exaggerated; ... protuberances and apertures prominent." From this base in his own body, he makes the leap (circa 1974) into the equally subterranean & mysterious cave-world (French *grotte*, Italian *grotto*) of the European Paleolithic, enters it (literally) crawling "on all fours," to find in the animal beings painted on its walls a first "construction of the underworld" by "Neanderthal and Crô-Magnon men, women, and children, who made the nearly unimaginable breakthrough, over thousands of years, from no mental record to a mental record." The work is by turns "ecstatic and comic" (Weinberger) — & just as often, grim & terrifying in its assessment of the present human state. It is carried forward further by a remarkable series of translations of modern predecessors (Césaire, Vallejo, Artaud, Holan), whom he calls (as an extension of his central image) "conductors of the pit" & with whom he enters into acts of both apprenticeship & struggle. And his still larger community — both external & imagined — takes form in a range of portraits & addresses to shades & spirits of the recent (& related) dead: Wilhelm Reich, Bud Powell, Bill Evans, Chaim Soutine, Frida Kahlo, Francis Bacon, Paul Blackburn, among others. Together with his germinal & aptly titled magazines (*Caterpillar* in the 1960s, *Sulfur* through the 1990s), the work becomes — as he would have it — the model of a renewed (renewable) "construction of the underworld."

2. The Practice of Translation

Translation alongside original creation is the great conduit for bringing new language and thought into a culture. It is also, for some of us who practice it but particularly for those who practice it as poets, a way of making poetry not unrelated to our ways of making poetry in any case. It is a testimony as well to the collective nature of the poetry project and to the desire on the part of many poets, contemporary and historical, to form against all odds a kind of visionary company. All of this, for those of us who approach translation in this way, enters into an assessment of any particular translation as an example of the translator's art and practice.

In judging the submissions for the 2008 Landon Translation Award, I chose from a small wealth of poetry books in translation, any number of which could have justifiably been selected. Yet if the award is to honor the translator alongside the poet being translated, one of the books published that year stood out from the rest in ways that are difficult to emulate. In *The Complete Poetry of César Vallejo*, the poet and translator Clayton Eshleman marks the end of a nearly fifty-year encounter with the work and life of one of the truly giant figures of twentieth-century poetry. That encounter, however, is far different from the lifetime work of a devoted scholar or even of many a poet who takes to translation as a kind of secondary profession. Such work can be of the utmost importance, and yet with Eshleman something else is going on for which I can find no easy equivalent. More than any poet I know he has pursued a dangerous path for a translator, a path on which the translation itself can be wrecked, diverted at best, by too close an identification with the translated poet. Yet Eshleman evades those pitfalls, while creating a narrative of interactions with his subject that is without precedent and with a deliberate consciousness of what he's doing and why, and of how he may fail in that effort. Toward this awareness an important feature of *The Collected Poems* is his Afterword, subtitled *A Translation Memoir*. This is the account – and not for the first time – of his struggle with Vallejo, not in the usual sense of a translator working on a difficult text but in a way reminiscent of Lorca's intuition that the greatest poetry results from a struggle with the *Duende*, the more-than-muse for poetry.

The description in Eshleman's *Memoir* goes back over forty years and describes, convincingly enough, "violent and morbid fantasies" and a dreamlike struggle with "a figure who possessed a language the meaning of which I was attempting to wrest away." Of those early imaginings, he writes later: "I thought Vallejo day and night, dreamed Vallejo," and in his poem "The Name Encanyoned River" (the title taken from Vallejo): "For fifteen years you have rivered my sleep, / as if I slept under your gun, / as if my dreams took place in the pipe / you flowed through." Or again and more vividly in the *Memoir*: "Now I was having dreams in which Vallejo's corpse, wearing muddy shoes, was laid out in bed between [Eshleman's first wife] Barbara and me."

This is hard-core poetry and may currently be unfashionable, but it makes of Eshleman's Vallejo translations an action story and the work of the translator an adventure in poetry. At the same time, and more than many, Eshleman is scrupulous in his working and goes to great lengths to get Vallejo *right*. As he tells it, speaking of advice given him by Cid Corman, an older poet/mentor, whatever the relationship might be to Vallejo or other translated poets, the act of translation was not to be an act of "interpretation," a freewheeling remake of the original poem. Rather: "Corman taught me to respect the original at every point, to check everything (including words I thought I knew), to research arcane and archaic words, and to invent English words for coined words – in other words to aim for a translation that was absolutely accurate *and* up to the performance level of the original (at times, quite incompatible goals)."

Take Eshleman's translation of Vallejo's short early poem, "The Spider," a figure central to Eshleman's own imagination, and see how authentic the language is and how close to Vallejo, as if to prove that poet and poet-translator have made a (nearly) perfect fit:

It is an enormous spider that now cannot move:
a colorless spider, whose body,
a head and an abdomen, bleeds.

Today I watched it up close. With what effort
toward every side

it extended its innumerable legs.
And I have thought about its invisible eyes,
the spider's fatal pilots.

It is a spider that tremored caught
on the edge of a rock;
abdomen on one side,
head on the other.

With so many legs the poor thing, and still unable
to free itself. And on seeing it
confounded by its fix
today I have felt such sorrow for that traveler.

It is an enormous spider, impeded by
its abdomen from following its head.
And I have thought about its eyes
and about its numerous legs . . .
And I have felt such sorrow for that traveler!

The resultant translations are quite remarkable as poetry and, even with-out the accompanying narrative/memoir, give a chilling sense of Vallejo's power. Yet Eshleman, who has translated other strong poets such as Césaire, Artaud and Holan (he is by now Césaire's principal translator) is here at the height of his powers as a poet-translator. If Vallejo truly found him in a dream and led him into poetry, the response as translation more than requites it.

3. Eshleman and Goya

First a poem, after Goya's *Caprichos:*

THE SLEEP OF REASON

Words imprinted on a sign
by Goya   glowing
white against a surface

nearly white:
the sleep of reason
that produces monsters.
He is sitting on a chair
his head slumped
resting on his arms
or on the marble table,
pencil set aside,
his night coat open
thighs exposed.
All things that fly at night
fly past him.
Wings that brush an ear,
an ear concealed,
a memory beginning
in the house of sleep.
His is a world where owls
live in palm trees,
where a shadow in the sky
is like a magpie,
white & black are colors
only in the mind,
the cat you didn't murder
springs to life,
a whistle whirling in a cup,
gone & foregone,
a chasm bright with eyes.
There is a cave in Spain,
a fecal underworld,   *for Clayton Eshleman*
where bats are swarming
among bulls,
the blackness ending in a wall
his hands rub up against,
a blind man in a painted world,
amok & monstrous
banging on a rock.

In my writings over the years, the work of certain contemporaries, like that of multiple generations of forerunners, has given me a series of touch-stones against which to test my own ideas and powers as a poet. With Goya, as here, the discourse has been all imagined, fictive, with no hope for a response except, again, in the imagination. By contrast, the dialogue with Eshleman, as with other contemporaries, remains ongoing and mutual: an interchange, in this case, that has spanned more than four decades and has fueled moves on my part, and possibly on his, that would have been impossible without such interaction. In writing through Goya's *Caprichos*, I was aware at a certain point that the direction the images were taking – both Goya's and my own – was bringing me into a territory in which I felt Clayton to be my companion and fellow traveler. I was then reading his *Juniper Fuse*, and when the "fecal underworld" came into my mind and into my digression from Goya, I thought, though it wasn't Clayton's phrasing as such, that I somehow heard his voice behind it. That seemed fair enough, given Clayton's own appropriation from Bakhtin of the lower body imagery and the sense of the grotesque that became a characteristic of his mid-life writing.

I believe that Clayton, at an early point, had made the decision to be totally relentless in this direction, as Goya was in his. I prized that relentlessness and his determination to pursue a poetry that would take him to his limits – and us along with him. There is with that a singular intelligence that emerges in the way he comes at a subject, an idea or an experience, and gives it an unexpected shape and meaning. This holds for his translations as well, the desire to get under the skin of the poet whom he's translating or to let the poet come to him in dreams. He also knows, when he writes about caves and the secrets they contain, that he must first crawl through their darkness in order to bring those worlds to light. In doing that – and so much else – he has allowed us to see and touch a world beyond our means, and for that I will be forever grateful.

[The first note, largely of my writing, appeared in *Poems for the Millennium*, volume 2, co-edited by myself and Pierre Joris and published in 1998 by the University of California Press. The second note was written in the course of judging the Harold Morton Landon Translation Award for the Academy of American Poets and was originally published by the Academy in American Poets, volume 35, Fall 2008. The third note appeared in *Festschrift for Clayton Eshleman*, A Canopic Press Book in 2006. —Jerome Rothenberg]

Jed Rasula

To Moisten the Atmosphere: Notes on Clayton Eshleman

The following notes make local points about the work. My strategy was to consciously avoid being swept along in the mode of commentary, exegesis, and hermeneutic probing, because I sensed that Eshleman's poetry compels, lavalike, an inevitable duplication if one tries to stay with it, reporting on it as it goes by. Many readers, I suspect, find themselves confused by Eshleman's work. I have always found it commendably direct in laying out its motives; but the imaginal texture is congested, thick, tactile. It requires not so much reading as digestion. *Gerere*: Indo-European root providing a basis for the words CONGEST, DIGEST, INGEST, SUGGEST, REGISTER, GESTURE, and JEST. Like Walter Benjamin's unfinished *Passagenwerk* on the arcades of Baudelaire's Paris, I feel as though the process of gesturing toward, digesting, and registering Eshleman's suggestive congestions and jests is an interminable project. What follows are episodes.

*

In a 1977 article in *Boundary 2,* I identified Jack Spicer's Hades in terms of his Orphic emancipation of pronouns. The way in which *I, you, he, she, it, we,* and *they* in Spicer's book cycles get activated as phonemic particles extends not only to pronouns (spear points of identity) in Eshleman's Hades, but to quantitative sections of language as biopsy, contusion, secretion, no longer even "speech act" in the

> dear unframed minds of poets each
> clutching their pieces of hemispheric
> erection with its crocodile basis, the fear of
> drying verb, of doors whose nouns will not turn,
> of wee wee tethered kneenuts, alleyoops of traceyfire,
> of nail notwiches mouthed by Gertrude, of garbage.[1]

It is possible to read Eshleman's work in terms of its periodic swings between the manifest, embodied "garbage" (the pure menacing play of language), and its opposite, most evident in the earnest diagrammatic expositions of what such play means. This latter pole is represented by those poems that pursue such concepts as "therio-explusion" and "the separation continuum" and that are dominated by a rhetoric of the image ("Visions of the Fathers of Lascaux" and "Hades in Manganese"). The former mode, a supple embodiment of language play (not only in the ludic sense, but as in the slack of a rope, excess *give*, Derridean supplement in his account of Plato's pharmacy) is most evident throughout *Hades in Manganese*, especially in "Sound Grottos," "Dot," "Hermes Butts In," and "Silence Raving." Although *Hades* and *Fracture* overlap, both temporally and thematically, they are clearly distinguishable in terms of the former's playfulness and seriality (note the many pieces sectioned by asterisks, pauses, and punning perturbations) and of the latter's related sobriety of purpose. In the selected poems, *The Name Encanyoned River*, there is a bias for the expository retrospection of *Fracture*, but in the final section (suitably titled "Antiphonal Swing") there's a return to infant burbling, multiphasic identities rising up through the textured voicings of the poems like so much laughing gas. In "Deeds Done and Suffered by Light" a further degree of hilarious solemnity is attained when the poet's dead parents start sputtering in their adjacent coffins, trying to get Clayton Jr. (then fifty) to stop staying out late at night, while the father's "GLADYS WHAT DO YOU WANT?" percolates up through the text over and over until it blurs to "GRADDISROTDRUDRURUNT."[2]

Eshleman's *antiphonal swing* (skimmed off the final line of Hart Crane's *The Bridge* – "Whispers antiphonal in azure swing") is literally what makes the poetry work. If it's serious, it must, somehow, get silly; if it's overcome with levity, it must submit to a sobering scene of instruction. This rhetorical oscillation keeps the language in view as event and obstacle both; it sustains wife Caryl, presents Gladys and Clayton Sr., along with many others as active eruptions rather than references; and most significantly, it gives the reader a place apart, a momentary sanctuary from the poem's inevitable compulsions, because there's always another mood, another bend in the road. When the air of the explanatory sarcophagus gets stale, there is bound to be some refreshment like "Eunice Wilson, over in Plot # 52541."[3] Eshleman's is a work in which "mature transformations / intermingled with the immature," in which

Words were walls worth boring through, worth
turning into combs, words were livable

hives whose centers, or voids,
sounded the honey of emptiness dense
with the grayish yellow light nature becomes
to the soul for whom every thing is a cave[4]

The first grotto of the Eshleman grotesque is the cave of being bound
by birth to Indianapolis (which Kurt Vonnegut, as I recall, dubbed the
asshole of the universe) in a characteristically middle-American family romance, epitomized in the image of twelve-year-old Clayton stuck in the
laundry chute, chatting with his mother, who prefers this arrangement
that puts the Bakhtinian lower body out of sight.[5] The second grotto is
pledge week in Bloomington, Indiana, Tenth and Morton Streets, Phi
Delta Theta, where "What is virgin or just beginning to be experienced
/ is destroyed before it is fully there."[6] This is followed by the recupera-
tive grotesquerie of Reichian therapy, lying naked in fetal position "under
the searching eye of a clothed adult."[7] Subsequent postures in the grotto
resonate with Bud Powell sipping "lunch on all fours" in a "rudimentary
turning, crawling / chorus after chorus."[8] The informing image is Blake's
engraving of Nebuchadnezzar with clawed hands and feet, his dripping
torso breaking out in spots of animal pelt. Possibly the theme of therio-
expulsion originates here; it recurs continually in images that duplicate
Nebuchadnezzar "crawling in place on a leash" (see "Sound Grottos" and
"Tartaros" in *Hades in Manganese* for a start). In this posture, the animal
body contaminates the human, and vice versa, as the separation of one
from the other becomes a traumatic continuum. A singular fifth eidolon
of this apparition is that of the doppelganger in "The Dragon Rat Tail,"
who turns out to be Robert Kelly blurting instructions for dealing with the
parents ("Find them in the grass!"[9]). The moment that Kelly speaks here,
the terms of ventriloquial companionship stand revealed: Eshleman is in
the grotto of *The Loom*, sliding through another man's entrails, vomiting
prophetic axioms of a helpless parasitology.

*

Paul Blackburn enters Eshleman's work as the guardian angel of his own rebirth as a poet (the first birth being not as a poet, but as an Indianapolis WASP pursuing a literary career against all odds). Blackburn died in September 1971; in October, Kelly began writing *The Loom* while living in the Los Angeles area. The Kelly / Eshleman companionship during this time was integral to both men. The knot of fused intelligibility, then, is a "covering cherub" of Paul impacting Clayton and Robert into coauthors of a Nachlass, an afterbirth of his death in their own work.

Much like Pound's surgical role in extracting *The Waste Land* out of "He Do the Police in Different Voices," Eshleman's maturation as a poet can be precisely dated from his role in guiding *The Loom* through inception, revision, to final publication. *The Gull Wall* is saturated with the reward, the privilege of the transference: stirrings of a third-person narration, an enhanced clarity of first-person avowal, and the downward-spiraling, convulsive tug of the shorter line ("Realignment," "Creation," "Portrait of Francis Bacon") that tightens the focus and speeds the delivery. It's intriguing to note how much it has been Eshleman, rather than Kelly, who has delivered on the promise of *The Loom*.

Eshleman's focus as a poet is deeply indebted to others, in ways so explicit as to make a mockery of Harold Bloom's "family romance" of traumatic lineage and the psychic distress of stylistic appropriation. (On the other hand, Bloom's psychotropic model is exactly to the point with respect to Eshleman's literal family romance.) It's because of this indebtedness/ embeddedness that his immersion in Kelly's *Loom* became Eshleman's own polar maelstrom, through which the spirit of Blackburn descends, corkscrews in, and makes the rounds as if it were a cherubic physician attending the legion of damaged souls in a personal-history clinic, patching them up so Eshleman can ventriloquize his own recovery through animated puppets (for puppets, think Hans Bellmer). It sounds like a hideous process – and it is. But I would suggest that it's just this grotesque commitment, unflinchingly faced at the time, that provided Eshleman with a mountain of useful debris to burrow through. What's more, because he was so assiduously burrowing, on all fours, subjected to the intertextual harrowing of Kelly-Blackburn-Vallejo, he was in the right position to feel the full impact of Paleolithic cave art during his first exposure to it in 1974.

This particular history I toss out as a challenge to anybody who would read Eshleman's work in conventional ontogenetic fashion, seeing a slow rise to maturity followed by a plateau of "major work." Such a canon-haunted perspective can never recognize what is most frightening about *Indiana*, *Altars*, or *Coils*; this is the work of a man so desperate to become a poet that if left unguided he will ruin his own life just to have suitable material (i.e., the conventional bourgeois romance of self-destruction for art's sake). The work of the 1970s-80s is the result of honoring the guides, the *daimons*, and attending to them when they came along.

*

Imagine Blake's image of Nebuchadnezzar as a portrait of Eshleman; those pelt drips off his flank are adhesive tentacles. Having carried much of other people's writing on his back (as translator), some of it stuck and has come off in chunks. The Vallejo phrase "the name encanyoned river" – swollen with sixteen years' translation of Vallejo's work – became a dense six-page poem. The elegy for Holan in *Fracture* is uncannily given over to the Czech poet's voice (Eshleman having cotranslated his extraordinary long poem "A Night with Hamlet"). Comparable but smaller tatters of others' works and voices swirl about in eddies at the margins of poems, but they are generally submerged in the vortex. Eshleman's style is monolithic in its onward surge, so that the contributing elements glimpsed in the flood appear as bits of human flesh borne downstream after a catastrophe. The force of the flow is emblematic of the larger, overriding disaster humankind has made of the world; compulsion is not strictly individualized, and in fact the sense of personal identity is always clotted with others (like Whitman in "Song of Myself" #31: "I find I incorporate gneiss, coal, long-threaded moss, fruits, grains, esculent roots, / And am stucco'd with quadrupeds and birds all over"). At its most distressing, otherness is laminated as a mask, directly onto the face – too close to see, too restricting even to properly breathe through. "The Dragon Rat Tail" thus becomes a most peculiar flare, an *ars poetica* (*ars* rhyming in bodily *grottesca* with arse), the plasmic interiority of his poetics accidentally revealed within the poem. In the presence of this disclosed procedural turbulence, this autopoiesis, he can only be

> hideously embarrassed by
> the closeness of the thing,
> whatever it was, to my
> own organs, that I was pulling
> myself inside out, that the poem
> I sought was my own menstrual
> lining.[10]

Eshleman has not only translated, but in his choice of originals has also managed to constellate a pantheon of uncannily related figures in Césaire, Vallejo, Artaud, and Holan. The French, Spanish, and Czech texts are gnarled, full of glottal impediment, ungainly, chunky, even difficult to pronounce – which is to say, much like the English of Eshleman's own poems. It cannot be overemphasized that the material intractability of his work is intimately related to the experience of translating seemingly "untranslatable" figures. It has enabled him to forge an idiom that speaks to virtually inaccessible sensations of personal agony, and this in turn facilitates an acute registration of tortures and deprivations going on around the world, entering his work (most notably with "The Tomb of Donald Duck") as part of an ongoing texture of privacy where the public can begin to hurt in a familiar voice.

*

To read Eshleman is to encounter a claim that prohibits browsing. You can't dip in casually; his is not a poetry of easy diversions. This demand has severely curtailed an adequate public reception of Eshleman, more perhaps than that of his contemporaries. Is it because most poets offer some ready-made cue, some starter kit for generating more poems, idiomatic plugs, or electrical sockets that can be tapped into for current? It is surely the case that Eshleman's work doesn't yield itself to this kind of poaching. His poetry provokes reflection, engagement, eliciting a bodily compulsion to either keep reading or else go on to something altogether different. It's exhausting to read, because it doesn't pander to any formulaic intimacy of disclosure. Nor does it conform to vanguard models, which can also provide the reader with an escape hatch (spot the method and move on). There is no pretense that it is habitable, in its concreteness, by anybody else than its author, its survivor.

Bob Perelman's taproot to César Vallejo in "The Unruly Child" (in *To the Reader*) provides a link with Eshleman as translator and, if followed out, affords one of the few glimpses of something like an Eshleman "influence" in a younger (and nonallied) poet. Where have we seen the mode of the political grotesque of Perelman's *The First World* before?

> Let language, that sports page of being
> mystify its appearance in all speech writing thought tonight
> so that the thing, that object of burnished flirtation
> can smuggle out of the self, that drill bit[11]

> Having taken off our corsets and 19th century
> headgear, how perplexing it is, to feel media
> slipping the power out of language as one might debone
> a chicken before the remaining flesh is roasted, eaten,
> done with[12]

This is not an isolated example, but a demonstrable precedent; which is not to deny Perelman's particular skills, his unique acrobatic contortions, but to breathe a sigh of relief that somewhere, somehow, the cauterizing precisions of the Eshleman *grottesca politica* have acquired a life of their own, a functionality not indebted to the quirks of his temperament and particulars of his own life.

The *New York Times Book Review* assertion that Eshleman is a poet who "will not cooperate with taste, judgment, aesthetic standards" is possibly the most useful statement on his work to have appeared thus far.[13] What it unwittingly says is that Eshleman is not one of those who *do* cooperate in every way they can, whose work settles benignly into a workmanlike poise, a determined but subservient professionalism. These "cooperative" poets resemble the legion of German artists who carried on during the Third Reich as if all those *others* who had fled the homeland where shirkers, misfits, or degenerates. In the *Times* formulation, "taste" is the watchdog of political hegemony. In literary politics, aesthetic "standards" are to the practice of poetry what bipartisan squabbles are to politics; both are masquerades, prosthetic compensations for something missing. Eshleman's noncooperation is exemplary, a much needed sensation of alarm on the phantom limb of the body politic.

*

How can you tell whether an Eshleman poem is "uncooperative"? Take "Junk Mail," for instance; to all conventional purposes, the poem replicates a familiar model: Poet as Tourist of Self-Authenticating Experience. Like any workshop poet, Eshleman sports with the provocation, spoofs it, takes it seriously, agonizes over it, but then, flagrantly uncooperative, turns himself into both spectator and spectacle. He schizzes. The poem bifurcates, and we're left with a self-diddling creature called Me unzipping his pants on the basement floor.

> Nothing, charmed from its nickel dungeon,
> eyes this little fellow like we frat rats used to eye
> a frightened, unsure, slightly ugly, clearly needy girl.[14]

Nothing, I might add, can compare with the abrupt and utter rudeness of this change of face, the slipperiness in which the convention of a unifying perspective is abandoned and a hideously partial aspect ("we frat rats") is taken on without irony. Or if it is, it's catachresis, a "mis-use" (uncooperativeness) of image or figure by being a *full use* of it. In the fullness of the time of "Junk Mail," we frat rats are all eyeing an unsure, frightened, needy girl. The rest is up to the reader, that newfound *she*, that oasis of migratory pronouns.

*

A book by Geoffrey Harpham, *On the Grotesque: Strategies of Contradiction in Art and Literature*, usefully focuses the notion of the "grotesque" not only as a tradition, but also with application to the "grotesque realism" of Bakhtin (important to Eshleman since the early 1970s), with its riotous intrusions of the "lower body stratum" into the patrolled estate of Apollonian clarity. The following passages have immediate relevance for reading Eshleman.

(1) "[T]he grotesque, and those who indulge in it, frequently encounter a backlash that takes the form of genealogical abuse with accusations of illegitimacy, bastardy or hybridization, terms that indicate structural confusion, reproductive irregularity, or typological incoherence. *Genre, genus,* and *genitals* are linked in language as in our subconscious."[15] Not only does the *Times* critic reproach Eshleman for his uncooperative untidiness, blurring the categorical certainties of aesthetics and the well-made poem (like a well-made bed, spit-shined shoes, and a clean rifle); but also I recall a comparably wild claim by another critic who accused Eshleman of printing his own photo on the cover of the 1968 Grove Press translation of Vallejo. A patent absurdity (the visage was recognizably Vallejo's to anybody who knew), this could only happen to someone like Eshleman, whose immersion in the grotesque incites a boundary delirium in others.

(2) "These figures can best be described as images of instantaneous process, time rendered into space, narrative compressed into image."[16] Think of "Tiresias Drinking," with its image of "mouths forever frozen / at the roller coaster's summit in wild hello."[17] This poem collapses successive images of the underworld until it hits this freeze-frame greeting. In *Hades and Fracture* the continual brooding on the underworld is an attempt to spatialize the Paleolithic, make it visible now. Or to make the cave-wall images – all that *is* visible now – a potent compression of the natural history of early humans, the narration of origins disclosed in a glance (and not just any glance, but one given by the flash of a nuclear bomb).

(3) "The grotesque is a naïve experience, largely contained within the context of representational art, art in which, however temporarily and provisionally, we believe."[18] Eshleman's work is abidingly representational, but its means of representation are constantly destabilized by the matrix of the grotesque. Eshleman's pledge: to submit to the metamorphosis, but aspire to the coherence, of selfhood; to honor lover and marriage as a functional resolution of two independent identities; to accede to reasonable statement and cultivated, nurtured images as being in themselves sufficient for communication and social bonding. Such notions are not naïve; no, they are grotesque. "The Color Rake of Time" is their anthem.

(4) "[T]he grotesque consists of the manifest, visible, or unmediated presence of mythic or primitive elements in a nonmythic or modern context. It is a formula capable of nearly infinite variation, and one which, rightly understood, illuminates the entire vast field of grotesquerie."[19] Eshleman's heraldic figures, like Tiresias or Ariadne, are calculated

incubations, "unmediated" presences, because they so saturate the poems with their insistently primitive nature. They are not classical statuary, but grotesque harbingers who reach up, pawing and fingering the present, contaminating it with the glow of *grottesca* as well. The mythic elements in Eshleman are diffused, not figurally specific so much as auras of an unfocused aurora borealis of the imaginal. Despite his preoccupation with spiders (his heralds), Eshleman's is really a bovine, ruminating imagination, feeding perennially on the same turf. Maybe he sees the spiders so clearly because in the Nebuchadnezzar / Bud Powell posture they happen to be local centaurs in the bovine gaze, up to its ears in sacred nutritive filth. As Harpham says, "meaning, which must go somewhere, migrates to the low or marginal."[20]

(5) Harpham, like Eshleman, is drawn to Blake's rendering of the shaggy Nebuchadnezzar. Such emblematic figures of the grotesque "are in a state of anarchy, producing an impression of atrocious and inappropriate vitality."[21] This is a useful description of Eshleman's poems, in which all forms of life are raffishly prolific and uncontainable; the dead parents won't stay dead, the frat rats' escapades from decades ago keep staining the present with their "abortioned ooze," the daily count of animals going extinct asserts itself in the desperate cycle of food-to-fecality and the semen-menses continuum. Anything organic, in fact, if given a suitably grotesque space – a tunnel, an intestine, a cave – blurts out indelicate promptings from the deep carnal appetite, the implacable gargoyle that howls, over and over, the permeability of any hydrocardon-based form of life, gnawing at "The Seeds of Narrative":

> at 15,000 BC our torso is already
>
> a slack empty loop, a kind of lariat falling
> nowhere, at the top of which is the bird head we've
> desperately put on to stop
>
> conformity to ourselves – already we are a mask
> atop a watery loop, heartless, organless
> but not sexless for, like a gash in motion,

our penis is out, without terminal, out on brown rock
blackness-bathing, pronged up as if it could match
the uterine hunger of

Who is that hovering above this little tentacle,
this little only thing we are putting forth?[22]

Eshleman's fraternity scenes are as graphic as Robert Capa's war photos.
But as language, they are more thoroughly self-portraits than a photo can
ever be. The grotesquerie is thus comparable to the work of Diane Arbus,
all of whose compositions seem self-portraits, hideously parasitical on the
visages of others. What is most disturbing in Arbus, as in Eshleman, is the
uncanny saturation of the whole world with the specificity of personal experience and idiosyncratic taste, as though everything – every extraneous
detail, any disaster however distant, and the most abhorrent urges – were
all in the family. The outer limit of this mode might be marked by the
photos of Joel Peter Witkin, whose cadaverous tableaux raise the model of
family and kinship to an unpalatable extreme.

*

In light of its research orientation, Eshleman's is a scholarly poetry,
improbably tethered to a churning language and a "fecality that wants to
be born" (see "The Seeds of Narrative" in *Fracture*). *Fracture* and *Hades in
Manganese* contain between them two dozen pages of prose contextual-
ization. This procedure of self-exegesis then escalates: *Hotel Cro-Magnon*
(1989), *Under World Arrest* (1994), and *From Scratch* (1998) add another
sixty pages, much of it in the form of detailed notes to the poems. Such
gestures are not self-important claims to seriousness, but a manifest care
that the text be a worksite, a research center, not a performance space
where the gladiatorial poetic ego struts. A ground of seriousness is provided for the reader and at the poet's expense.

*

Many of Eshleman's poems function like sanctuaries, safe houses for
eye-witnesses on the lam, on the run, forced to change name and residence and even identity, simply to stay alive after giving testimony. But

the poems are sanctuaries also in the religious sense of the confessional. To consider the integrity of this space, this sanctuary, note how many Eshleman poems undergo a healing toward the end, a sobering up after the Bacchanal, a suturing of exposed parts. The act of closure is rarely elegant in Eshleman; this is not because (as it may seem) he is a poet of middles – which after all would be entirely appropriate to his gastronomic poetics – but because the spatial organization of a sanctuary is strict, inside is kept strictly separate from outside, and the transition is abrupt, instantaneous, like coming out of a cave. In the lines that conclude "The Loaded Sleeve of Hades,"

> you are closed and opened
> in the multiple ambivalences of your fracture,
> and no resolution is sincere.[23]

In the preface to *Hades in Manganese*, Eshleman confesses an urge to divide the book into sections, "one for poems dealing more or less directly with Paleolithic imagery and one for poems which do not. Then I realized that such a division would be against the way I try to write. I have no interest whatsoever in writing poems 'about' the caves, or even doing poems that can be identified as 'poems with the Paleolithic as the subject.' It is the present itself, with all its loop backs and dead-end meanders, that is precious to establish."[24] However, this has not kept Eshleman from aligning himself with a procedural method all too easily mistaken for the genre poem of tourism, set theme, direct treatment of the "thing itself," and so forth. Some of his most eloquent poems are textbook topical in just this way, from "Hearing Betty Carter" in *What She Means* to "Permanent Shadow" and "The Lich Gate" in *Hades in Manganese*, "Magdalenian" and "The Inn of the Empty Egg" in *Fracture* and "The Man with the Beard of Roses" in *The Name Encanyoned River*, to cite a few. Not to mention the ongoing series of "portraits," "still-life" framings, or the travel poems (location given, date attached). For a reader inclined to the Brooks and Warren or Ciardi version of the poem as self-regulating and well-behaved cultural artifact, Eshleman's work glitters with many exemplary pieces that could be lifted out of context, slapped together into a book that even *The New York Times* might find compliant with its standards of taste and judgment. Impeccably crafted and envisioned pieces such as "Ira," "The Crone," and "The Color Rake of Time" come to mind. But these are really sleights of hand within the larger panorama, which incline to process, image-based rhetoric, and an angular associative logic rooted in the "weird" chords for which bebop was legendary. I trust the tangible, marked progressions most in *Hades in Manganese*, its many poems in sections like oranges, opening out on the hinges of their asterisks concentric, sweet, segmented, partial. By contrast, a monstrosity like "Visions of the Fathers of Lascaux" abandons this formal integrity and simply gushes, on and on, almost to no purpose (or rather, for the purpose of invigorating its author's imagination – a legitimate end, if less rewarding for a reader).

*

One of the signals of a new level of rigor in Eshleman's work of the early 1970s is a commitment to personal integrity (rather than aesthetic constraint) within the poems. "The Cogollo" is a prime example. The poem sustains an acute vision of orgasm commercialized as the Big O (c.f., the self-help industry Stephen Heath exposes in *The Sexual Fix*). Eshleman's "orgasm as gargoyle" is profusely illuminated with grotesqueries, but rather than rising in summation to a final, overpowering image, there is instead an ebbing of the disturbance, the poem ending:

> love, made, keeps me living in the poem and the poem,
> to remain pregnant in birth, tumbles me out on the shore
> to illuminate, with Caryl again, antiphonal.[25]

This is not an aesthetically attractive or even cogent ending. It doesn't begin to fulfill any of the literary establishment criteria for closure. But the personal integrity it abides by is a singular model for a renewed aesthetic attention, where the old saw of the separation of life and work is broken down, overcome, cast aside. Caryl's presence here is as necessary as the many dedicatory prose notes explaining her role as auditor, mate, companion, insistent ever on "what she means."

What She Means is a terribly forthright title for a book of poetry, uniquely responsible to its ground, background, fact and act, motives and motifs. For in every book since *The Gull Wall*, Eshleman has done more than dedicate the work to his wife, Caryl (in *Under World Arrest* the concluding section of notes titled "Gratitude and Annotation"); he has pointed insistently to the work as consecration of the marriage. The nature of what is said in the text is conditioned by, seasoned by, someone besides the author. This is properly *what she means.*

As a title, *What She Means* also reflects the heredity of male poetry, exposing an unclaimed veil of companionship that is most assuredly there, but too often mystified by talk of the muse. There is much to be gained by looking beyond the traditional specter of literary continuity as a coterie of male bonding (and not only to discover the obvious neglected resource of the female writer). *What She Means* is a sure-footed contribution here, opening the male poet to an order altogether different from Phi Delta Theta. The antiphonal engagement with Caryl makes of the marriage a literary event, and makes the poet a "pledge" or initiate of something worthier than brotherhood.

*

Since the preceding notes where published in 1987, Eshleman has published three more books, big ones (another 550 pages), constituting not only a body of work, but a salutary model of what investigative poetry can be. His encounter with the Paleolithic has been sustained in ongoing visits to the Dordogne caves (the title *Hotel Cro-Magnon* honors his principle residence in the region, in Les Eyzies). The work continues to be involved with imaginative precursors, and increasingly preoccupied with painting (in the twenty-page poem "Soutine's Lapis," in *From Scratch*, Eshleman has found the perfect complement to his own imaginal contortions, resulting in one of his most enthralling pieces). It now seems clear that the studio environment of a visual artist is somehow germane to Eshleman's working habitat, and that his body of work may intimidate some because its tactility is borrowed from another medium. To read Eshleman, think Rodin (via Rilke's first-hand observations). Eshleman's aptitude at translation made a furtive leap into wholesale invention in the 1970s as he began writing and publishing poems under the name Horrah Pornoff. While I never doubted that it was his work, he always denied it. But he finally relented and included the Pornoff corpus in *Under World Arrest*. These poems have a character apart and make a convincing case for Eshleman as a partial author of heteronymy in the model of Valery Larbaud or Fernando Pessoa. His work has often been involved with masks, not in the sense of impersonation, but as a ritual gesture of the carnivalesque. (Eshleman's *hibernaculum*: squatting studiously in the excavated carcass, feasting on the glow of burning fat that provides warmth, light, and nourishment.)

The work in *Hotel Cro-Magnon*, *Under World Arrest*, and *From Scratch* is dedicated to examining (while continuing to occupy) the masks of investigative countenance. This has meant a humbling exposure to critical reflection ("'You're pigging out on underworld hooey'"[26]), which has had an enlivening effect on the work, making it more humorous and accessibly at ease. This is not to say that Eshleman's insistence on exposing himself to political horrors ("the monster composed of daily news"[27]) is compromised in any way – the very title *Under World Arrest* speaks to a decidedly fin-de-millennium condition – but the poems are less cocksure (to use a term associated with D.H. Lawrence), more open to starting *from scratch*. There is even a kind of pledge undertaken in "The Sprouting Skull": "I knew that poetry now was more a prisoner of this world / than an alternative to it – and this is why / I have drilled holes in my poems."[28]

The holes themselves are variable. The recent books pointedly include poems resembling drafts, abandoned worksheets; and their presence helps ventilate the suffocating intensity of neighboring poems. But Eshleman's self-exegesis in accompanying notes and annotations amplify the ins and outs, the conduits through which the reader is led *and* in which the reader is read. In "Postentry," Eshleman is haunted by a dream of reading to an audience concerned only with listening to themselves, which he construes at first to reflect his "inability to have the book I thought I had written."[29] The resulting vision is an extraordinary reckoning with the interface between author and reader. The encounter is charged with the mute plea reminiscent of Robert Duncan's punning remark that *responsibility* means ability to respond:

> Many in the audience had copies of things that looked like mine, a booked audience that shows up as all authors to hand to the bookless speaker volumes that appear to be his but turn out to be their own prayers. I'd call this blizzard weather, or books as flakes, a gyre in flail: who has come to hear who? Should I stand by the podium and listen to the three hundred read from books with my covers but books whose pages are more attached to the audience than to me? Plasmic pages, like loose skin pulled forth, a stomach furl gripped, held forth, and read? Why not? *Read the sun*, I once heard,

becoming a poet is the process of learning to read into, around, and through, anything. To read the moon is to imagine the moon. To imagine the moon is to speak as moon. To be a mooner! So the audience is exposing various parts of their flesh which they read hearing me, or hearing my rustling looking for my book. I read, and they hear me as themselves. Shouldn't that be an occasion of great appreciation, even joy? They experience what I read as part of their own flesh. I am the man I suffered I was *theirs*. But it doesn't work this way anymore, does it? Holding forth a leaf of skin they fail to realize that the words are not theirs, these translators, they hear me as themselves and my presence translated into their pulled-forth selves is, upon translation, simultaneously erased.[30]

Ecce homo: to read is to be read, and to be read is to undergo translation – that is dismemberment. Eshleman, among the most adept and dedicated translators, teases out the implications of his art only to find, like Orpheus before him, his head on a plate, wearing the cap of mortality. But his question remains, and remains most pertinent to readers: Shouldn't this work, this great labor, be an occasion of joy?

So the holes are consequential. In *Under World Arrest* Eshleman finally assimilates himself to an elegiac consistency. Previously, the prospect of elegy had been attenuated by obligation, hesitation, or most often by being rerouted toward the heroic insistence of self-making (writing as rescue). Here it's as though elegy arises, weirdly vigorous, from a source close to fatigue; not malaise, but a forgetfulness hatched by indifference to the distinction between poem and note, poetic line and genreless jot. One consequence is that the political shock references stand out as somehow inept (Indianapolis insisting on its Protestant indignity, oblivious to the baroque Catholic sprawl of the underworld). More moving is the sense of simple vacancy – nothing to do, nothing to say – that begins edging into the work, having no place (no set themes, no objective correlatives), but by virtue of that condition deflects the elegiac potential of the poems from headline atrocity to the less flamboyant, but no less immediate, drama of homelessness – by which I mean the dislodged condition that is the very ground of poetry for Celan, Vallejo, and others. A life in poetry constitutes itself *as* dwelling, and poetry too has to submit to its ends beyond that particular habitation.

Watch out for unity as you age,
　　it's in cahoots with reduction

Be as these rocks not deluged,
just gleamy in their lenten instant

　　　Myriad-glimmered
reason surfing the tectonics of dream,

Mallarme's "throw" still tumbling in the air,

poetry as shipwreck,　　oceanic page,
"a throw of the dice"　　the gamble of alchemical research
"will never abolish chance"　　no way
　　to predetermine reception –

Unless a work of art is its own shipwreck
a master is proposed outside the maelstrom

Surf looks more perfect than I can imagine a god,
perfection that if not seen through
　　dwarfs imagination –
seen through,　　nature *is* imagination,
roving tooth breast
　　on which I row
60 years a second[31]

*

CODA

　　Serendipitously, *Juniper Fuse* was published just as I was proofreading
this chapter. Subtitled "Upper Paleolithic Imagination & the Construction
of the Underworld," *Juniper Fuse* instantaneously infuses thirty years of
Eshleman's work with a precipitous destiny. Decades spent visiting and
revisiting caves largely in southwestern France; assimilating the archaeo-
logical scholarship; writing poems to and through the cave experience; but,

120

above all, anchoring life's work to the deepest (temporally most remote) grottos of human experience, Eshleman has wagered himself in the lines and specks on fissured walls with a sapience poised somewhere between Mallarmé's astral shipwreck and the tumbling dice of the blues. Even Wallace Stevens comes to hand with canny assurance in an epigraph: "The poetic act ... is an illumination of a surface, the movement of a self in the rock." Although undertaken with different motives than the public service role envisaged by Ed Sanders in *Investigative Poetry*, Eshleman fully realizes the potential of such investigation in *Juniper Fuse*. Inasmuch as *Juniper Fuse* includes some forty poems, most of which have appeared in earlier books, it might be misconstrued as a topical culling, a sort of "selected poems on the theme of." Given Eshleman's incessant drive to revision, they might even be seen as *new and improved* versions. But to do so would belittle the project, which is a genuine fusion of diverse modes of investigation (including, besides the poems, 130 pages of prose, 40 pages of notes, more than 60 illustrations in color and black and white, along with a detailed index, all of which transfigure the apparition of a "poetry book" altogether). *Juniper Fuse* makes an implacable claim for poetry as a necessary investigative prerogative. The shift in emphasis here is decisive: Paleolithic cave art, in *Juniper Fuse*, is clearly not a "theme" capable of generating poems, but a challenge to poems to justify their existence in the face of insuperable pressures from outside – not an easy preposition where the caves are concerned, for they involve an *inside* that's *outside* historical reckoning, possibly qualifying the poet as the most reliable technician of these (pre-) "sacred" spaces. Not for nothing does Eshleman cite Rothenberg's stance, contra Adorno, that "After Auschwitz there is only poetry."[32] Literally, or metaphorically? For Eshleman, such a choice is a smokescreen, for "to be human is to realize that one is a metaphor, and to be a metaphor is to be a grotesque (initially of the grotto)."[33] Grappling with the "grotesque archetype" concrete in rock, "this wall" that "can sustain our marks / and send them back into our bodies / vibrations of the end beginning anew in us?"[34] The question mark – like *Juniper Fuse* as a whole – is a jaw, gnawing on the future of the past, greeting us all "at the roller coaster's summit in wild hello."[35]

[1987, 2004]

Notes

1. *Hades in Manganese* 50

2. *The Name Encanyoned River* 232.

3. *The Name Encanyoned River* 232.

4. *The Name Encanyoned River* 233.

5. *The Name Encanyoned River* 231.

6. *What She Means* 63.

7. *Hades in Manganese* 107.

8. *The Name Encanyoned River* 139. This poem, "The American Sublime" in *Hades in Manganese*, was retitled "Un Poco Loco" after Bud Powell's tune in *The Name Encanyoned River*. In general I cite from the later volume because of its revisions (Eshleman is an immaculate, and fanatic, reviser).

9. *The Name Encanyoned River* 99.

10. *The Name Encanyoned River* 99.

11. Bob Perelman, *The First World* (Great Barrington, MA: Figures, 1986) 46.

12. *What She Means* 68.

13. *New York Times Book Review* (October 11, 1981).

14. *The Name Encanyoned River* 198.

15. Geoffrey Harpham, *On the Grotesque: Strategies of Contradiction in Art and Literature* (Princeton: Princeton University Press, 1982) 5.

16. Geoffrey Harpham, *On the Grotesque* 11.

17. *The Name Encanyoned River* 155.

18. Geoffrey Harpham, *On the Grotesque* 18.

19. Geoffrey Harpham, *On the Grotesque* 51.

20. Geoffrey Harpham, *On the Grotesque* 74.

21. Geoffrey Harpham, *On the Grotesque* 6.

22. *Fracture* 57-58.

23. *The Name Encanyoned River* 151.

24. *Hades in Manganese* 12.

25. *The Name Encanyoned River* 107.

26. *Hotel Cro-Magnon* 146.

27. *From Scratch* 163.

28. *Hotel Cro-Magnon* 156.

29. *From Scratch* 188.

30. *From Scratch* 188-89.

31. *From Scratch* 72-73.

32. *Juniper Fuse* xiv.

33. *Juniper Fuse* xxiv-xxv.

34. *Juniper Fuse* 148.

35. "Tiresias Drinking" quoted here from *Juniper Fuse* 67.

Pierre Joris

Over Coffee, Alone: Some Notes on reading C.E.

Over coffee, alone: often, over the laſt 40+ years have I sat thus, reading, writing & translating. Alone, but often inhabited by someone else's thoughts & words: the one I'm reading, the one I'm translating, the ones in mind even if elsewhere right now. I would thus extend the line and say: *over coffee, alone — in the company of.* Thus, this morning, as on many mornings over the years, over coffee, alone, but in the company of Clayton Eshleman, whose line that is, *over coffee, alone*, the firſt line of *The Book of Yorunomado*, though a line that appears altered at the ſtart of "Webs of Entry," the poem that opens his great book-length poem sequence *Coils*, the summa of the firſt part of his work/queſt, where it reads: *alone, over coffee.* Three words & one comma: Eshleman's care visible right here, as he shifts that tiny phrase, sounding emphasis, deciding difference matters, rewriting as he always does. No *espontaneo*, he, no quick dash into the touriſt-crowded ſtreet to swipe the flower from between the bull's horns, empty braggadocio geſture, even if elegant & crowd-pleasing. No, Eshleman is the solid worker, the careful craftsman forging his lines in a smithy of drafts, alterations, refashionings of the firſt (yes, possibly spontaneous) outpouring. Something I always ſtood in awe of & tried to learn from: his absolute care for the poem & his self-doubt re firſt ejaculations. "Firſt thought, beſt thought," (as Allen Ginsberg has it) is not for CE, who, no matter how much of the Dionysian bull he rides, will tame it with Apollonian bridle — no, not tame it, but guide it, lead it on, teach it a complex dance & have it walk ("meander") through territories, psychic & other, rarely if ever explored.

...This crude clay / ... this hand of bloodsmeared Indiana wall... The personal side of these notes needs to be made clear: I have known Clayton Eshleman since late 1969, & over the years this friendship has informed my own sense of poetry & its possibilities, as well as my praĉtice of translation. There was something deeply fascinating for me — who had juſt arrived in New York with the aim of becoming a poet in the

123

American language, if not a 100% American poet (too much Euro-dreck ßticking to my ßticks for that, probably) — in his early poetry as it delved into the heartland psyche of an Indiana boyhood. Like any young man, "self-expression," i.e. the poem exploring the "I" of the poet, was one core engine of my own apprentice work. Though back in Europe, having come to poetry via Celan, Michaux, Benn, Mallarmé, the various 20C avant-gardes, & finally the Beats & Pound, I already knew that a Bukowskian or similar display of brutalized and brutalizing ego did not make a fertile ground for a life's work in poetry, but would only lead to ever more limiting & ßtultifying repetition. Eshleman's ex-plorations of self were at another level altogether, no cocktail chatter "verse" here recounting inßtances of facile Freudian angßt to be over-come by coating them with a few glib closing lines of wit or fake wis-dom. No attempt to corset vague bourgeois feelings of inadequacy & cultural & political precariousness in the safety net of traditional poetic forms. No. Eshleman's work was a ferociously honeßt exploration of the true disaßter of white American maleness ßtunted by the reaßtionary proteßtant religiosity & cultural atrophy of Eisenhower's America. An exploration that needed to expose & explode those (Blakean) "fetters" that bind mind and body, i.e. the cultural & sexual shackles that dimin-ish human possibilities. Blake thus became central to Eshleman's own queßt or in/queßt (to use Nicole Peyrafitte's useful punning term for such a push in personal poetics & poethics). You can sum up the pro-gram of CE's queßt in Blake's lines: "To cleanse the Face of my Spirit by Self-examination, /... I come in Self-annihilation & the grandeur of Inspiration/... To caßt off the rotten rags of Memory by Inspiration, / .... To caßt aside from Poetry all that is not Inspiration." In a late piece ("Eight Fire Sources," gathered in *Archaic Design*) Eshleman sums up what Blake gave him as follows: "Reciprocity, I discovered via Blake, is the daily, human goal."

Powell compassionately extended his tongue, / licked my laid out senses. Not that the poßt-war Europe I grew up in was necessarily a more enlight-ened place, ßtuck as it was in the cultural morass that had moßt recently brought Greco-Chrißtian Euro-culture after 2000 years of firßt, reli-gious, then humanißt, then scientific & democratic "progress" to the totalitarian abyss of Nazi genocide. It was difficult to see how to ex-traßt oneself from that quagmire, though for some of my generation the wide open American space — not only its geographical space, but also its art, music & poetry — beckoned as a possible escape from those stupefying historical fetters. It was therefore exhilarating to discover how hearing jazz, Bud Powell specifically, showed a way out (there was a piano in the Eshleman house — cf. the poem "The Bison Keyboard" in *Hotel Cro-Magnon* — on which young Clayton learned to play). As he writes in "Eight Fire Sources:" "I listened to [*Tea for Two*] again and again, trying to grasp the difference between the song line and what Powell was doing to and with it. Somehow a vague idea made its way through: you don't have to play someone else's melody — you can improvise (how?), make up your own tune! wow — really? You mean I don't have to repeat my parents? I don't have to 'play their melody' for the rest of my life?" That was 1951 Indianapolis — & when I read a first Eshleman Bud Powell poem in the early seventies, it brought me right back to 1961 Ettelbrück when I discovered Charlie Parker, who also showed a way out, & led to my first piece of published writing. Jazz, that 20C cultural depth-charge, jazz as life-line, jazz as able to show, as making available another way of hearing, of experiencing, of rhythming, of imaging the world. In the lines from *The Book of Yorunomado*, "This crude clay,/... this hand of bloodsmeared Indiana wall..." I hear a pun on his first name. Rereading these lines today, they suddenly propose that the "crude" Indiana boy will begin to recede under the influence of the second syllable of the name, the "ton" as it discovers "tone," to make for a new Clayton(e) — make that a French "e muet" at the end — able to riff & improvise on complex psychic cords, while remaining deeply anchored in clay, earth, loam, rock, that is, in his telluric base.

Unlike Olson / I do not 'hunt among stones.' / I hunt inside stone writes CE in the poem "Cemeteries of Paradise," & indeed their hunts have different quarries (pun intended). Olson's hunt, even if remembering Rimbaud's quest ("Je chasse parmi les pierres") sets out with the Poundian aim of trying to locate an ur- yet already city-shaped center of Kulchur, via a central figure (Coatlicue or Ullikummi, say) or image, & seems to remain hooked on singularity, on the one — as he wrote to Robert Kelly: "not imageS but image." This will inevitably lead him to the transcendent (& to Rimbaud's "chasse spirituelle"?), albeit in its gentlest & least oppressive guise, in the figure of the Angel of Sufism, in the final Maximus volume. In "Notes on Charles Olson and the Archaic" Clayton comments as follows on his own reworked Olson line: "In other words, I have gone back to the ice, as it were, before there was a city, to the dark of caverns, as an archeologist of the wee* hours, right before dawn, and before any heaven." To a place thus where no government of either a heavenly city or an earthly city has been able to reduce the Milky Way abundance & lushness of images to the fixity & immobility of the One. A rhizomatic space that is immediately & always an endless maze of hollows, conduits, meanders of every shape, where those nomadic hordes of images retain their iridescent hues & fuses, where those changeling images (as mistyping the word gave me suddenly "mages," "i mages," "I Mages" – amans of the self?) are part of & inextricable from the geomorphings of rock itself. These images – grotescas, one could say, deturning one of Eshleman's favorite terms – become a, if not the, core meditational investigation of his work, not only as specific subject matter but also as core constituent & medium of the poetry. So that I would venture the suggestion that Eshleman is the one poet who has continued to explore & deepen the original insights of "deep-image" poetry as first laid out by Jerome Rothenberg & Robert Kelly (& that have nothing to do with the cheapened version peddled for some time by Wright, Bly & Co.) If, without necessarily relinquishing the gains of their thinking about image, Rothenberg & Kelly have gone on to other investigative foci in their poetics – sound & syntax most immediately come to mind –, Eshleman has persisted with an image-based poetics, where image transformations impel the poem forward, expanding Kelly's early insight that "the rhythm of the images constitut[es]... the deep structure of the poem."

(* in that Scottish "wee" I hear a young boy's glee, besting the father figure by sneaking out before dawn if only for a wee moment or a quick wee in the garden, to both frighten & exalt himself with the images his mind projects on or extracts from night's waning darkness – I can see the gleam in Clayton's eye, a flare of that mischievous, puckish humor rarely recognized but, I believe, often present in the work)

All of life is present every moment and that is what makes for the baroque grotesca of his art, not some dis- or mis-formation of things or thoughts, & certainly not some willed blending/bending into misshape, but that exact experience: *all of life is present every moment*. This

126

realization (both as the act of becoming aware & of actually making, of achieving facture) does indeed distort the clean, Euclidian perspective of the 3-dimensional object, but it does so in order to permit those other, connected things, objects, shapes, *images* always present to reveal their presence & kinship. In the poem "Cooking," to use a very simple example, the act of scrubbing & looking at the chicken carcass being readied for cooking, this *Ding,* to use the Rilkean term, links to a not at all Rilkean presence / image / sensation, namely "the cold under [his mother's arms] as I carried her into the hospital toilet." We are all familiar, to some extent, with such associational events, but have been taught to repress, sublimate & dismiss them more often than not — especially when they touch on the taboos of our culture. Yet it is precisely the artist's job to track & trace such chains & associational linkages, especially those that can challenge our cultural taboos & certainties by venturing into the minefields of our psyches. There is a level at which such chains of associations & transformations can run amok, accumulate *ad infinitum,* crust over from an overload of both the perceiver's psyche and the original *Ding*: This would be psychotic crackup, such as experienced by Artaud (a core figure in CE's universe) who did indeed go through such breakdowns & paid the price in hospitalizations & electroshocks. For Eshleman this is of course not the case: the association ladder he climbs up to gather & select, like the agile Indiana cave-dweller shaman that he is, is a solid & well-earthed construction. The ability to select, of knowing the difference between the real & the imaginary, is exactly what I would call the health of the artist (or anyone's health, for that matter). To know & to work that difference, to know how to follow the image I'll again call the "deep image," i.e. the one that has *duende,* the vibratory charge that enlivens, enriches human & poem, this indeed is the poet's job.

Must poetry become infected to truly live? Eshleman raises this question in his 1994 poem "Nora's Roar" (a powerful memorial piece for his friend, the artist Nora Jaffe). He has just been thinking of Charles Baudelaire & thus some Baudelairian sense of the need for great modern poetry to be "infected" by some malady, psychic or physical, as a sort of leaven to make the dough rise & the "flowers of evil" bloom. Which brings to mind an exchange of letters from the early 70s — not to hand, but somewhere in our respective archives — where we speak of the psychic stress that both burdened & underwrote the lives & work of two poets we were deeply engaged with: Antonin Artaud & Paul Celan. I have to admit, somewhat shamefacedly, that, unable to consult the letters, I no longer remember what Clayton had proposed, but it was my contention that both these poets' psycho-pathologies were an integral part of the European condition, that it was this condition that had infected, & finally killed them. (That they had been "suicided by society" as Artaud put it in relation to Van Gogh in a poem Clayton translated). Thus, no matter how essential their work, how major their impact on our contemporary perception of the advances poetry had to perform to be an accurate witness to the century & beyond, we should not, could not, see them as models. This was so, I thought, not only because trying to imitate these poets or their poetics was both impossible & out of the question — even though their *poethics* did provide powerful guidelines. That, I went on, is what I was after by leaving behind the Europe of Artaud & Celan where "infection" was endemic in order to come into a vastly more open, newer, not yet psychically & artistically over-cathect-ed field. In a poem of that period (*The Book of Luap Nalec*), I saw "the strong body of America arched / night over an ephectic Europe." A vi-sion, thus, of the open field of America as a healthier place or at least a place where health was possible (where, as Olson put it, there was room to breathe), where an Olsonian/Duncanesque open-field poetry could unfold without those European psychic strictures. Over-optimistic, this young starry-eyed romantic *On the Road*-er, yes, possibly — & in hind-sight, certainly, given the political developments of the decades since. Eshleman's work (& here lay one of its immediate attractions for me) both questioned & proved, worried & endorsed this possibility, & thus its great usefulness for me as I started to find my place in the American space.

Reciprocity... is the daily, human goal, this quote from an earlier note sud-denly comes back to me as I think on how to address the question of Eshleman as translator. "Reciprocity" may be the best word to frame the activity of translating, or at least of the kind of translating Clayton has been committed to all his working life. He often spoke of translat-ing César Vallejo as an apprenticeship & this relation (a dynamic I'll confirm via my own 1/2 century apprenticeship to Paul Celan's work) has indeed to be based on a reciprocal engagement in order to bear

128

fruit — even, & maybe exactly because, one of the two is dead. The idea is not to use (as all too often happens) the famous dead as leverage for a literary career, not to "colonize" another, often minority & "foreign" language by breaking it in & taming it into the current imperial lingo. As Hölderlin claimed he wanted to write "Greek in German" when translating the great tragic poets, so the idea is to open the "target language" up to new possibilities, using the foreign language to reveal one's own language's limitations, to show its fault lines & hairline fractures, widen them to enable new perceptions, new thoughts, new configurations to slip through the cracks. It is a question of exploring one's lacks & limitations in the acid-test of a powerful oeuvre & learn to open up one's own poetics to the challenge of a dense, often "dunkel / dark" matter — Celan speaks of a "constitutional, congenital darkness of the poem." A humbling yet exalting experience, one in which Clayton has been a steadfast master, guide & compañero.

the stamina of his wound is what CE meditates on regarding Paul Celan today. The word "stamina," a rich, strong 3-syllables, bears a closer look. It refers most directly to the "physical or moral strength to resist or withstand illness, fatigue or hardship," it says endurance. It comes to us via the Latin stamen, referring to a thread, the thread of life spun by the fates or Norns. One of Celan's poems is called *Fadensonnen* & reads: "THREADSUNS //above the greyblack wastes. /A tree- /high thought /grasps the light-tone: there are /still songs to sing beyond / mankind." I described the Celanian landscape proposed thus: "Neither u-topia nor dys-topia, as has at times been argued, Celan's topos is a visionary-realistic land- and language-scape mapping the second half of the 20C from the devastating aporia constituted by World War II, its extermination camps and nuclear wastelands, and reaching beyond Celan's own dates through that fin-de-siècle into the mauled dawn of the 21C." Of those threadsuns I wrote that any single sun (see above re single image) as source, *arche* or *telos* of our world has, under the pressure of the multiple & the many, been changed, has ex- or im-ploded: these multiplied suns are threads now, thin elongated – lines of flight. Threads are fragile, they can break: we can no longer barter our own finitude for the possible transcendental infinitude of the sun-circle, helios or Yahweh whatever name it was given. Our, man-and-woman's, finitude is our measure – and, as the expression has it, it hangs, we hang by a thread. The thread spun by the fates, or their Norse counterparts, the Norns – these latter dwell, as it happens, in a northern scape, a place, in Celan's phrase, "north of the future." Yet all is not loss. These threadsuns fold into the word that gives their elongation – the "Faden," the thread – something more, something which in English is still there in the word "fathom," which comes to us via the indo-european root *pet and germanic *fathmaz: "the length of two arms stretched out." The thread thus a way — based on the human body itself— of measuring space, or of "sounding" depth (the poem also speaks of a "Lichtton" a "light-tone" or sound) and, maybe, of a measure, or a new measure for the world & for poetry. But "stamina" has not yet exhausted its charge: that "stamen" is also the male reproductive organ of the flower, grounded in the Indo-European root -stā which means to stand, bringing back a Celan poem that goes: "TO STAND, in the shadow of the stigma in the air. / Standing-for-no-one-and-nothing. / Unrecognized, / for you / alone. // With all that has room in it, / even without / language." A difficult act, indeed, & how to keep that stamina, that ability to stand, over the years? In April 1970 Paul Celan wrote in a letter to his friend Ilana Shmueli: "When I read my poems, they grant me, momentarily, the possibility to exist, to stand." Two weeks later Celan gave himself over to the drift of the Seine, exhausted after having stood tirelessly, selflessly for the possibility of a new life.

...he neither allowed it to flow at full vent, nor did he brilliantly cicatrize it at the right hour is how CE qualifies the "stamina" thought & I'm not sure how to read this, wondering if Clayton isn't asking too much of Celan, hoping that the latter could have made the wound flow or cicatrize at will. Could that be an excess of American self-confidence in the individual's ability to control and direct one's fate? Is it a matter of "allowing" something of that extremity to happen? (Or does it suggest that Celan was in control & knew how not to allow it to flow?) Celan did cauterize — very carefully & in many ways better than many survivors — his survivor's wounds, though starting in 1960 the Goll affair did rip the crust that had formed off the wound, reinfecting it again & again. Celan tried to stem this infection & he fought to the last. Post *Todesfuge* & especially throughout the late work, all the way to the final weeks of his life, there is a powerful attempt to create a new, inhabitable world — despite Auschwitz, Hiroshima, Vietnam. So I can't &

won't judge, can't suggest that he may have been able to — I wouldn't know what. I agree with Clayton when he says that Celan "worked it (his wound) as a muscle as long as there was any strength left in it" but I do not know what "other energies" he could have set in motion "that might have given him reason to live at the point that the wound ceased to ache," as Clayton suggests. Whenever I think of Celan's death — or any similar death — lines from a Robert Kelly poem I read the very year of that death come to mind: "in front / of the agony of any being / we are stupid mute."

...a condition in which there cannot be poetry and in which there can only be poetry is another way in which Clayton describes Celan's situation— though that, I feel, also describes the situation of all poetry that wants to be of essential use at this jointure. There is a phrase by Celan defining the state of poetry today that I believe can be applied usefully to Eshleman's work, namely: "La poésie ne s'impose plus, elle s'expose." The German philosopher Peter Sloterdijk, in one of his Frankfurt poetry lectures points out that this sentence is a witty French word play which gets lost in his German translation even if in the English version — "Poetry no longer imposes itself, it exposes itself" — it survives, malgré a loss of elegance. Sloterdijk, for whose ear the French line "also strikes the right tone," suggests that it corroborates & fortifies a Romance idea of poetry: "The freedom of art is dependent on it not becoming domineering / Die Freiheit der Kunst hängt daran, daß sie nicht herrschaftlich wird." Noting that the *exposing* considered here does not have a grammatical object, he argues that this is not happenstance, because, when poetry exposes itself, it doesn't do so primarily to public judgment, to the praise or blame of its contemporaries, to analysis or to posterity's miscomprehension. The way Celan sees poetry as exposing itself, does not have to do with the matter of communication or the lack thereof, ("it doesn't exhaust itself in the play of sending & receiving," Sloterdijk says) but it makes of poetry nothing less than an "an analogy of existence — an objectless, open risk." (Sloterdijk's word, "Wagnis" also suggests "dare," even "wager.") Poetry, in Celan's sense, has thus to lay itself open & be an existential wager, as a testing of the possibility of true life, & demands that stance (same root — stā — as stand & stamina) as he put it in the already quoted phrase: "... my poems... grant me, momentarily, the possibility to exist, to stand." It has

always been clear to me that Eshleman's relation to poetry is of a very similar & of as exacting a nature, even if due to obvious geographical & historical reasons, the realization of this exposure is profoundly different. As he put it in "Nora's Roar:" ... to live / in near obscurity, happy / within the frame of imagination, this word / we mob, // it is our only refuge."

Mas d'Azil: A name, lovely in its vowel-consonant music, that appears a number of times in CE's work dealing with the prehistoric. A village, lovely in a *vieille France* sense, we drove to this morning to visit its famous cave. As is nearly always the case when thinking, talking, walking about prehistoric sites & art, Clayton will not be far from my mind — as was indeed the case this morning as Nicole & I drove to Mas d'Azil. The visit of the cave (no art in there, at least none that is approachable, only a cave-warren) that now explicitly connects itself to contemporary art, was however a sadly Disney-fied preamble to nothing, except a gorily lit up "temple" room (a vast cathedral-like space that would have been awe-inspiring if left to its own unadorned & silent devices) in which loudspeakers assaulted us with tinny extracts from Mozart's Requiem. The only surprise was one of the two contemporary artists who were making use of the space: Gary Hill. As we climbed the metal stairway towards the upper cave system, we started to see a projection on top of the site's reception building's roof, which Nicole immediately read as a river running counter to the actual river, the Arize, just ten feet below. This virtual river carries along a whole range of modern flotsam & jetsam, the cultural detritus of our techno-times. We stopped & watched & wondered. A strange sound, like the hushed drone of an airplane or an electronic siren overlaid the sound of the river(s). What to make of this?

... *anything can be anything as long as it sells. Image has gone into apocalypse.* Hill's video is appealing, and indeed an interesting response, though the white, slightly abstracted & near-ghostly shapes these objects of our everyday life were given, made for too aesthetically clean/cleansed/ sterile a set of images. Both of our immediate thoughts were that actual, used & stained McDonalds hamburger boxes & wrappers & the like would have made images with a stronger & more urgent appeal. I did wonder what Clayton would have made of it, had he been along for the ride. His piece "Postentry" came to mind, where an imaginary publisher tells him: "The images we buy are critic-coded, their stories all reflect existing missings, pop-up audience zones or prestige perks." This could function indeed as a criticism of much of the aestheticized imagery of both the visual arts & of poetry (his "still strung on transpersonal chains manipulated by your missing story"), as very consciously countermanded by Eshleman's work on & from the cave materials & other image-troves. Or, to cite parts of the image-string of his auto-definition in that same piece: "So I'm like an alchemist, I guess, an antiquated beaker bubbling away in a Swiss hut... observing my spider, cooking up a storm... translating my baby book, an octopodal radio giving off all the right signals... Theseus slumped drunk in a cul-de-sac, a labyrinth in effect, a sun-oiled tunnel when it comes to night."

Is it our work to push doghouses, jeans / and waffle irons into earth's orifices, / to shun them as soon as we use them? The first lines I came to this morning as I opened *The Grindstone of Rapport*, speak of exactly such a montage of junk & detritus used to create art (the two Detroit houses assembled by Tyree Guyton). CE contrasts this late 20C work with Rilke's sense of things — of his Ding-Gedichte, for example — & the latter's complaints in 1925 that "from America, empty, indifferent things are pouring across, sham things, dummy life..." One way of seeing Eshleman's work is as an attempt to bring back / dig down to whatever numinosity the images of our "American century" may contain, with as the back-wall of his imagination, the images of our Cro-Magnon ancestors.

Imagination is the keelson of paradise: The opening line of the 40-page poem called *The Jointure*. A superb example of late Eshleman, I wrote in my blog entry when it came out, this 2011/2012 poem is a perfect entry point into the late poetry as it returns to & transforms core materials in Eshleman's psychic realms. Kenneth Warren accurately sees *The Jointure* as "a brilliant 'I-beam' that illuminates the stack of androcentric figures through which his opus is staked to man's collective psychic force. Eshleman's primordial intention in *The Jointure* is contact with the ancestral realm. Among totems honored are Yorunomado, the daemon of Eshleman's first breakthrough poem written in Kyoto, and Xochipilli, the Aztec prince of hallucinogenic plants. Painstakingly refined in *The Jointure* are the precise pivot points through which these perpetrators of soul muſt come and go in order to realize the fate, form, and integrity of a lifetime given to the imagination." (I quoted on Nomadics blog, & as it ſtill reads like an excellent, exaȼt description, I'll let it ſtand here.)

Imaginal love: I have been reading — & rereading — *An Anatomy of the Night* with great, & indeed, increasing pleasure. It is vintage Eshleman, that is, the ſtrength & power of image-making, always his forte, & the muscular & nervous dynamic that organizes & drives these knotted metaphorics, have in no way diminished with time — & combine to make for the rich & dense writing we as readers of CE's work have grown accuſtomed to over more than forty books. To speak of an Eshlemanian *Altenſtil*, literally juſtified for an author in his late seventies, even one as continuously & energetically prolix as CE, is however meant here foremoſt as a positive comment on the quality of this part of the *oeuvre*. The writing now seems more leavened & thus — if not, if never relaxed or loose — moving away from the extreme density of much of the earlier work, a density that may at times have worked againſt his readers, certainly againſt younger generations coming to Eshleman's work for the firſt time. He achieves this leavening by inserting / collaging prose seȼtions, either his comments on, say, the caves' material the poems are dealing with, or journal-like entries, with citations from his wide readings (Róheim, Hillman, Kühn, Djuna Barnes, etc.) to create a tapeſtry that unifies the book, making it more than a simple collection of diſtinȼt poems, creating a weave, a *textum*, in which one ſtrand of the writing refleȼts on the other, enriching & commenting on the other ſtrand(s). In that sense I see the book — beyond the sheer pleasure & information it is providing me — as an excellent point of entry into CE's work for new readers. If "night" & its mares or dreams are a ſtaple of poetry, in Eshleman's hands any simple surface ghoſtliness is dismissed in favor of an in-depth inveſtigation — a *mano a mano* ſtruggle, often — of the psychic energies both dreams & insomnia propose. The darkness of night is mother/siſter to the darkness of the prehiſtoric caves that have been such an essential part of Eshleman's poſt-Indiana work, and the skills required for navigating through both spaces are closely linked — juſt as the images CE's psyche throws up in those siſter-realms are closely linked to each other while rhyming with other spaces, the aȼtual and psychic basement-caves of the poet's Indianapolis childhood home. These notes — which will keep on elsewhere, as I'll keep on reading Clayton's work as a necessary & strength-giving food against the lethal superficiality of much of our world & art — have now to be brought to an close. Let me do so with a poem from this late collection, a poem that presents a (at least momentary) resolution of the demonic hauntings, the darknesses various nights involve, through Caryl, the loved woman, & Clayton's companion for half a century:

[16]
   Imaginal love
   incorrigibly infected by violence,
            the damnation strut in the human,
   fuse of extinction   formless horizon:
      now the daily telepathy

   I listen to Caryl breathe.
               Why cannot her being
   bless the world? Bless it to awaken from the doomcraft
               that is religion—

   The dark sloughs its "d" and the ark of dawn,
   first in my heart, then in the fuzzy edge of the window
      blind,
   reveals Caryl's recumbent profile.

   Blind edge, road of awe, world axis that allows me to
      contemplate her breathing.

                              [Bourg d'Oueil, August 2013]

Additional Resources

Paul Celan, *Breathturn into Timestead: The Collected Later Poetry of Paul Celan.* Translated & with commentaries by Pierre Joris (New York: Farrar Straus Giroux, forthcoming 2015).

Pierre Joris, *Le Livre de Luap Nalec* (Le Castor Astral, 1986).

—, *Poasis (Poems 1986–1999)* (Wesleyan University Press, 2001).

Gary Hill & Allan Packer, *Sanctuary for reverse Engineering (R.E.S.) Exposition Grotte du mas d'Azil* (les Abattoirs FRAC-Midi Pyrénées, 2013).

Peter Sloterdijk, *Zur Welt kommen — zur Sprache kommen* (Suhrkamp Verlag 1988).

Eric Mottram

The Poetics of Rebirth and Confidence:
An Introduction to *Coils*

The peristaltic movement which Eshleman notes from Wilhelm Reich in the introduction to *A Caterpillar Anthology*[1] is one entrance to a main purpose in his work up to and including *Coils*: the nature of *being* reborn and *getting* oneself reborn, the interaction of nature as *letting be* and human nature as education and intention. It is this major business which, properly enacted, gives Eshleman's work its power, and the poetry itself is not really in need of exegetical unpackings and simplifications. But it might be useful to trace some of the exploratory action leading to *Coils*, and then to say something about the structure of that book. How to read the process of this purposive poetry is where one is likely to find oneself battling with Eshleman himself, if one ever had the temerity to contact him as well as his work, since his tenacity of purpose extends rightly to ensuring the proper attention of his reader. The particularity of his poetry has that personal and social urgency. One confronts a rare kind of work, courageously presenting itself in the bloody intellectual and physical process of discovering of the self and its honest registration. Eshleman speaks, in the anthology introduction, of Olson's performance at Berkeley in 1965 as the inspiration of a poet who "took on his Selfhood," revealed the "heart / mind of a poet" and "worked through the Hydra-head of inner vs. outer reality, of public vs. private, those hideous distances that have plagued poets immemorially."[2] Eshleman's achievement is to have his own way of performing the process of discovering selfhood, without being trapped by art as substitute for life: "often when the artist says the art is my life, he sadly means, implicitly, that the art realized the life which was not realizable in itself."[3]

Eshleman provided *Caterpillar* 3/4 (1968) with an epigraph from Reich which read in part: "Truth is full, immediate contact between the Living that perceives and Life that is perceived. The truthful experience is the fuller the better the contact … truth is a natural function in the interplay between the Living and that which is Lived." In *Caterpillar* 5 (1968) Eshleman notes this implication in Duncan's *Bending the Bow*: "Not to

136

fear the romance, the romantic feeling that man would enter into but fears to at the cost, he fears, of reason and virility" – adding that Duncan and Ginsberg have "in our time ended the cult of the need to be masculine that would freeze the heart of the poem to a stony core." He criticizes Carol Berge's *Poems Made of Skin*: "Unimaginative in that her poems are … one-dimensional and have an academic sense of metaphor (that is not real). Tight. On a leash. Much feeling here never expressed. And bitter. Unforgivingly bitter." Reviewing Blackburn's *The Cities*, in this same issue, Toby Olson uses Wittgenstein's *Philosophical Investigations* to state the principle that words are part of the event – "the man who speaks is a central variable: his particular history. That's a kind of specific location: the man, where he is in his head and the world, talking. Paul Blackburn has always risked this participation… His is not a poetry of control, prediction or reduction to the manageable… He rightly recognizes language as a *form of life*: for each man what finally comes out of his mouth from where he is." These qualities inform Eshleman's own poetry and he knows that this kind of verse cannot be found without considerable dislocation of old self. Writing of *Reich Speaks of Freud*, he gives some account of his own therapeutic experience with a Reichian analyst – a minute of child-wildness, enforced "dynamic reliving of incidents rather than talking about them," which causes a discharge of anguish. The purpose is to release the body's armoring, to be able to yield to sexual loving, "to experience another person fully," to reach "man's only truly powerful valve of social self-regulation." Eshleman advised every poet to learn something about himself through Reich's *The Function of the Orgasm*; it could at least show the possibility of release from making poetry around unhappiness, being nourished by it rather than confronting what Blake know as "the Satan of unacted desire" (it is a much needed counter to the popular suicidal-confession school of poetry and its irresponsible critical advocacy).

For Eshleman's poetry, contrary to superficial appearance, is not confessional: it is not that kind of self-regard in verse. In *Caterpillar* 7 (1969), in consideration of an exchange with Robert Kelly over his discovery of Reich, he shows a condition beyond that kind of wallowing: "a base, or a shelf as I would prefer to call it, has been dropping away; the universe is less and less without that particular restriction; it is more as one sees everywhere…" More particularly: "I have begun to experience my endurance… the land has opened, cracked, as if to make me visible. 18 January 1967." The same issue contained part of Reich's 1967 *People in Trouble*, a major work which discusses the nature of entering the Living: "consciousness means turning one's attention towards one's origin, one's own organizations, one's own stagnation." And Eshleman's review of *The Teachings of Don Juan* notes the "scary-difficult" moment in Reichian therapy when the "neurotic structure begins to crumble and one is standing naked 12 year old with all that fear facing present day adult New York." Eshleman's poetry had also to articulate that kind of learning through experience, not by "watching or hearing or reading." In *Caterpillar* 8 / 9 (1969), in a passage which became in *Altars* a parenthesis between parts two and three of "An Ode to Autumn," he speaks of creating Yorunomado and Niemonjima as "male female forces" out of "bedrock yin / yang" and Blake's Los and Enitharmon – symbolic forces to be used where life could not be expressed directly. The poetics of Eshleman's work begins to be stated precisely at this point: "Now if symbolic forms are related to repression how does one make an imagined world if one's energies at large are being expressed? / But it also makes sense to me that never do we dwell in such a state that could be honestly believed non-repressed."

The energy in symbolic forms could still be drawn on for development, that struggle Eshleman noted in Artaud's "chant babble" written in Rodez, "to make a movement," and which he relates to Don Juan's movement through the crack in the world: "I hear 'out of this world' for a poet as 'toward a created world' in realizing *this world*." That his is not to be some closed privacy is clear in "An open letter to George Stanley..." in this came issue of *Caterpillar* in which he claims that power which all artists want: "this power realized as a HUMAN Act" by a visionary man. This need is also inflected as: "my sense of power, or possession, wch I learned thru the making of a poem called *T'ai*, is a magic, miracle (with the root *mira!* See!), the power to induce speech, the sense that there is no repetition... Force implies alternation; creation affirms the way things ARE, not forced to be. We want to exercise not force but our power. To allow our work to perform its possession." This power energizes Eshleman's sense of what revolution could mean. In a letter in *Caterpillar* 10 (1970) he quotes Duncan's "a new order is a contention in the HEART of existing orders" and Reich's "revolution is to go to the CORE of things," as against Leroi Jones' force or violence: "any man who urges revenge, given the fact that war is the father of us all, is in direct contradiction to, simply, intelligence... Reich argues that under the rotational sense of revolution is the core of killing, and he names this The Emotional Plague... It seems to me that revolution as it is practiced today in the world, the rotational kind of revolution, might be seen by the imaginative eye as that sword which man keeps revolving about him to hide paradise. Such revolution is the way we keep ourselves occupied so as not to have to deal with paradise." (In *Caterpillar* 15 / 16 (1971), Eshleman believes that "if Bataille wld reveal his own sexual 'disturbance' his work on the *erotic* could be more felt.")

Caterpillar 17 (1971) uses *Jerusalem* plate 88 on "mutual interchange" of the "Human Four-Fold Forms" in both "intellect" and "emanation," which constitute "the Fibres of Brotherhood." The following issue (1972) contains Eshleman's first translation of *Artaud Le Momo*, a major text in which a man expresses in Eshleman's words, "the discrepancy between vision and existence," and once again exposes "the fall" as the attack on human life by a priest-cult 4,000 BC – "about the same point in history that Blake and Wilhelm Reich locate as the moment of 'the fall.'" The issue is a choice between being a man and a mad man: "At that moment the imaginative or creative potential in man became a 'fall-hauntedness' and whoever continued to possess this potential became in effect a 'spectre of the dead.'" In a note on his translation of Vallejo's 1937 "Hymn to the Volunteers for the Republic," Eshleman writes of how the poet "fully opens himself to the conflict, and thus to death," (*Caterpillar* 19) and his commitment to the Peruvian poet is total and clear in his translation of *Poemas Humanos*, a central metaphoric act of his life in the Sixties. (During this decade, Eshleman published a series of important *Caterpillar* books – works by Césaire, Blackburn, Frank Samperi, David Antin, Jackson MacLow, Corman on Zukofsky, and his own work. The editor's announcement carried this statement: "The *Caterpillar Glyph* is a small napalmed Vietnamese child. Until the end of the war this black caterpillar.") The translating of Vallejo involved him in the life and work of a man totally committed to the complex of poetry, revolution, Christianity and the nature of suffering: "In Vallejo the amount of physical suffering is the alteration that it seeks; he poses the problem for the poets who follow him even more crucially than Blake: given the fact that man suffers and that I, as a poet, am always responsible for suffering, what can I do to lessen this suffering – as a poet?" So that: "Vallejo's sickness is not a matter of literary concern – it leads directly to Wilhelm Reich. This Peruvian, revealing the crack in the foundation of his armature, tells us: You must get well. / So was I charged. Utter enlightenment working out over the years" (Foreword to the translation dated 17 January 1968).

A noted to *Altars* dated 20 March 1971 reports that in the Autumn of 1966 "I left my family (on two levels), and began Reichian therapy. Immersed for a year in Vietnamese War protest and anger and grief, the energy which I was able to rechannel fall of 1967 and started *Caterpillar* magazine."[4] *Indiana* (1969) publishes poems composed between fall 1963 and 1968, a large and firm representation of Clayton Eshleman's gaining of poetic power: to find a way of presenting the self as the intersection of information from history, society, psychological analysis and family inheritance, not as a stasis but as a process whose purpose is movement in total commitment, in the sense that these paragraphs have attempted to document, what the poet calls "inch by inch progress." The poems afford the privilege of following a man's self-haul towards what he takes to be a necessarily reborn self, with no more self-regard than is needed for poetic transformation of experience into power and for the maintenance of what dignity a man must sustain in this decade and through such a rebirth. In one of his finest books, *The House of Ibuki* (1969), he writes:

> I am seeking to
> explain to you that State wherein a man becomes
> serious, that is, starts to let the world through,
> Tsuruginomiya was my lodestone, starts to be
> elsewhere at once
> "show everyone to everyone"[5]

In *Bearings* (1971), the energizing and control from Reich takes this form at one point: "that to live means one aggressively seeks striving for that other – for someone who is special, who one feels very tender toward – one is cheating primarily."[6] This striving "keeps the anguished striver clean, keeps *perception moral.*"[7] Earlier considerations of war and violence now appear as: "War, William Blake said, is Energy Enslaved, and I would translate that on an individual plane: *violence is blocked energy.*"[8] The experience of Artaud is: "the existence of the priest and the politician are a surly froth on the unhappy seething of life – could we become self-regulatory – and that, self-regulator, is Reich's term ... the politician and the priest would simply dry up."[9] The figure of birth becomes even more controlling as Eshleman moves into the 1970s – a man can "birth" his creative work, a woman, himself, and he is only "now beginning to understand" this fact and dare to think of it. Naturally, he has been accused of the sexist use of a woman, but it is clear the *mutuality* of birth is at the core of his work, even if one partner takes an initiative in the necessity, and that person is the creative artist whose record we participate in. Home, he writes, is not a system: "no freedom without freedom for all mankind."[10] His work shows him *learning* these facts and their ecology, beginning, for instance in *Indiana*, where he writes: "I am either a friend of myself or nothing."[11] It is clear from *Bearings*, for instance – at the age of thirty-five – that what he works for is a poem which does not hide, but at the same time does not flaunt, the action of the young self reaching manhood, a poem between the puritan and the flamboyant. So that he can write with and without symbol, in clearing the body and the intellect for their training, in *Altars*:

> The poet does not
> go for broke, but
> respects craft's double gate,
>
> not mythical man   & not myself,
> man kneeling,
> all he has come thru
> now floods, condenses[12]

The figure of Hart Crane haunts the procedure as a homosexual and suicidal poet of power:

> *conversion at solstice*, my cell work
> to be restructured by Crane's Broken Tower
> the beautiful fisheyed Adonis of our
> species, eating his thin wrists & tasting
> his battered cock on my tongue, nearly
> choking in the stinking heat, in the cistern
> Cancer makes light as the great
> circle of creation now comes to stop,
> as mill wheel suddenly to stop & push
> back to source...[13]

In *Indiana*, after mentioning Crane at one point, Eshleman speaks of "getting from being a middle-class youth in a fraternity with a convertible to an artistic consciousness," and his fear of remaining on the threshold of that passage through. He speaks, too, of the trite condition of early sex life – the conventions of woman as cunt, distrust of boys and men, telling homosexual jokes, married life based on "respect" for the wife and masturbation out of tension. Later in the same book he gives his experience of Crane (and Soutine) as like that of hearing Bud Powell – as sex: "he fucked me, all the way up thru my anus thru my eyes; how can you not praise & praise a person who began to unthaw you, to restore some of what you know is your humanity."[14] Poetry itself was "a wall through which I've tried / entrance … Book thrown up to shield me from another's sight." Translating Vallejo was one way through: "I believe my connection with Vallejo is partially sexual."[15] The next task, the job of *Altars*, is "to live within the conflict of the experiential & imaginative life"[16] – a year's poem in sections ordered through the *I Ching* and Dane Rudhyar's astrological work *The Pulse of Life*. The thirty-five year old poet realized that "the time had come to live my life less in resistance & and more in cooperation" – and resistance is again given as "a wall I had erected against which to feel my own weight as well as to test others' truths."[17]

The first poem dramatizes the crucial necessity of self-forgiveness, preparatory to rebirth and the future action of a man of power (in the sense, now, that Olson recognized from Keats' letters):

> this chaff
> the bundle of your 34 years
> modeled on personality
> must fall…
>
> … I have lived, ever since I can remember, in the dramatic
> alone of my ego[18]

And "Ode to Autumn" concludes with the voice of a female form to be abandoned in order to leave that ego:

> I am that form which fucks with your mind,
> which you idealized as partner out of wanting to be
> hurt. You have chosen me many times because you
> distrust yourself as creator…[19]

"The Mountain" (originally in *Caterpillar* 10 (1970)) uses the possibilities of Tantric discipline whereby the serpent-power of Kundalini is moved upward through the chakras in the transformation of energy, and Reich's therapeutic release from rigidity by breaking the segmental rings of armoring. The next group of poems concern Olson, and his death, the film-maker Brakhage, and the "agony of Capricorn" which is the breaking of order and the structuring of rebirth – "phrases as pieces of film, held up, rejected or spliced in," and Capricorn as "ultimately the State but as imagination it is majesty of Civilization."[20] Olson appears as a figure of rebirth, both in himself and in his readers, presented in Blakean terms (described in more detail in one of the important notes in the book).

Altars then proceeds, through materials of ritual suicide, a woman severing a man from deadness, and the dissolution of Capricorn order in the experiential process of Pisces, to the center of the poems, an ode to Reich, who is invoked as the tutelary spirit through whom is enabled that "diminution of the traces of original sin" that Baudelaire defined as "real civilization" (which the poem quotes).[21] The ode cites *People in Trouble*, a work written in exile, and exile within the State becomes a main theme of the poem. Blake's Lavater marginalia against the precept of "Woman's Love is Sin"[22] is linked to the embrace of the poet and his wife, within the knowledge of Reich and the other guiding spirits in Eshleman's work, as the generative center of the Blakean Eden. The poem ends with Reich explaining to Vallejo:

> that poetry is translation not just of language
> but the passing of a psyche into new form.[23]

This can then be placed with the poet's own statement at the end of the autobiographical note to *Altars*: "my poetics are the oldest and most engaging human adventure: the emancipation of the self" – and with his attempt in *Caterpillar* 7 to identify a change in American poetry which "has to do with mind letting go, going with its glow, raga-fabric, a kind of Romantic Abstract (Blake-Pollack), something that is not strictly European-American... first signaled in the syntax of Allen Ginsberg's *Howl*... it means, whatever it is, the natural falling away, the crumble, at last, of the old universitarian 'way.'"[24] Reich enables sexual and social understanding which the poet may use in his life-work, the perpetual action of destruction and birth. Such is a small part of *Altars* in summary form, making no attempt to do full justice to the book's detailed structuring of "Eros in the poem," and the nature of Eshleman's dedication to the serious function of the poet in society.

That seriousness is there, too, in *The Sanjo Bridge*:

> Some people simply do more than others, know more, are more –
> some people actually DO expand their consciousness (rather than
> make power-bullshit out of their claim that they have), do see MORE
> of life than others.
>
> I feel that the supreme way a man indicates that he HAS expanded his consciousness from what he was given to something much
> more is by making an art. A way to define art is to say that it is a
> record of what a person has seen.[25]

The basis is not "how well he meshed with what everyone else was thinking," or how "far out," but his "difference" of vision, "how much one person... could manifest and bring through life." Eshleman's examples here are Theodore Enslin and the Fellini of *8½* as against Bob Dylan...

Indiana, New York, Peru, Japan: the locations are specific. Throughout the period of working on the Vallejo, living in Japan, and the years covered by the paragraphs above (1962-72), Eshleman worked at a book at first called *The Tsuruginomiya Regeneration* and actually published as *Coils* in 1973. "Tsuruginomiya" translates as "Sword Shrine," the place of work, of building. But out of *Altars* reappears *seppuku*, a ritual disembowelment which is, in *Coils*, placed with the image of a spider, the figure of a generation / regeneration out of degeneration that "cutting into oneself, which is also a shaping act, of making the poem / as regeneration, the very place of cutting transformed into an outgoingness, or a spinning out of oneself, thus the spiderwork." The whole book moves towards the final and title poem – in fact *Coils* is a whole, plotted as such also by prose commentaries before each of the seven sections, from the dedication to the poet's mother – "my first source of power" – and the epigraph "I Sing the Body Electric," to the concluding metamorphosis of materials. In a sense, therefore, it is meaningless to quote, but perhaps a measure of Eshleman's achievement can be offered here fragmentarily. We can begin with "Coils" itself.

The poet understands that the forces in his life which he "must oppose to keep on learning are not a woman,"[26] that the mother is finally to be buried and is buried, that the feminine in himself and in his wife can

144

be truly figured as iridescent newborn creation. In "the intense Okumura Garden," he experiences the configuration of the persimmon, "the pregnant red spider's web," and his wife Caryl.[27] The praise performed here, at the end of the book, truly concludes the years of exploration and pain which it articulates so clearly. Eshleman is explicit, direct and ecstatic in his own rhetoric of long lines, evolved from Blake, Whitman and other sources:

> I love you as a man & as an imagination
> the sacrifice poetry demands is not abstinence nor a shedding
> of personality but the sharing of one's penis or one's vagina
> with the cornucopia of the ages while one takes in disembowelment
> & emanates silk. The beloved who is true, the lover who is true,
> do not disembowel each other, yet both love each other & are
> thus open to the world which is obsidian to the virginal body of
> love; yet the world is also a perceptive field ever-widening to
> an awakened person. I love you is my happiness with you &
> at the same time a vibration sent forth against the opacity
> clogged in my body & mind against this flowing persimmon...[28]

The achievement of *Coils* is to have found a form for the detailed performance of the total autobiographical experience of ten years, not to reuse the ecstatic or the suicidal, the needed orders of psychology and literature or the day-to-day struggles of the body against inertia and towards birth. The work gives the poet the right of access to "Coils." The mythology and iconography of the work are partly invented, partly renewed, and they are fully functional in the enterprise of discovery and invention of form. *Coils* needs no additional commentary from judgmental criticism. At a third reading even it stays as a region of dense, sacral activity, which could easily be repulsive to the reader nurtured on the tenets of minimal feeling, minimal inventive form, maximum ironic timidity and maximum absence of risk in both form and experience. The Eshleman event is strong enough to carry its faults and scars since they are the troubles of urgency, prolificity, an abundance in the structuring of energy, and an innate knowledge that a finicky, eliminatory procedure simply imitates that puritan regressiveness his work challenges at source – inside the body and at its edges.

We have nothing like *Coils* in British poetry because we have been trained to fear explicit emotion, inventive vehicular forms for the developing of experience, and the communication of abundance rather than scarcity. *Coils* defines the decrease of a man's space which is endemic to puritan capitalist society. We have lost Blake's sense of potency in expansion of consciousness. *Coils* renews that potential and tells us we do not have to be stoic, ironic and constipated in our culture, nor do we *have* to redress anecdotal explicitness with injections of surrealist method or conceptualist impersonality. There is another way – a buoyant egocentricity and fearless autobiography, placed at the disposal of responsibility to self and society in a state of revolution, as initiatorily defined in Reich, Blake, Vallejo, Whitman, and Crane – those great figures who energize Eshleman's courage, his aggression against the training and inheritance of bourgeois America through research into the prophetic springs of poetry.

He does not offer tidy end-products. He invites you into a poetry confident of human evolution out of inertia and consumerism, through anguish and revulsion, to ecstasy and that essential entrance on a path of educated understanding. In the absence of a supportive community, it is a lonely process. "Adhesive Love" gives the degree of information and ability reached (dated March 1973). He links arms with Ginsberg through common usage of a passage from Whitman (in *Democratic Vistas*):

> It is to the development, identification and general prevalence of that fervid comradeship (the adhesive love, at least rivaling the amative love hitherto possessing imaginative literature, if not going beyond it) that I look for the counter-balance and offset of our materialistic and vulgar American democracy and for the spiritualization thereof… I say democracy infers such loving comradeship as its most inevitable twin or counterpart, without which it will be incomplete, in vain and incapable of perpetuating itself.

Eshleman then makes his distinctions through both Whitman and Blake:

> *Amatory* love is a state of love in which not only are man and woman at war but so are man and man, and woman and woman. *Adhesive* love implies a sense of the human in which love in its variations and forms becomes the *adhesive* force in all its relations… it is human and not sexual. One approximation might be Blake's "The human is four-fold, the sexual three-fold," which is

Blake's distinction between the third level of archetypal consciousness, Beulah, or erotic love, and the fourth (and in Blake's work, the highest) level, which is Eden, or creative love.[29]

Historical separation of spirit and sexuality is an error responsible for conflict. Van Gogh and Vallejo witness the terrible power of art in men "burdened with the 'adhesive,'" needing to create "*in order to be human.*"[30] The necessity is to end "what we have always had, *imagination compensating for our essential impotence and ignorance confronted with existence,*"[31] partly by recognizing the operative truth of Reich's peristaltic biological principle, and the reality of Don Juan Matus's ability and vision. "The House of Okumura VII" in *Coils* begins: "I had not been fucking./ I had not been able to write…" and initially continues by recording a change from impotence:

> The world begins in our biology
> Before we are born, but that birth is
> As nothing Poetry is all about being reborn
> Fucking keeps us flowing
> If we stop forces riot over which
> We have no control
>
> Blake: "War is Energy Enslaved"
> O sweet sweet revolution! …[32]

"The Golden String" presents some of the ecstasy in the revolution of the body against withholding. The poet dreams of a paradise in which life energy in all creatures is creatively freed:

> Thus the energy of my dream reverberates down the golden coils
> of the imagination, this paradise wch is not mine alone fans
> & deepens with the churring of the orange monarch's wings…[33]

In one of the most powerful poems in the book, "The Octopus Delivery," "octopus" is metamorphosed from a horror associated with shit coils in childhood and adulthood, and "the festering / deposit of the populace of / Imagumano, the collectivecoil," to "the Japanese octopus mermaid / coiling out of ocean affirming sexual desire," and the necessarily slow rebirth from "the coils of time."[34] The poems therefore move from lines in the first poem of the book, "Webs of Entry": "My language is full of dirt and shit. / Is it too great a thing to imagine / I can conceive myself?"[35] A pregnant red spider and a ripe falling persimmon epiphanize natural (automatic) birth; the poet is hooked on his own flesh and, through apprehension of his wife's pregnancy, understands some of his fear "of possibly never being born."[36] *Seppuku* (in "The Duende" and "Niemonjima"), under the fearful guidance of Vallejo, is a necessary cutting into inertia. Part II continues the exploration of a "suppressive relation" to energy, a classic process of coming to terms with the relationship of birth out of death, maggots out of garbage, sexuality and death, with fake and true brotherhood, and with the opening of inertia to suffering:

> but the female
> gate in man must open, yet the horrible
> suffering if it opens & something else does
> not open! But there was no cure or cause
> to who Vallejo was, perhaps it was the enormity
> of what he took on, the weight of his people
> to utter, & I shuddered to think of Indiana,
> and what it would be to cast Indiana off…[37]

The poems use both people in the poet's life and an adaptive mythology of Japanese origins as the field of striving for creative change – women, poets, Blake's characters, Japanese figurations – and, in part III, the wild garden of the Okumura house, and a spider – "an energy spirit, a power gift, the first connecting up of language to my body… the metamorphosis of my disembowelment."[38] "The Tsuruginomiya Regeneration" is commenced; therapy proceeds; a marriage ends; the poet learns not to judge. In part IV, Reichian "streaming" and Reich's writings move "The Tsuruginomiya Regeneration" into *Coils*, a work of a man learning how to "assume responsibility" for his energies, to trust his life and his imagination as "the creative process" and a "balanced energy-household."[39]

Hart Crane moves to the center of the poetic action; the inference of T'ai, the hexagram for peace, is imagined; the difference between the promise of false freedom of spirit in scientology and Reichian therapy is understood – the latter enables an alteration in life which does not conclude or enslave the spirit. Yorunomado and Niemonjima are joined by

Origin, the figure of a necessary stern father to the "emerging son-self" (the presence of Cid Corman) and Coatlicue, Aztec mother of the gods:

> now a man gave
> me a power to see my soul,
> this is Origin,
> I was possessed by this
> gift, was the Collar
> of Yorunomado,
> I imagined a man to be
> free of a father,
> Yorunomado was born of the wars of
> Coatlicue & Origin
> Coatlicue is a force
> Coatlicue is an imagining of mother,
> having no mortal mothering poem mind
> seeks its bedrock, seeks beyond
> Indiana, beyond ethic a mother, a spider
> watched in the year fearful fortified
> pregnant castle, ringed with skulls
> devours its mate, goes as far
> back as I can imagine, this image
> inception of the second birth...[40]

In part VI the figure of Caryl begins to shape as the woman in her own right through whom the poet may gain his life, beyond mother, earlier marriage and sexual experiences of a necessary but transitional kind. But the need for rebirth as a whole – not separating poetry and orgasm, not simply intellectualizing, and not simply lust – violently haunts the action still: "baptism without desire." Indiana and parents still have to be understood and released from. In the final section of *Coils* the pregnant spider is the figure of birth, the victim spinner of form from the body, the female which creates and may then die or be swept away, the generational which has to include the destructive, the parents to be released from. It is Eshleman's power that the single image can contain this load. The four poems reshape the book's action and bring it to the shape of a conclusion in the sense that poetry holds processes of experience which can be presented and then moved away from. The erotic in life and in art is fused with powerful resource:

> I stood in Creation the air
> like yolk each form like running
> blood I gave way like my wall
> & loosed my nature…[41]

So that in the final poem, "Coils," praise is in order, since the awakening has been earned. The whole poem ought to be quoted because it is the peak of Eshleman's achievement to this point in his career. The awakened self remains in "the collectivecoil." The long cadences have the confidence of a man who has passed through and can afford poise in his knowledge: "knowing I am, a murderer in the collectivecoil" is accepted responsibility.[42] The coils of Coatlicue are to be lived in, not spurned. The figure of bottomless coils is part of the universal iconography of the serpent and the maze, the chambered shell and the coiled germ, the great mythology of the spiral. But there is no question of abstract drift into images from "the collective unconscious." The poem concerns what is means to say "I love you is my happiness with you & / at the same time a vibration sent forth against the opacity / clogged in my body & mind against this flowering persimmon."[43]

[1974]

This essay was previously published in Poetry Information *and* Margins.

Notes

[1] "Introduction," *A Caterpillar Anthology* xii.

[2] *A Caterpillar Anthology* xiv.

[3] "A Note on Carolee Schneemann's *Fuses*" *Caterpillar* 2 (1967); reprinted in *The Price of Experience* 13.

[4] Biographical note, *Altars*.

[5] "New Guinea, ii: Becoming Serious" in *The House of Ibuki* 48.

[6] *Bearings* 12.

7   *Bearings* 12.
8   *Bearings* 13.
9   *Bearings* 15.
10 *Bearings* 19.
11 *Indiana* 95.
12 *Altars* 52.
13 *Altars* 96.
14 *Indiana* 83.
15 *Indiana* 57.
16 *Altars* 108.
17 *Altars* 108.
18 *Altars* 12.
19 *Altars* 15.
20 *Altars* 112-3.
21 *Altars* 70-3.
22 See David V. Erdman, Ed. *The Complete Poetry and Prose of William Blake* (Berkeley: University of California Press, 1982) 601.
23 *Altars* 73.
24 "Review of Robert Kelly, *Axon Dendron Tree*" in *Caterpillar* 7 (1969) 252.
25 *The Sanjo Bridge*, non-paginated.
26 *Coils* 146.
27 *Coils* 147.
28 *Coils* 147.
29 "Adhesive Love" *Caterpillar* 20 (1973); reprinted in *Realignment*, *The Gull Wall*, and *The Price of Experience*. See *The Price of Experience* 71.
30 "Adhesive Love" in *The Price of Experience* 72.
31 "Adhesive Love" in *The Price of Experience* 76.
32 *Coils* 50.
33 *Coils* 110.
34 *Coils* 133-4.
35 *Coils* 12.
36 *Coils* 13.
37 *Coils* 32.
38 *Coils* 40.
39 *Coils* 54.
40 *Coils* 91-2.
41 *Coils* 137.
42 *Coils* 139.
43 *Coils* 147.

John Olson

Eshleman's Tjurunga

A poem by Clayton Eshleman is so much more than just a poem. It is a psychic journey. Anarchic apparitions diffuse the perfume of musk in a geography of the underworld: the murmur of subterranean rivers, stupefying incisions in the membrane of reality, the smell of volcanic sulfur, the bubble and hiss that is the rapture and torment of creation. A delirium in the blood awakens calamities of divine perception. An immersion in Eshleman is a saturation in clay and claw and the ineffable grace of Upper Paleolithic art: animals of stunning grace painted on chthonic rock. We can see into the depths of a hidden, primal reality, peer over the abyss into an underworld of shadows and passions buried in the rubble of our beleaguered imaginations. One emerges from the experience of hearing or reading one of Eshleman's poems feeling explicit and reproductive. It is as if one's consciousness had been illuminated by the light of an ancient flame.

The best way to read Eshleman is with an animal eye. Eshleman's aesthetic is one of animistic integration with primal realities. It means being alive to one's skin, the flesh and blood and bone you inhabit, acknowledging your impulses, desires, feelings, however disquieting or contrary to polite convention they happen to be. Facing taboos, conflicts, ineffable longings. If there is a wolf in you be a wolf. Enter the poem with the eyes and teeth and ears of a wolf. If there is a worm in you enter the poem as you would encase yourself in a chrysalis and hang in silent reverie, evolving into an imago of agitation, breaking from the encasement and spreading wings lurid as the profligate colors of paradise.

"Images are bodies," observed James Hillman, "Animal images in art, religion, and dreams are not merely depictions *of* animals. Animal images are also showing us images *as* animals, living beings that prowl and growl and must be nourished; the imagination, a great animal, a dragon under whose heaven we breathe its fire."[1]

Eshleman's totemic animal is the spider. "It all began with a gorgeous red, green and yellow spider centered in her web attached to the persimmon tree in the Okumura backyard," Eshleman avers in his essay "Companion Spider." "The orbed web with a female spider at center is a compelling metaphor for the labyrinth," Eshleman observes later in the essay. "The male spider, with semen-loaded paps, muſt make his way to the center without signaling via the wrong vibrations that he is prey, inseminate the much larger female, and then skedaddle before she seizes and devours him." [2]

Eshleman elaborates an essential aspeſt of his *poiesis* in the paragraphs that follow:

> In the Cretan labyrinth a hybrid man-bull, the Minotaur, lies in wait at the center for those who attempt to pass through. In one version of the myth, Theseus with a thread from Ariadne (whose name relates to Arachne, the weaver turned into a spider by Athena) kills the Minotaur, exits the labyrinth, and with others transmutes its turns into a weaving dance. The alchemiſt Fulcanelli writes: "The piſture of the labyrinth is thus offered to us as emblematic of the whole labour of the Work, with its two major difficulties, one the path which muſt be taken to reach the center – where the bitter combat of the two natures takes place – the other the way the artiſt muſt follow in order to emerge. It is there that the *thread of Ariadne* becomes necessary for him, if he is not to wander among the winding paths of the task, unable to extricate himself."

> Fulcanelli turns the web-become-labyrinth into a transformational arena. This triple overlay may offer some useful leads in underſtanding self and other. Jung offers considerable information on his view of the self in *Psychology and Alchemy*. He calls the self the union of opposites *par excellence*, the opposition between light and good on one hand and darkness and evil on the other. He proposes that the self is absolutely paradoxical, representing in every aspeſt thesis and antithesis and, at the same time, synthesis. It is the totality of the psyche, embracing the conscious and the unconscious. It is the *lapis invisibilitatus*, a borderline concept, and ultimately indeterminate.

> The red spider pierced my heart as an extraordinary gift. Did it beſtow a self? Working through Jung, I would have to say no. It confronted me with an extreme otherness that has taken years to

process, and its presence, and absence, muſt have bled into "the bitter combat of the two natures" that I engaged in with the obdurate *Poemas humanos*. Fulcanelli tells us a bit more about this "bitter combat," describing it as a battle between an alchemical Eagle and Lion who tear at each other until, the eagle having loſt its wings and the lion its head, a single body (referred to as *animated mercury*) is formed. As a hybrid, the Minotaur consiſts of a grotesque synthesis prefigured by mating spiders. Both conjunctions emit a lethal aura. [3]

The mind, teeming with words, extrudes a web of concentric elegance. It is a web whose filaments are secreted from a *Materia Prima* in which the conflicts and contrarieties of the evolving psyche churn in a ſtate of unbridled and indiscriminate chaos, the silk of dissonance, the movement of eight supple legs creating a pattern of solace for the war within, a luſtrous thread of labyrinthine reverie woven out of the appetency of one's loins.

Géza Róheim, in *The Gates of the Dream*, notes the similarities of the spider's method of issuing a web to the trance of the shaman, describing "a kind of magical rope that medicine men are believed to possess within their bodies and that confers great powers."[4] The Kabi in Auſtralia's Queensland, more properly known as the Gubbi Gubbi, believed that a Rainbow serpent lived in unfathomable water holes in the mountains. It is there that an initiate to shamanic tradition would go to sleep and become aware of a prickly sensation in his limbs. This was a sign of an imminent journey to the underworld. The Rainbow serpent would come and take the neophyte into the creature's domain, extract from his body sacred pebbles called *kundir* and give in exchange a magical rope that the initiate would keep within his body and that conferred great powers. This rope is called *maulwe* and is used by medicine men for many purposes in the same manner that a spider uses his webbing thread. It is sung out of the teſtes and attached to trees so that the medicine men may walk across the air.

Words are made for dreaming. It is not hard to think of a joining of words as a process similar to the making of a web. The intricacy of the pattern, the fineness yet ductile ſtrength of the ſtrands bear analogy with the supple endurance and infinite nuance of language. And what is more like writing than the hypnogogic sensation of emitting a fertile connectivity out of the conflicts and emotional turmoil of one's being, the exaltation of the poet in her/his war againſt the literal, againſt the cloddish, utilitarian values of commerce and Cartesian split from nature, and the conversion of lived experience into the hallucinatory splendor of poetry and fiction? In the delicate employments of spiders and the myth of Ariadne we find something vital revealed about the passageways of the human psyche.

"Jung's method of interior imagining," observed James Hillman, "aims at healing the psyche by re-establishing it in the metaxy [middle ground between the worldly and divine] from which it had fallen into the disease of literalism."[5]

Eshleman notes a strong parallel between shamanic tradition and the agonies and creative triumphs of Antonin Artaud:

> Making his way between biology and classical myth here may be the ur-poet shaman, who at the center of his or her initiation undergoes symbolic torture, dismemberment, and rebirth. While the animal-masked dancing shaman originates with prehistoric hunting peoples, in the 20th century there are intriguing parallels between the career of a shaman and the life and work of Antonin Artaud. Both share a nervous crisis, a painfully isolated initiation, symbolic death – in Artaud's case, a ninety-minute coma after electroschock – and rebirth, a new name and new language, chanting, gesturing, drumming, and detailed accounts of their spirit world adventures with allies and demons. The material here is much more complex (and utterly unintentional on Artaud's part) than those associations that cropped up in the understandably disputed "white shamanism" of the 1970s.[6]

Poetry is dangerous. It is a rag of infinity ripped from the wall of time. As a product of the imagination, it is, as poet Philip Lamantia marvelously phrased it, "a miracle of words." But as a mode of survival, even as a mode of social contribution, it is more apt to be a target of abuse and mockery than a thing to be marveled at. It isn't just that you can't make a living at it, it's because of what it does to you. It's a drug. It raises your consciousness. It opens your self to deeper levels of being. You find yourself wandering the planet gathering moon shadows and mugwort. The trajectory of your life is marvelously deformed into a search for chimeras and fame, signs of divinity, time spent unraveling the perspectives of interior mirrors, spellbound by a swirl of universe in the verdigris of a doorknob. It's nuts, I tell you.

Even among communities that give support for sanctioned, transmundane activities, following the transformative path toward spiritual awakening can be a painful and hazardous experience. In *Tristes Tropiques*, Claude Lévi-Strauss describes the quest for spiritual power as a thorny ordeal:

> Among a great many North American tribes, the social prestige of the individual is determined by the circumstances surrounding the ordeals connected with puberty. Some young men set themselves adrift on solitary rafts without food; others seek solitude in the mountains where they have to face wild beasts, as well as cold and rain. For days, weeks or months on end, as the case may be, they do not eat properly, but live only on coarse food, or fast for long periods and aggravate their impaired physical condition by the use of emetics. Everything is turned into a means of communication with the beyond. They stay immersed for long periods in icy water, deliberately mutilate one or more of their finger-joints, or lacerate their fasciae by dragging heavy loads attached by ropes to sharpened pegs inserted under their dorsal muscles. When they do not resort to such extremes, they at least exhaust themselves by performing various pointless tasks, such as removing all their body hairs, one at a time, or stripping pine branches until not a single needle remains, or hollowing out blocks of stone.

> In the dazed, debilitated and delirious state induced by their ordeals they hope to enter into communication with the supernatural world. They believe that a magic animal, touched by the intensity of their sufferings and their prayers, will be forced to appear to them; that a vision will reveal which one will henceforth be their guardian spirit, so that they can take its name and derive special powers from it, which will determine their privileges and rank within the social group.

> Have we to conclude that, in the opinion of these natives, nothing is to be expected from society? Both institutions and customs seem to them like a mechanism the monotonous functioning of which leaves nothing to chance, luck or ability. They may think

that the only means of compelling fate is to venture into those hazardous marginal areas where social norms cease to have any meaning, and where the protective laws and demands of the group no longer prevail; to go right to the frontiers of average, ordered living, to the breaking point of bodily strength and to the extremes of physical suffering. In this unstable border area, there is a danger of slipping beyond the pale and never coming back, as well as a possibility of drawing from the vast ocean of unexploited forces surrounding organized society a personal supply of power, thanks to which he who has risked all can hope to modify an otherwise unchangeable social order.[7]

"The Tjurunga," a poem of some 120 lines, is particularly representative of Eshleman's oeuvre. Inspired, in part, by an essay by Robert Duncan that appeared in *Caterpillar #1* in 1967 titled "Rites of Participation," and which is included in the collection of Duncan's prose titled *The H.D. Book*, the tjurunga refers to a sacred object in Australian aboriginal culture. It is an object of tremendous significance. The tjurunga "begins as a digging stick, first thing the Aranda child picks up," Eshleman's poem begins.[8] This is accurate. "The Aranda say that a newborn child is crying for his tjurunda," observes Géza Róheim, "and in order to pacify the infant the grandfather gets the tjurunga from the cave."[9] The object is best described as an oblong piece of stone or wood. "As far as the women are concerned," Róheim continues, "the tjurunga is called a *papa*, which is really the name of the little stick the children hold on to when they first stand erect." Róheim further elaborates:

Of course the children are crying for their mothers, and therefore we might suspect that the tjurunga brought from the cave, with the concentric circle on its surface, represents the mother. The same applies to the little sticks, the first object the children hold on to after the mother. A tjurunga, however carefully encased in string to prevent the women from seeing it, is actually placed in the cradle. Mysterious powers are supposed to emanate from it and to further the child's growth. When the young man has been circumcised he receives a nankara tjurunga, the mysterious body of his maternal totem ancestor, which henceforth accompanies and protects him in his wanderings. When he is already a married man the grandfather leads him to the sacred cave, shows him the tjurunga of his totem ancestor, and says "This is your body, *nana* (this) *unta* (you) *iningukua* (the same). Do not take it to another place or you will feel pain." So long as this tjurunga is in safe custody the personal security of the individual is not in danger. The tjurunga represents a mystical bond between him and his totem ancestor.

Every person has two bodies: a body of blood and bone and fingernails and skin, and one of stone or wood. Skin doesn't separate us from the world, it connects us to the world. Our first contact with the world is immensely tactile. We feel everything. We must touch everything. We must put things in our mouths, suck on them, taste them. This is why, later in life, when we engage with writing and poetry, we want to be in an active relation with the image. Desire fuses with its object. Words express qualities of living perception, scriptures in the fog, sermons in stones, books in brooks.

Robert Duncan makes a great imaginative leap and thinks of the first toys the infant comes into contact with: "The toys of the nursery are not trivia but first given instruments of an extension in consciousness, our creative life. There is a travesty made of sacred objects when the building blocks that are also alphabet blocks, the animal and human dolls, the picture books, are rendered cute or babyish."[10]

The third stanza of Eshleman's "The Tjurunga" gets personal:

I had to create a totemic cluster in which imagination
could replace Indianapolis, to incorporate ancestor beings
who could give me the agility
– across the tjurunga's spider's web –
to pick my way to her perilous center.

Perilous because transformational. Because death. Because the poet may be eaten after fertilizing his own creation, his labyrinth. Devoured, then altered out of the dream state into divine scintillation, hallucinations of language in which an imagery of mutation and convulsion mimic the sublimation of the alchemical alembic, metaphors mixed and bubbling over a blue flame.

We find a cluster of totemic reference beginning in the 26th line:

These nouns are also nodes in a constellation called
Clayton's Tjurunga. The struts are threads
in a web. There is a life blood flowing through
these threads. *Coatlicue* flows into Bud Powell,
César Vallejo into sub-incision. The bird-headed man
   floats right below
                  the pregnant spider
         centered in the Tjurunga.

Coatlicue is Nahuatl for "Skirt of Serpents." She is the Aztec earth goddess who gave birth to the moon, stars, and a pantheon of gods, including the feathered serpent Quetzalcoatl, Huitzilpochtli, the bloodthirsty warrior, and Xochiquetzal, a daughter who would teach the world to spin and weave, to paint and carve, and give to humankind the secret of the cycles of life and the pleasures of the body. Coatlicue is a formidable figure, containing within her both a womb and a grave. A necklace of skulls adorns her breast, amid live, pulsing hearts.

Bud Powell is the legendary jazz musician, known for his innovative technique and sheer intensity.

Of particular significance is César Vallejo, whose collected works were translated by Eshleman and published by the University of California Press in 2007. Eshleman has had a long and labyrinthine relationship with Vallejo and the trials and tribulations of getting Vallejo's work into published English translation has been an intricate and delicate process whose perplexities and frustrations, exposed to the vagaries of human irrationality and conflict, reveal a process not unlike a spider sending out a dragline and evolving, by trial and error, a concentric pattern of tensile strength and exquisite delicacy. The spinning dope contained in the silk glands of the spider is a flagelliform silk protein rich in particular amino acids, depending on the task at hand. There is something remarkably internal and spider-like about Vallejo's poetry. It is fiercely, unabashedly intricate, nuanced as Peruvian opal, and yet resonant and extreme in its emotional confrontations. Its syllables hang threaded together, trussed in a syntactical web whose thrust nimbly formulates, with bizarre images and preposterous neologisms, a being-in-the-world ecstatically trembling over an abyss of meaninglessness. In the web is a fecund possibility of the most primordial kind of knowing, which is Being in and of itself. Raw, unmitigated Being.

Eshleman describes Vallejo's evolution as an intimate mixture of incendiary emotions and materials from the unconscious "as well as those untoward regions of human experience that defy rational explanation." Once again, it is the journey and ordeals of the shaman. "I saw Vallejo, Arthur Rimbaud, Antonin Artaud, Aimé Césaire, and Vladimir Holan as examples of these poetics."[11] "It is worth noting," Eshleman remarks, "that Vallejo's poetic development is quite unusual. Coming from the conventional, if well-written and passionate, rhymed verse in *Los heraldos negros*, the reader is completely unprepared for *Trilce*, which is still the most dense, abstract, and transgression-driven collection of poetry in the Spanish language."[12] "Vallejo's development in his post-Peruvian poetry," Eshleman continues,

> involves taking on an ontological abyss, which might be briefly described as follows: Man is a sadness-exuding mammal, self-contradictory, perpetually immature, equally deserving of hatred, affection, and indifference, whose anger breaks any wholeness into warring fragments. This anger's only redeeming quality is that it is, paradoxically, a weapon of the poor, nearly always impotent against the military resources of the rich. Man is in flight from himself, as the worlds of colonial culture and colonized oppressiveness intersect. At the core of life's fullness is death, the "never" we fail to penetrate, "always" and "never" being the infinite extensions of "yes" and "no." Sorrow is the defining tone of human existence. Poetry thus becomes the imaginative expression of the inability to resolve the contradictions of man as an animal, divorced from nature as well as from any sustaining faith and caught up in the trivia of socialized life.[13]

"The Tjurunga" concludes (as will I) with a short narrative whose chief characters are Foreskin, Guardian Ghost, and Bud Powell:

> Foreskin wandered out of Indianapolis. Saw a keyboard, cooked
>   it in B Minor.
> Bud walked out of a dream. Bud and Foreskin found a waterhole,
>   swam.

Took out their teeth, made camp. Then left that place, came to Tenochtitlan.

After defecating, they made themselves headgear out of some hearts and lopped-off hands.

They noticed that their penises were dragging on the ground, performed sub-incision, lost lots of blood.

Bud cut Foreskin who then cut Bud.

They came to a river, across from which Kyoto sparkled in the night sky.

They wanted to cross so constructed a vine bridge.

While they were crossing, the bridge became a thread in a vast web.

At its distant center, an immense red gonad, the Matriarch crouched, sending out saffron rays.

"I'll play Theseus," Bud said, "this will turn the Matriarch into a Minotaur."

"And I'll play Vallejo," Foreskin responded, "he's good at bleeding himself and turning into a dingo.

Together let's back on, farting flames."

The wily Minotaur, seeing a sputtering enigma approaching, pulled a lever, shifting the tracks.

Foreskin and Bud found themselves in a roundhouse between conception and absence.

They noticed that their headgear was hanging on a Guardian Ghost boulder engraved with breasts snake-knotted across a pubis.

"A formidable barricade," said Bud. "To reach paradise, we must learn how to dance this design."

The pubis part disappeared. Fingering his sub-incision, Bud played "Dance of the Infidels."

Foreskin joined in, twirling his penis making bullroarer sounds.

The Guardian Ghost boulder roared: "WHO ARE YOU TWO THE SURROGATES OF?"

Bud looked at Foreskin. Foreskin looked at Bud.

"Another fine mess you've gotten us into," they said in unison.

Then they heard the Guardian Ghost laughing. "Life is a joyous thing," she chuckled, "with maggots at the center."

Notes

1 James Hillman, *A Blue Fire* (New York: Harper & Row, 1989) 68.
2 *The Grindstone of Rapport*, 287.
3 *The Grindstone of Rapport*, 290.
4 Géza Róheim, *The Gates of the Dream* (New York: International Universities Press, 1969) 247.
5 Hillman, *A Blue Fire*, 58.
6 *The Grindstone of Rapport*, 291.
7 Claude Lévi-Strauss, *Tristes Tropiques* (New York: Penguin Books, 1974) 39-40.
8 See *The Grindstone of Rapport*, 223-227.
9 Géza Róheim, *The Eternal Ones of the Dream* (New York: International Universities Press, 1945) 237.
10 Robert Duncan, *The H.D. Book* (Berkeley: University of California Press, 2011) 158.
11 César Vallejo, *The Complete Poetry*. Ed. and Trans. Clayton Eshleman, 684.
12 César Vallejo, *The Complete Poetry*, 686.
13 César Vallejo, *The Complete Poetry*, 687.

Andrew Joron

Earth Diver

The farther back one goes in time, the more things begin to resemble one another – until the mind resembles a cave, until light itself looks dark, pulses of ghost-particles populating the void.

According to an archaic logic, going back is the same as falling to the center.[1] Rebirth requires an impossible topology. Unsayable word, coiled within a stone's intestines.

Earth-embryo enwombed in water & air.

"If the cave was charged with a dreamlike womb atmosphere, we can imagine that the person crawling into it, groping from one unknown object to the next, perhaps in total darkness, entered fantasies in which he or she played a fetal role and sought, in some fashion, to be reborn." These words of Clayton Eshleman from his book *Juniper Fuse,* a work that seeks to retrace the mind's passages through the Underworld, may serve as an ars poetica for Eshleman's own poetic practice.

In modernity, poetic practice conventionally begins & ends where language does. Eshleman, however, re-members the sign that was dismembered from its earth-root. A cry raised beyond meaning became the first song, its chant that enchantment of the body that is consciousness. Language allows the animal literally to jump out of its skin.

In modernity, poetic practice conventionally begins & ends with the social subject. The human sphere has been insulated from the heat of its matrix. What is wild about the body—including the body of language—is that it conserves this heat, the birth of the earth out of the sun. Thus Eshleman, crawling backwards, devolving all desire, finds words in their first frenzy: "They are the waaah and no of breath / that enable spirit to appear."

Crawling down into the source-cry, the poet discovers the moment when making was One: one art, the sulfurous Whole Art, where all the senses meet in one convulsive *gestus*, one synesthetic act. For the cavemen blew their images onto the walls with reeds or directly with their mouths, sing-ing painting, using hallucinogenic pigments. Here, the genetic code of SING is mutated to SIGN. In this sense, the origin of speech was simultane-ous with the origin of writing, of music, and of art.

This "spray technique," where the mouth rather than the hand is used to paint pictures—magically conjuring the visual through the instrument of the vocal—was first scientifically documented by the French prehistorian Michel Lorblanchet in his study of Australian aboriginal art.

"During my stay in Australia," Lorblanchet stated, "I learned a great deal about cave art through my contact with the aborigines. Thanks to this fieldwork, I could subsequently look upon the Paleolithic art in France with new eyes. I understood better how the representations in French caves might have originated. Thus, in attempting to reproduce the art work, I blew the colors directly onto the wall with my mouth, a technique that the aborigines of the Northern Territories still employ. The pigments are chewed and then 'sprayed on' directly with the mouth."

Lorblanchet, using infrared photography, found that the stippled patterns of the cave paintings in France had also been produced in this way: "We know now that the spray technique was used not only at Pech Merle, but also in many other caves such as El Castillo or Lascaux.... The spray tech-nique appears to have possessed an extraordinarily symbolic significance: it is the human breath that, in the truest sense of the word, breathes life into the cave wall by creating an animal or a sign there. There can be no more direct or closer unity between the creator and the work. As a result, the cave paintings may be interpreted as totemic or shamanistic works."

Lorblanchet further argues that the process rather than the product of this making held the highest priority for its practitioners: "This experi-ment [of reproducing the Pech Merle paintings with the spray technique] refutes the presupposition according to which the artistic end-product was the primary aim of the artist.... On the contrary, it is quite possible that in many cases the cave-wall image represents only the trace of a creative process whose importance was equal to, or even greater than, the end-product."

The idea that this "creative process" involved a synesthetic, perhaps shamanistic experience is given credence by Lorblanchet's investigation of the chemical composition of the pigments that were used. "This investigation," he writes, "has incidentally revealed how poisonous many of the [chewed and partially ingested] pigments used in stone-age art were. Manganese dioxide, for example, can cause disturbances of the nervous system, including hallucinations. The hypothesis of shamanism, according to which paintings were rendered in a state of altered consciousness (as comparative ethnography has attested as well), is supported by this discovery."[2]

While Lorblanchet's work is not discussed in Eshleman's book *Juniper Fuse: Upper Paleolithic Imagination and the Construction of the Underworld*, the French prehistorian's findings seem to complement and confirm the American poet's approach to cave art. Indeed, decades earlier, Eshleman had published a volume of poems entitled *Hades in Manganese*, the results of his initial poetic foray into the prehistoric Underworld.[3] The title itself calls out the mind-altering ingredient of the cave-painting pigments.

Lorblanchet and Eshleman both understand cave art to be the product of shamanic activity. However, in contrast to Lorblanchet's reconstruction of the spray technique—as expression of oral *verbum* into visual figure – Eshleman, at least in his earliest book of poems inspired by cave art, views the pictures as the result of *drawing*, of handiwork infused with dream-energy – or, more ferociously, as trance-actions of sexualized violence carried out by the hands. Eshleman writes, in the introduction to this book, "The fact that many of these [figures] are struck again and again with lines that look like arrows or lances (or possibly ferns – or fern/lances, ambivalent plunges/withdrawings, desires hooked on kill and live), suggests a testing of the drawn image, a wonder in attempting to make 'it' go away – can I kill what I have made?"

In "Winding Windows," the question is posed of the shaman-artist: "What can he wound in the rock?"

Once an outline is gouged, wounding
the rock becomes a wild satisfaction,

to daub wall, to try to bloody it,
to finger rock as if it were
the flesh of separation…

The word "separation" holds special significance here, recalling the separation of the human from the animal re-enacted, in Esleman's view, in the cave paintings, whose production was "the result of the crisis of paleolithic people separating the animal out of their thus-to-be human heads…what we call 'the underworld' has, as its impulse, such a catastrophe behind it."

Here, in the introduction to *Hades in Manganese*, Eshleman first broached the theory of the "construction of the Underworld" (based on an essay by the Jungian psychologist James Hillman). According to this theory, the early humans turned the caves into a sort of dream-laboratory in which they could process the effects of the construction of Mind itself – i.e., the separation of the human from the animal, and the resultant stratification of consciousness. The night-world of the caves corresponded to an inner world of dream and imagination, a zone temporarily liberated from the day-world's survival-driven activities. The autonomy granted to desire in the "dreamlike womb atmosphere" of the caves allowed the incipient imagination to fully access the primal drives of Eros and Thanatos. The pictures created in this liberated zone still burn as original realizations of the vitality of sex and death.

This descent into the Underworld can serve as a paradigm for all creative/poetic activity. Authentic art's radical renewal of perception must always, in some way, recapitulate the birth of consciousness itself – the moment when the Cry reorganized as Voice, when the Sign took on a life of its own, when the dream escaped from the inner into the outer world. Even with the advent of civilization and its systems of repressed desire, the artist could be seen as inspired with (as Plato famously put it) a "divine frenzy," possessed by a power not entirely human. Thus, poets prehistoric, antique, and modern may be characterized as, in Eshleman's phrase, "conductors of the pit," channeling and transferring the original energies of the Underworld into conscious activity.

In the introduction to his book of translations, *Conductors of the Pit,* Eshleman wrote: "The pit, the abyss, the unknown that Baudelaire proposed poets are to penetrate, the penetralia, the recesses of the mind, the darkness of political domination, the gulf between worlds. To conduct the pit, then, versus the orchestra of the living, is to induct and order materials from the subconscious as well as from those untoward regions of human experience that defy rational explanation." For Eshleman, poetry "lets... abyssal power glare into the language. And receiving the abyss is only part of the charge that [certain] poets have taken on: they have conducted chaos in such a way that it has been symphonically bound into their writing. In this sense, they are not conductors of the orchestra, but conductors of the pit, snake-charming its depths, drawing up figurations that sway in rhythm to, or against, their own processes."[4]

Our human world is bounded, above and below, by a crawling chaos of incomprehensible forces that, while threatening to overwhelm us, are also responsible (in most mythologies, including the scientific one) for generating our existence. American avant-garde poetry (since the middle of the last century, at least) has significantly failed to take this cosmic condition into account, either in its theory or its practice. Eshleman's work stands as a rare exception to this trend: for him, poetic production entails the conduction of a cosmic chaos, a penetration and (re)construction of the dark potencies of the Underworld (at once subverting and inverting that neo-Platonist poetics, dominant from antiquity to early Romanticism, according to which inspiration emanates as light from an Overworld).

In his work as a translator, Eshleman has crawled down the throats of other poets; in his own, cave-art-inspired poetry, he has attempted, by performing what he calls a "cosmogonic dive,"[5] to enter the (w)hole of the earth, to hear:

the hum of pre-poetic vocality,

where the human, twisting its
animal imperative, wrenched
free into narrative.

In the works that followed *Hades in Manganese,* Eshleman would continue to poetically exercise as an earth diver, returning (as witness) to the depths where an animal bloodmud first convulsed into humanity.

Notes

[1] Eshleman writes of "the archetypal pattern in which psychic movement is depicted *as vertical streams of energy revolving around a center*" (his emphasis), in *Juniper Fuse* 234.

[2] Michel Lorblanchet's writings on cave art remain largely untranslated into English. The text quoted here appeared in the German-language newspaper *Die Zeit* (January 31, 1997); my translation of it was published in *Sulfur* 42 (Spring 1998). For an example of Lorblanchet's more recent writing on this subject, see *Les origines de l'art* (Paris: Pommier, 2006).

[3] All my quotations from Eshleman's poetry herein are taken from this volume.

[4] *Conductors of the Pit* xv and xvii.

[5] *Juniper Fuse* 207–209.

Kenneth Warren

Archetypal Configurations in Clayton Eshleman's Underworld Poetics

Throughout the 1980s, the relationship between poetry and archetypal psychology achieved a distinctive register in Clayton Eshleman's underworld poetics, an opus of fantastic poetry, free-ranging scholarship, moral protest, and mythological vitality. Articulating a traumatic vision of imagination through animal magnetism, somatic discharge, and soulful sign play, Eshleman's underworld poetics is palpably grounded in his travels to Cro-Magnon caves in the Dordogne, his intellectual engagement with psychologist James Hillman, his editorship of *Sulfur: A Literary Tri-Quarterly of the Whole Art,* and his extraordinary commitment to translation. Just as John Clarke, another poet steeped to a considerable degree in the soul psychology of Jung, Hillman, and Corbin, emerged decisively in the 1980s as Olson's true successor in the upward thrust of imagination into the celestial realm of Sirius, so too did Eshleman become in the 1980s Olson's true successor in the downward thrust of imagination into the archaic realm of Tartaros. In such poems as "Notes on a Visit to Le Tuc d'Audoubert," "Visions of the Fathers of Lascaux," and "Our Lady of the Three-Pronged Devil," Eshleman generated an artistically complex and emotionally charged advance in American poetry that has not yet been fully appreciated for the light it casts backward and forward on human imagination, myth, and species communication.

By approaching the imagination of Cro-Magnon caves through Hillman's revision of Jung's psychology, Eshleman extended the mythopoetic tradition of Olson and Duncan into a potent archetypal reflection of the poetic mind historically situated in the 1980s. At a time when Language writing was emerging as a kind of Titanic shadow of abstraction, linguistic intricacy, and theoretical excess to the Dionysian emotional body of the New American poets[1], Eshleman managed with passionate brilliance to capture and elaborate this creative tension in *Sulfur,* publishing in addition to Hillman other archetypal psychologists such as Wolfgang Giegerich and Robert Avens, along with such poets as Charles Bernstein, Lyn Hejinian, and Ron Silliman. Suffice it to say, Eshleman's intensive sensory experience of self-artistry in Cro-Magnon caves was the strange attractor that constellated during the 1980s a mythological field of warring gods whose poets are still speaking through personifications embedded in canons, computers, and coteries. Against the present day digital drift of poets into social network fanaticism and uploaded self-preservation effects, the complex forces of attention, interaction, and personality contained in the 46 issues of *Sulfur* feel exquisitely elemental, inspired, and numinous.

First named by Hillman, archetypal psychology is a cultural movement of image, imagination, and soul-making that hit stride during the 1980s and that gave an informed psychic perspective to Eshleman's underworld poetics.[2] Archetypal psychology, explains Hillman, "starts neither in the physiology of the brain, the structure of language, the organization of society, nor the analysis of behavior, but in processes of imagination."[3] Against such scientific and social conceptions that reduced longstanding notions of authorship, self, and soul to fictions, archetypal psychology offered Eshleman an oblique phenomenological process that de-literalizes attitudes in order to recover "the world as a place of soul."[4] According to Hillman,

> Archetypal psychology *axiomatically* assumes imagistic universals, comparable to the *universali fantastici* of Vico, that is, mythological figures that provide the poetic characteristics of human thought, feeling, and action, as well as the physiognomic intelligibility of the qualitative worlds of natural phenomena. By means of the archetypal image, natural phenomena present faces that speak to the imagining soul rather than only conceal hidden laws and probabilities and manifest their objectification.[5]

Initially Hillman entered into Eshleman's awareness through Robert Duncan and Robert Kelly. After meeting Hillman during the mid-1970s, Eshleman read *The Dream and the Underworld* (1979). In an interview with Keith Tuma, Eshleman explained: "In the late 1970s I read James Hillman's *The Dream and the Underworld* as a way to help me de-literalize the animals to be found on cave walls."[6] In the preface to *Hades in Manganese* (1981), Eshleman noted that Hillman's writings on dreams, eventually published in *The Dream and the Underworld*, spurred him to imagine that the caves, too, were "an autonomous realm, an archetypal place that corresponds with a distinctive mythic geography—in short, an underworld that is not merely a reflection, i.e., a diminution, of an empirical sense world."[7] The title poem "Hades in Manganese," written in 1979, was dedicated to Hillman.

Like Charles Olson, Eshleman demands to be read psycho-poetically. That is to say, Eshleman's underworld poetics must be read through the structure and dynamic of the psyche, which purposefully enfolds mental, emotional, and spiritual contents of the self and collective unconscious into a mythopoesis that proclaims the fantasy of "the Whole Art." With an emphasis on the unconscious and man's contentious bond with nature, Eshleman's underworld poetics contains roots in the 18th century Romantics, most notably William Blake. In order to realize an underworld poetics, however, Eshleman must thrust outward and down, pressing out of himself and into the earth so energetically that any likelihood of cultural containment within Romantic introspection, Christian subjectivity, and even Olson's Catholicity is determinately negated. Clearly, Hillman's archetypal psychology supported Eshleman in such determination.

Whereas the analytical psychology of Jung offered Olson a modern, scientific perspective on the modalities of ego and self, the archetypal psychology of Hillman offered Eshleman a postmodern phenomenological revision of both the empiricism and Kantian idealism specific to Jung's formulation of such archetypes. To read Eshleman psycho-poetically, as *Novices: A Study of Poetic Apprenticeship* (1989) would propose, requires bringing the modern formulations of Jung and the postmodern revisions of Hillman to bear upon "that labyrinth in whose folds struggle between self and other is said to lead to the transformation of personality and significant art."[8]

Situated in an emotionally-drenched complex of alchemy, archetype, and apprenticeship, the psychological crux of Eshleman's underworld poetics is outlined in *Novices: A Study of Poetic Apprenticeship*, a training manual for beginning poets originally conceived while he was attending a seminar on alchemy presented by Hillman. Drawing image and insight from the alchemist Fulcanelli about the place where "the bitter combat of two natures takes place."[9] Eshleman proposes that "there is an archetypal poem, and its most ancient design is probably the labyrinth."[10] Here, as Fulcanelli suggests, "the thread of Ariadne becomes necessary for him"[11], thereby making a fecund connection through the wife of Dionysus to both animality and love, two essential dimensions in Eshleman's underworld poetics. Placed in "Tartaros," then, Eshleman's "archetypal poem" needs to be understood psychically through the Orphic conception of the birth of Dionysus—"the god in opposition to the Titans; as the most repressed god throughout Western culture; as the god of women, of wine, and of tragedy; and as a god with a strong relation to death."[12]

Becoming a poet, suggests Eshleman, requires an initiation into the dark forces of an underworld where both Dionysiac and Titanic forces battle over propitiations. Shaped by "the archetypal poem," Eshleman must deliver hellish insight into the forms of deformed personalities that are rooted extensively in evolution and prehistory. Within Eshleman's underworld poetics, "the bitter combat of two natures" is connected to a primary complex related to the conflict between Dionysus and the Titans. In "Tartaros," a poem from *Hades in Manganese*, he writes:

> Covering Shaman, you are the Tartaros-enchained Titans I approach every moment of my life. When you juggle my sex, tomb and excrement as desire, I talk Kali. When you crouch horned in the cul-de-sac of my will, I talk Minotaur. When you scatter my flesh, my son weeps Set. In essence, you are me with the abyss over your head, so looking at another, I see myself through the abyss, and that other seems to be alien—and is, as am I.[13]

Eshleman's descent to the realm of the dead requires, paradoxically enough, a life-affirming mastery of affective art through an intentional respect for the poet's conscious and unconscious connection to others. In other words, the inexhaustible filament of a Dionysiac love emotionally binds Eshleman's journey through the labyrinth to "the thread of Adriadne." For it is only through an emotional connection to others that one might enter the dynamic process of self-creating reality, which demands through relationship an alchemical surrender of the conditioned ego to the master archetype of the poet.

In "The Feeling Function," Hillman observes that "the cooperative relationship between ego-consciousness and unconscious dominants—is, as a relationship, largely a function of feeling."[14] The deep feeling that animates Eshleman's engagement with the Upper Paleolithic imagination amplifies, in an elemental sense, the meaning and practice of "one saturation job," which he absorbed from Olson's advice to Ed Dorn: "Best thing to do is to dig one thing or place or man until you know more abt that than is possible to any other man."[15] Inasmuch as the element of feeling is water, Eshleman's "saturation job" in Upper Paleolithic imagination drips into the postmodern world of alienated and repressed emotions a relational solvent from an archetypal order of belonging.

In "A Discussion with James Hillman on Psychology and Poetry," originally published in *Sulfur*, Eshleman presents through Dionysus and Apollo his grasp of Jung's organization of psychic energy, which classifies the external, objective motivation of the extroverted attitude and the inner directed, subjective motivation of the introverted attitude

> My experience has been that Jung's oppositional categories are backed up by the majority of significant twentieth-century poetry. Few poets would use Jung's terminology, but most would participate in some form of oppositionalism, whether it is Dionysus vs. Apollo, Romantic vs. Classical or experimental vs. traditional. The tendency is to believe that there is a kind of Blakean antimony between the "prolific" and the "devouring," Devils vs. Angels, that is an essential aspect of poetry itself, and that this "war" is played out from generation to generation, with each side accusing the other of not really being what they propose to represent. While it may be that a yin/yang coherence of the new warring with the old is essential to imaginative movement, the poetic product always seems to be heavily indebted to one of the two sides.[16]

Eshleman's dialogue with Hillman about the diametrically opposed modes of psychic energy through which poets relate to the world is packed with implications concerning typology and the poetry wars of the 1980s.

Although filled with the soul-making aspiration of archetypal psychology, Eshleman's physiological exertion into Cro-Magnon caves supplies the crucial clue to the "meanders" that wind through "an archetypal poem." In "Decanting," a poem from *Hades in Manganese*, for example, Eshleman initially encounters "Our Father of the Caves."[17] Then he doubles back from "Caravaggio's beautiful jaundice lime Dionysus / gathering himself into his fawn cluster" in order to recollect in prose a memory of unblocked respiration and somatic release that allows him to stream energetically from his own animal body toward the outside world.

My basic exercise was to lie on my back, naked, knees raised, legs falling out and being brought back together in coordination with breathing amply in and out (at "out" the knees flopped to the side—at "in" they were together) AND to stay in eye contact with Dr. Handelman while one of us talked. The more I stayed in eye contact while doing this kind of breathing, the more I felt my body—which led me into severe emotional corners. After a year of this exercise, with all its consequent meanders, I started to feel a streaming sensation in my feet and fingertips, which, over the second year, gradually passed through my body to the point that near the end of the therapy a bracing streaming would take place throughout my entire body after commencing the exercise. To be naked, on one's back, knees raised, under the searching eye of a clothed adult, evokes what is earliest in us, not only our infancy, but also being suffused with feeling and inducting and responding to whatever is outside.[18]

Consequently, the outward flow of sensation from the Dionysian emotional body ripples freely throughout Eshleman's underworld poetics. Inasmuch as his underworld poetics is concerned with the self-regulation of grotesque lower body psychosomatics, Eshleman must actually crawl into caves in order to confront the gouging of his own archaic discontents in rock. By dragging his body down to "real bedrock—a genuine back wall," he can render an experiential account of "Cro-Magnon metaphors" that pushes far beyond Olson's initial archaic and projective deposit.[19] At the Cro-Magnon "back wall," he drills into the raw material of projection that operates in both poetry and psychology. There "Upper Paleolithic people began to separate the animal out of their about-to-be human heads and to project it onto cave walls," as he notes in the introduction to *Juniper Fuse*.[20] With visionary sensitivity, he sees the immense significance that animal imagery played in marking the site of a traumatic rupture that gave rise to art, conscience, imagination, self-knowledge, and shadow.

Hillman's postmodern reinterpretation of Jung's theory of archetypes collapses any empirical, rational, and scientific claims within the domain of psychology. Whereas Jung posits an objective link between body and psyche as well as between instinct and image[21], Hillman departs from such factual assertions. Favoring image-rich platforms of dreams, fantasy, mythology, and poetry, Hillman provides Eshleman with the archetypal perspective that inspires him to honor Dionysus and Hades through an un-flinching penetration of the Cro-Magnon cave. In the line to Eshleman's underworld poetics, then, Hillman provides this rich passage:

> There is an imagination below the earth that abounds in animal forms, that revels and makes music. There is a dance in death. Hades and Dionysos are the same. As Hades darkens Dionysos toward his own tragedy, Dionysos softens and rounds out Hades into his own richness.[22]

The deep psychic texture that Hillman proposed in *The Dream and the Underworld* offered a way for Eshleman to bear down on the implications of the Cro-Magnon possibility field initially outlined in Charles Olson's "The Chiasma, or Lectures in the New Sciences of Man," put together by George Butterick, and published in *Olson: The Journal of the Charles Olson Archives* (Number 10 [Fall 1978]). In these lectures that alerted Eshleman to the potentials within Cro-Magnon, Olson elaborated "the science of the image" through *Essays Toward a Science of Mythology: The Myth of the Divine Child and the Mysteries of Eleusis* (1949/1969) by Jung and Kerenyi.[23] Both "physiological and mythological evidences"[24] are cru-cial to Olson's "science of the image." In this respect, Olson's "science of the image" is rather closely attuned to Jung's empirical viewpoint as well as to his notion that the archetype is an objective inherited pattern. To be sure, Hillman's archetypal psychology dispenses with such Jungian claims. From an archetypal perspective, then, Olson's "science of the im-age" and "physiological evidences" can only be embraced as fantasy-based expressions that concentrate our perspective on the depth of imagery and soul-making potentials that might be experienced by the poetic mind. Underscoring the imaginative space that he inhabits as poet, Olson pro-vided a quote from *Webster's Collegiate Dictionary*, 5th ed. (1945): "the for-mation of mental images of objects not present to the senses."[25] Therefore, it is not hard to see that once Olson returned himself as poet to his roots in the imagination his location is well within the preferred domain of ar-chetypal psychology.

From Olson's viewpoint, the Cro-Magnon possibility field is substan-tially hinged to "spoken language."[26] Olson suggests "that it is possible that most of our psychic devices trail back to him; the cave, the dance, the Malinowski point on myth as living reality, thus the man-anima(1)-divine connecting, possible (my own hunch) spoken language."[27] Thus Olson's "science of the image" is ostensibly the imagination absorbed in the linguistic complex. With postmodern chops from archetypal psychology, Eshleman argues that Olson's version of Cro-Magnon development is hobbled by "an over-emphasis on speech, and a failure to make the connection between tools and image making."[28] Nonetheless, Eshleman detects the "shamanism" within Olson's recognition of "'the poet's ability to hear through himself and access 'secrets objects share.'"[29] Pushing through Olson's initial signals on "motion," then, Eshleman finds in the Cro-Magnon cave that "an enduring and catastrophic 'separation continuum' was set in motion ... by initial image-making."[30] Again, Hillman's archetypal psychology prompts Eshleman to drill further into the archaic grain that speaks through Olson. While Eshleman's charge to animate the Cro-Magnon cave with imagination rather than history can be seen advancing from both Olson and Hillman, archetypal psychology enables him to spring animal presence from humanistic captivity. His engagement with Hillman thus generates an underworld poetics that activates conscious understanding, critical insight, ethical regard, experiential depth, imaginative genius, and mythological fantasy.

Within the space of Upper Paleolithic imagination, Eshleman is initiated into the hot-spit cross-modal vulva of Apollo's pre-historical optics. "Silence Raving," another poem from *Hades in Manganese*, answers the call to Cro-Magnon "back wall" of consciousness:

> Patter, pater, Apollo-globes, sound
> Breaking up with silence, coals
> I can still hear, entanglement of sense
> Pools, the way a cave would leak perfume—
>
> In the Cro-Magnons went, along its wet hide walls,
> As if a flower, way in, drew their leggy
> Panspematic bodies, spidering over
> Bottomless hunches, groping toward Persephone's
> Fate: to be quicksanded by the fungus pulp of
> Hades' purple hair exploding in their brains.[31]

Eshleman's brain is, likewise, enveloped in signals from Hades and rooted collectively in a primitive projection process that generates images of liminal beings elemental to feeling and intuiting the way back to

> Dionysus
> the plopping, pooling words, stirred
> by the lyre gaps between the peaks of flame,
> water to fire[32]

To participate with the images of Cro-Magnon caves requires a cooperative relationship with feeling and intuition—"water to fire," as Eshleman writes. Associated elementally with fire, the function of intuition occurs primarily at the unconscious level. In *Psychological Types*, Jung described intuition "as perception by way of the unconscious, or perception of unconscious events."[33] For Jung, "the primary function of intuition is simply to transmit images, or perceptions of relations between things, which could not be transmitted by the other functions or only in a very roundabout way."[34] The alchemical marriage of water and fire is equally the typological combination of feeling and intuition that produces the Divine Child of Dionysiac psychology—the mythological image presented by Jung and Kerényi in *Essays Toward a Science of Mythology: The Myth of the Divine Child and the Mysteries of Eleusis*. From this initiation into an elemental consciousness that joins feeling and intuition, then, Eshleman can see himself in Dionysus. Thereby he can approach "the madness inherent in the womb of the mother," which is the feral side of creation perceived by Walter Otto in *Dionysus: Myth and Cult* (1965/1981).[35] Thus "Silence Raving" concludes:

> the animals led in crossed
> a massive vulva incised before the gate
> the power that came up from it was paradise, the power
> the Cro-Magnons bequeathed to me, to make an altar of my
> > throat.[36]

In *The Thought of the Heart & the Soul of the World* (1981/1992), Hillman describes the role that sulfur plays in alchemical psychology. Hillman's description of sulfur gives a sense of the projective fire-power of the imagination that can be "thrown outward, ahead of itself."[37] As an alchemical matter of the heart's desire, Eshleman's engagement with publishing a literary magazine named *Sulfur* is joined to Olson's "projection of archetypal force onto language."[38] For sulfur is, according to Hillman's reading of Paracelsus "that which sticks, the mucilage, 'the gum,' the joiner, the stickiness of attachment."[39] Hillman suggests from Jung that "it is enough to recognize compulsive projection to be a necessary activity of sulfur, as the way in which this heart thinks, where thought and desire are one."[40] When Hillman connects sulfur to "the animal heart," the meaning of "the Whole Art" invoked for the magazine can be better appreciated in relation to Eshleman's underworld poetics:

> The animal heart directly intends, senses, and responds as a unitary whole. Wholeness in the act, as a quality of act.[41]

Launched in 1981, *Sulfur* included in its first issue Hillman's essay "Alchemical Blue and the Unio Mentalis." Amplifying blue works of imagination, communal existence, and mythological precedents, Hillman's essay underscores the link between Dionysus and Hades. Aligned respectively with emotion and essence within the invisible textures of archetypal psychology[42], Dionysus and Hades are crucial archetypal configurations in Eshleman's underworld poetics. Again, as editor of *Sulfur* for 46 issues, Eshleman was situating the personified forces of poetry wars within a lucent mythological field. Indeed, "the background against which *Sulfur* proposed itself is anchored in the Dionysian 1960s," as Eshleman himself noted in the final issue.[43]

In *The Postmodern Condition: An Enquiry into the Origins of Cultural Change* (1990), David Harvey, after having written about "the various counter-cultural and anti-modernist movements of the 1960s", cites an announcement by the editors of PRECIS 6 (1987) that "the culture of the advanced capitalist societist has undergone a profound shift in the structure of feeling."[44] Indeed this postmodern "shift in the structure of feeling" is a psychological insight that must be brought to bear upon the poetry wars of the 1980s, an historical moment when the poetic mind was increasingly absorbing Titanic templates of abstraction, formalism, and linguistic excess—expressions of human nature especially evident among Language poets, whose theoretical exuberance was fiercely opposed to Dionysiac deposits of emotion, image, life force, and primal mystery.[45] To be sure, Titanic mentality locates in language what could otherwise be located in the body. Such Titanism does not completely rule Eshleman's underworld poetics, however. In an exchange with Rachel Blau DuPlessis in *Sulfur 22*, he explains:

> But language is not the source of my experience; it is a mediational tool that is a result of symbol-making and symbol making itself is anchored in my <u>Foetushood.</u> Language is a kind of slippery taffy that I use to wire the outer to the inner.[46]

Inside the back pages of *Sulfur* tensions over the Titanic excess of theory flared symptomatically from time to time, marking this postmodern "shift in the structure of feeling" across any number of exchanges between poets. "I knew, of course, you'd have a mass of theory," Burns scolds Bernstein in *Sulfur 9*.[47] Objecting to "the newspaper cliché of 'the baby boom,'" Barrett Watten responds to Don Byrd in a way that allows us to appreciate both the elemental dynamism of *Sulfur* and the Titanic war powers evoked by that "baby": "I was reading in the paper today about 'friendly fire' (bombs from our side that drop on the troops) as a not unfriendly preliminary to a criticism of your article in *Sulfur 8*."[48]

Perhaps Eliot Weinberger's "A Final Response," appearing in *Sulfur 22*, after a heated exchange with Michael Davidson over "the technocratic prose of the 'Language' poets"[49] is the quickest way to capture a sense of the Eros lost in this postmodern "shift in the structure of feeling," a psychic fact which certainly informed the practice and reception of Language poets. Weinberger wonders: "One can only imagine how they will react to Rachel Blau DuPlessis, in her statement above, raising words like 'pleasure,' 'transcendence,' 'passion,' 'feeling.'"[50] For Weinberger, Robert Duncan, who had died on February 3, 1988, the day before "A Final Response" was written, personified such emotional gifts. From the perspective of archetypal psychology, such emotional gifts are attributed to Dionysus. Weinberger continues:

> For me, a model of the life and work of a poet was Robert Duncan, who died yesterday—a poet who embraces all the words of Rachel's list and much more—curiosity, pluralism, history, indignation, spirituality, social and moral accountability.[51]

Eshleman's deep sensitivity to the transpersonal energies that were streaming from Tartaros allowed him to channel through *Sulfur* the mythological tension between Titanic poets and Dionysiac poets that so well depicts the poetry wars of the 1980s. To be sure, Eshleman's immense productivity as editor, poet, and translator partially binds him to the world of Prometheus, a Titan who was not exiled to Tartaros. Nevertheless, in the battle of mythological mentalities, *Sulfur* was magnificently situated for imaginative reflections through archetypal psychology. From the perspective of archetypal psychology, then, *Sulfur* is an enormously rich mythological field that enables readers to appreciate more soulfully how the Dionysiac deposit of Robert Duncan and Norman O. Brown requires an opposing Titanic force. Consequently, Robert Duncan's "In Blood's Domaine," the poem that opens *Sulfur* 3, is followed by Ron Silliman's "Skies". From Tartaros, then, the Titanic extension of Language poetry reaches upward through Sillman's report: "THE SKY IS A GREY PLANE tending toward white, without, depth, barely with light."[52] As editor of *Sulfur*, Eshleman pulls down "the shimmer of a spider's thread in the plum tree light"[53] from Sillman's "Skies II" into a charge that sustains the feeling function so crucial to the Dionysiac transfer of emotional and relational force, which remains largely repressed in postmodern cultural production. In Eshleman's underworld poetics Ariadne's thread unwinds from *Sulfur* — that glorious 20th century cave of poets where the fantasy of "the Whole Art" could contain nothing less than a few rounds of Titanic "friendly fire" aimed at the god of the archetypal way of life.

[2012]

Notes

[1] See Raphael Lopez-Pedraza, *Dionysus in Exile: on the Repression of the Body and Emotion*, 2000.
[2] See James Hillman, *Archetypal Psychology: A Brief Account* and *Re-Visioning Psychology*.
[3] Hillman, *Re-Visioning Psychology* xi.
[4] Hillman, *Archetypal Psychology: a Brief Account* 25.
[5] Hillman, *Archetypal Psychology: a Brief Account* 19.
[6] *Companion Spider* 311.
[7] *Hades in Manganese* 10.
[8] *Companion Spider* 4

⁹ *Companion Spider* 20.

¹⁰ *Companion Spider* 20.

¹¹ *Companion Spider* 20.

¹² Raphael Lopez-Pedraza, *Dionysus in Exile:on the Repression of the Body and Emotion* 3

¹³ *Hades in Manganese* 81.

¹⁴ James Hillman, *Jung's Typology* 83.

¹⁵ Charles Olson, *Collected Prose* 306-7.

¹⁶ *The Grindstone of Rapport* 265.

¹⁷ *Hades in Manganese* 106.

¹⁸ *Hades in Manganese* 107.

¹⁹ *Juniper Fuse* xi.

²⁰ *Juniper Fuse* xvi.

²¹ See Andrew Samuels, et alia, *A Critical Dictionary of Jungian Analysis* 26.

²² Hillman, *The Dream and the Underworld* 45.

²³ *Olson: The Journal of the Charles Olson Archives* 10 (Fall 1978) 18.

²⁴ *Olson* 10 (1978) 32.

²⁵ *Webster's Collegiate Dictionary*, 5ᵗʰ ed. (1945).

²⁶ *Olson* 10 (1978) 13.

²⁷ *Olson* 10 (1978) 13.

²⁸ *Archaic Design* 235.

²⁹ *Archaic Design* 226.

³⁰ *Archaic Design* 233.

³¹ *Hades in Manganese* 55.

³² *Hades in Manganese* 55.

³³ C.G. Jung, *Psychological Types* 518.

³⁴ Jung, *Psychological Types* 366.

³⁵ Walter Otto, *Dionysus: Myth and Cult* 143.

³⁶ *Hades in Manganese* 55-6.

³⁷ James Hillman, *The Thought of the Heart & the Soul of the World* 14.

³⁸ See Charles Stein, *The Secret of the Black Chrysanthemum: The Poetic Cosmology of Charles Olson & his Use of the Writings of C.G. Jung* 119.

³⁹ Hillman, *The Thought of the Heart & the Soul of the World* 140.

⁴⁰ Hillman, *The Thought of the Heart & the Soul of the World* 15.

⁴¹ Hillman, *The Thought of the Heart & the Soul of the World* 15.

⁴² Hillman, *The Dream and the Underworld* 44.

⁴³ *Companion Spider* 275.

⁴⁴ David Harvey, *The Postmodern Condition: An Enquiry into the Origins of Cultural Change* 39.

⁴⁵ Raphael Lopez-Pedraza, *Dionysus in Exile* 3.

⁴⁶ *Sulfur* 22 (1989) 194.

⁴⁷ *Sulfur* 9 (1984) 215.

⁴⁸ *Sulfur* 9 (1984) 168.

[49] *Sulfur* 22 (1989) 182.
[50] *Sulfur* 22 (1989) 201.
[51] *Sulfur* 22 (1989) 201.
[52] *Sulfur* 3 (1982) 6.
[53] *Sulfur* 3 (1982) 149.

Jay Murphy

Eshleman's Caves

Almost from its very inception Clayton Eshleman's work broached the notion of double worlds. This strenuous process of pitching a rope between them is called the mission of poetry in one of his early poems, "Ode to Reich" (1970), in that "poetry is translation not just of language / but the passing of a psyche into new form." This could be the signal given by the liberation of his first poetry collection – the Tibetan wrath god on the cover of *Indiana* – the outer oppression or intolerable imperial extension, and the inner often poisoned, gutted, or dislocated core that was its correlate. Eshleman's poetry was an investigation that was more than a protest; it also plumbed a reclamation or reconstruction of nature. This despite the violence done to it, all the shocks the journey entailed in its reconstitution, and notwithstanding the new insular, almost unusable and shrunken character of "nature" – that now as he put it "Mother nature has become man's problem child." Agreeing with his friend Adrienne Rich that "modernity itself drives people into terror," Eshleman saw an overwhelming need to reach back, to the "caves as Lascaux, Niaux, and Chauvet … the cemeteries of the Cro-Magnon paradise." These shadow plays and gropings into the Upper Paleolithic wind throughout Eshleman's *oeuvre* and its traces of transformation. This fascination and urgency towards the geological (that is sometimes at once a geo-poetics and geo-politics), what Eshleman called poetry's "backwall" had as one of its most immediate and significant predecessors Charles Olson, whose 1946 "La Préface" had strikingly parlayed:

"My name is NO RACE"   address
Buchenwald   new Altamira cave

presenting Eshleman with the remarkable synchronicity that the majority of the known Upper Paleolithic caves were only discovered (and Altamira's antiquity officially recognized though it was discovered earlier) between 1900 and 1940. For Eshleman, Olson's own undeveloped project on the Paleolithic remained a potent suggestion of a literal perhaps salvic resurfacing of the Paleolithic in the midst of greatest crisis, a reminder that outer ecologies mirror inner ones.

The eventual result of Eshleman's head-on confrontation with these double-worlds and more than thirty years research into the "nearly disintegrated Atlantis" of the ancient cave paintings of southwestern France was *Juniper Fuse*, for which it is difficult to see any contemporary equivalent. In that book Eshleman combined poetry, psychoanalytic and philosophical speculation, art historical summation and musing, and often perilous, nothing if not visceral, personal wrestling with the psychic forces conjured up by his various experiences spelunking throughout the caves. *Juniper Fuse* is a rhizomatically structured source book where a prose discussion of the origin of image-making 10 to 40,000 years ago turns into poetry, and sets of poems around the Cro-Magnon merge seamlessly into thoroughgoing if idiosyncratic metaphysical exploration or packed, visionary reminiscence. The territory of *Juniper Fuse* ranges from Eshleman's "cobra" experience in Reichian therapy, to speculations on the original whirring, spiraling lines of the labyrinthine swastika sign, to the occult meaning of the "Whore of Babylon" or "honey-moon." He seems to have taken to heart the injunction of Antonin Artaud, who advised, in Eshleman's translation, "to be someone, / you must have a BONE, /not be afraid of showing the bone, / and of losing the meat on the way." Ezra Pound would have understood this project, certainly Olson would have. As would Robert Duncan, with his researches into the Kabbalah, medieval and early Renaissance alchemy, and Michael McClure, whose series of poems, *Plum Stones*, was largely inspired by the "physics of nothingness" of the ancient Chinese school Hua-yen.[1]

In taking on the immense task of a poet's treatment of the caves, Eshleman was especially inspired by Olson's notion of the "saturation job." As Olson wrote in a 1955 letter to the then young poet Ed Dorn: "Best thing to do is *dig one thing or place or man* until you yourself know more abt that than is possible to any other man. It doesn't matter whether it's Barbed Wire or Pemmican or Paterson or Iowa. But *exhaust* it. Saturate it. Beat it." For all their importance, Eshleman found that few other poets or writers had really delved into the issues of Ice Age art, this puzzling, potent "primordial underworld." There were tantalizing brushes. We know Picasso visited Altamira in 1902. And T.S. Eliot visited a similar cave in the Pyrénées, coming away with the blithe impression that "art never improves." Ezra Pound passed by them (without stopping) in his 1912 *Walking Tour of Southern France*, and they ſtirred Henry Miller, who never entered them but nevertheless proclaimed in *The Colossus of Maroussi* that the caves of Dordorgne "give me hope for the future of the race, for the future of earth itself." The cloſeſt experiment to Eshleman's remains Georges Bataille's 1955 *Lascaux, or the Birth of Art;* some of its theses – the human as the transgressive animal – also went into his later *Eroticism.* Eshleman doesn't follow Bataille's lead here, rather Eshleman is obsessed with nothing less than the advent of "that cataſtrophic miracle called consciousness," the myſterious, mournful separation of the human from the animal, the haunting impression that humanity is an "anguished attempt to center a ceaseless duplicity conjured by the evidence that each ſtep forward seems to be a ſtep backward." Often drawing on a lot of early psychoanalytic theorizing (Freud, Ferenczi, Roheim, Reich, and Jung, though not Lacan), Eshleman draws out some of the possible consequences of consciousness' gain in liberation from the "seamless animal web," and the concomitant loss of vital sexual energy now transformed into fantasy, dreaming, and imagining.

Compared with other contemporary interpretations, for inſtance those of the philosopher Jean-Luc Nancy, the radicalism and extremity of Eshleman's projeſt is all the more profound. Nancy looks at Lascaux and only sees "the geſture of the man tracing the contours of the apparition that nothing either supports or delimits … the simple ſtrangeness of presentation." Rather than a mere evocation of being, however monſtrous, Eshleman is aswim in what he calls the "basic thesis of occultism"—Blake's assertion that that the Creation *was* the Fall, that only mental things are real. In this he follows closely and ſtrongly the writings of Kenneth Grant, an acolyte of Aleiſter Crowley, who asserted the ancient myſtical poſtulate that the ſtream of life (exiſtence) is illusion, and the ſtream of death (being) reality. Eshleman charaſterizes Grant's interpretations as extremely "liquid'" which "often differ, depending on the context," based on an erudition ſteeped in African, Arabic, ancient Egyptian, Greek, Gnoſtic, Hebrew, Sanskrit, Tibetan and voodoo teachings. Clearly, Eshleman's projeſt involves nothing less than what Grant calls the "willed effort to Cross the Abyss" and "resolve the antimonies of mundane consciousness." Eshleman's speculations are never far from but in faſt always linked, and fused tight, to his experiences in the ſtone wombs. At one point exploring the caves in the summer of 1996, Eshleman finds himself in total darkness for a half-hour:

At first I closed my eyes (wondering if it would make any difference; it didn't), and rubbed my eyelids with my knuckles creating the dazzling diagrammatic millrace known as phospenes. Then I opened my eyes and stared into the dark. After some 10 minutes, pinpoints of light appeared like a fine snowfall holding in place. I thought of the three levels of light in the dark I felt myself inhabiting: the light in my head, the light in cave dark, and the stars in the night sky above. At some point in prehistory (possibly for navigational charts), they had become "heavenly bodies" configured as creatures, humans, and objects. Dürer's 1515 zodiacal map evokes a night belly with an intestinally entangled creature world. Animals are above us and below us; they know more than we do and less.

At another point, in Le Tuc d'Audoubert:

> at times I wanted to leave my feet behind, or to continue headless in the dark, my stomach desired prawn-like legs with grippers, my organs were in the way, something inside of me wanted to be
> *an armored worm,*
> one feeler extending out its head,
> I swear I sensed the disintegration of the backbone of my mother now buried 12 years,
> Entangled in a cathole I felt my tongue start to press backwards, and the image force was: I want to *choke myself out of myself,* to give birth to my own strangulation, and then nurse my strangulation at my own useless male breasts – useless? No, for Le Tuc d'Audoubert unlocks memories that bear on a single face the expressions of both Judith and Holofernes at the moment of beheading, mingled disgust terror delight and awe, one is stimulated to desire to enter cavities within oneself where dead me can be heard talking –

Those who looked askance at Bataille's Nietzchean mythologizing about the Lascaux caves, are likely to find Eshleman even further beyond the pale. But the striking sensory descriptions in Bataille's account are even further amplified here to a power-pitch, combined with a remarkable precision, with the form of Eshleman's book following what he calls the St. Vitus dance of one's posture and pilgrim's progress through the caves – as if portraying the stages of life – "birth channel expulsion to old age, but without chronological order, a jumble of exaggerated and strained positions that correspondingly increase the *image pressure* in one's mind."

Eshleman indicates how some of the images strike one like lightning. One 30,000 year-old Aurignacian engraving shows a large horse head and neck, on which is superimposed an equally sized vulva – shades of Lautréamont's umbrella and sewing machine or Allen Ginsberg's phrase "hydrogen jukebox" from "Howl." Some images are poised such that a viewer must contort his or her body into the position of the depicted action to see it, arching one's back along small crevices or ledges. The caves, after all, are not just metaphorical but veritable labyrinths. In what is virtually a kind of processual paradigm where one synapse relays to all others *ad infinitum,* Eshleman writes:

> Inching along walls and through tunnels, sometimes on my
> knees or waddling, occasionally on my belly, the cave and my
> mind became a synesthetic 'salad' of splitting overlays. Sensations
> and associations amassed and crumbled, bent and extended, died
> then flashed again, in ways that made me feel I was being pro-
> cessed through them rather than the other way around. Standing
> before large compositions in which the realistic, the fantastic,
> and the unreadable are in overlapping juxtaposition, I have felt
> myself drawn into a vortex of shifting planes which afforded no
> place for a perspective or a terminal.

Here is no paradisiacal return to undifferentiated origins but rather the "incubational pit," a "womb of stone," enough to make one *"sweat one's animal"* giving way to supercharged poetry:

> The moment we touch anything that touches us
> the entire body becomes a pipeline of inverse fire hydrants
> wrenching shut the feeling valves,
> for to connect with even the stain of an image is fearsome,
> a cog to cog moment in the interlocking
> twister of an enrapt reporter calling up
> the abandoned elevators of the lower, simian body
> derailed in Africa, those rotting luncheonettes

visited only by hyenas and ferocious ſtriped worms,
those bleached cabooses individuation pretends
to have left behind but which lurch open onto our brains
in dream to keep us open to
the fugal future of an earth
awesome, infinite, coiled in hypothesis.

Eshleman has written of the "Ice Age imagery" of the Upper Paleolithic imagination as an "undifferentiated paradise, a primordial underworld of unchanging perpetuity." Yet much of the agony of *Juniper Fuse* teſtifies that this is an impossible fusion. And herein lies the link to much of Eshleman's work as a translator, not juſt a poet – of César Vallejo, of Césaire, but especially as the foremoſt English translator of the notoriously difficult "late" or "final" work of Antonin Artaud. Artaud had returned to Paris in May, 1946, after nine tortured years in asylums, as what Eshleman described as a "cratered psyche ... affirmatively ghaſtly in its power to at once protect and organize its loathed and beloved cores." For all of the parallels to shamanic initiation Artaud offers, and to which Eshleman often refers, Artaud's "body without organs" conſtructed as a double or "outside" body in the asylums and proclaimed in his final, banned radio broadcaſt *To have done with the judgment of god* (1947–8) is no unified organism or even experience. Although many commentators have projected a holism onto Artaud, this "new body" is no reſtoration of some prior unity, or as Artaud writes "reintegration of a sensitivity misled." On the contrary it exploits the gaps and fissures between modes of sensory perception, between sight and sound and speech and touch – fueling the void, the grand engulfment into which Artaud aims to draw the world in a work like *To have done with the judgment of god*. Artaud's use of the scream, of the unrepeatable geſture, is to achieve a kind of permanent liminality, ultimately projecting himself into immortality – Artaud predicted his "present body" would "fly into pieces / and under ten thousand / notorious aspects / a new body / will be assembled / in which you will never again / be able / to forget me."

Artaud's writing is no return to any supposed bliss or resolution of undifferentiated origins but rather the far ſtranger emanation what he terms in his famous 1947 essay on Van Gogh "direct creation." This is a "semipiternal tempeſtuous transmutation," a "revolving force," akin to nature – Artaud compared the power of Van Gogh's paintings to a hail of atoms – but of a different sort. In fact, Artaud writes, "no one knows … what strange force is in process of being metamorphosed." Enigmatically enough, Artaud claims this is "the myth of reality itself, mythical reality itself which is/materializing." The transformations of "direct creation" go far beyond "apparent reality" and at the level of consciousness are a "stage of illumination in which disorderly thought surged back through the invading discharges of matter, / and where thinking is no longer existing…" In this apocalyptic fervor no thinking can subsist. One can call attention to the shamanistic parallels to Artaud – his vision quests, use of magic cane, profound loss of identity and possession by doubles, glossolalia, spitting and chanting in androgynous falsetto, death and resurrection experiences, obsession with fabricating a new body – though even these wither, as Artaud so ferociously demands to be taken on his own, invented terms and without any input or support from the surrounding community. A shaman without a community is an oxymoron. As Eshleman claims, in many aspects Artaud is more of a "Kafka man, put through a profound and transfiguring ritual while finding out, stage by stage, that it no longer counts." Yet his traces remain, some of his most crucial work salvaged for the English reader by Eshleman with the assistance of Hungarian-French poet Bernard Bador. Artaud poses in the starkest of terms the dangers and pitfalls as well as possibilities of a metamorphosis rooted in the "incubational pit" of the body. What Eshleman in *Juniper Fuse* describes as "vortex of shifting planes which afforded no place for a perspective or a terminal" as continuing trail of synapse and perception without the option of being ensconced in myth.

Eshleman in his translations of Artaud and others writing in extremis – as in the collection *Conductors of the Pit* – has provided his own elective affinities. Poetically it is difficult to point to Eshleman's contemporaries – perhaps Maggie O'Sullivan in her verbal inventiveness that seems to summon up buried languages, a willingness to drag the bloody carcass across the floor, to re-create poetry in ritual conjuration and incantation.[2] As an aesthetic project, it is usually visual artists immersed in our electronic sensorium, itself a kind of efflorescent, painted cavern, in film and video, who have most delved into similar issues – one thinks of the physical convulsions and exploration of blindness and smashed particles of language in Gary Hill, for instance.[3]

In a poetry world perhaps more smooth than striated, Eshleman makes a resounding case for lived experience, for the tortuous growth, however partial or fragmented, as rooted in self-suffering as modes of vision and dream. For all his ambition, Eshleman does not overstate any of these processes. Even famous 19th or 20th century examples of poetry's wedding with mystic experience – Rimbaud's "illuminations," Ginsberg hearing the recitation of Blake – are for Eshleman starkly limited, almost stillborn experiences. They lack the crucial "context" and development only experienced today by specialists of particular inculcation in the Fourth World. As Artaud wrote to Breton, "Who does not want to initiate himself to himself there is no other who will initiate him." Since so much of *Juniper Fuse*, for example, deals with the fungible remains, the creative dilemmas of dealing with the realization that leaving the darkened cave may mean realizing you never left it, it is not credible to accuse Eshleman of getting lost in an Dionysian cul-de-sac. He also at several points takes up Adrienne Rich's suggestion to him that he explore the invariably gendered implications of the material, that, in her words "the abyss surely = woman even when she's absent or unnamed." We are reminded in *Juniper Fuse* of the medieval *hagazussa*, the witch who sits on the *hag*, or fence, separating the village from the wilderness or "outside." Eshleman realizes that today's marginalized poet is a near-parody of "the one riding the fence," a messenger between worlds perhaps indirectly related to Lascaux's bird-headed man with a ritual staff. Yet Eshleman by his own example demonstrates that this task of a "semi-demonic" being "who participated in both worlds" or the double worlds remains an open call.

Notes

1 Conversation with Michael McClure, May, 2004.
2 See for example Maggie O'Sullivan, *Palace of Reptiles* (Willowdale, Ontario: The Gig, 2003); it is not for nothing that O'Sullivan's work seems to call for live soundings, that it is intimately related to performance.
3 The peculiar gaps and entropic limits in our synapses between sight and hearing and touch and word-language, mind and bodily perceptions have been a rigorously pursued program in virtually all of Hill's work from its inceptions. It's especially dramatized perhaps in a work like *Crux* (1983-7), where cameras are mounted on different body parts of the artist in the shape of a cross, so instead of visuals of body parts created and pinned down solely by eye-vision which is usually the case, the artist-as-cameraperson walking through the woods and his image are one and the same, presented in a real-time physical process. In a work like *Withershins* (1995) an environment is presented of a

large maze facing a large screen; any number of people can enter into this sound-based interactivity; depending on whether one enters from the left or the right, one hears a man's or woman's voice, the content of the text depends on the topology of one's movement. At one point in the maze, the sound text is six layers deep, so even if a viewer walks back and forth the text will continue to unfold in a different way; one area of the maze is symmetrical where the text is only one or two layers deep, yet even here the alternating phrases mirror each other. In his series of works like *Dervish* (1993-5), *Midnight Crossing* (1997), or *Reflex Chamber* (1996) he similarly if far more dramatically explores experiences of aphasis, blindness, apotheosis and breakdown in a sort of highly pitched, electronic "theater of cruelty." This is true even when Hill interrogates the human figure in cross-cultural migrations like *his Accordions, the Belsunce Recordings* (2001-2). Hill draws us toward a prior a- or prelinguistic state, or more dramatically forward to extinguishment. It's no accident that for the collaboration with the Amazon tribe of Yanomani Indians sponsored by the Fondation Cartier in Paris that Hill went the full distance doing psychotropic drugs with the indigenous shaman elders, resulting in his *Impressions d'Afrique* , 2003. As Steven Shaviro has written of *Reflex Chamber*, it "lures us into a kind of embodied thinking, one that has no conclusions short of our own death" (Steven Shaviro, "Fringe Research: Gary Hill," *ArtByte* vol. 1, n.4 (October/November 1998): 14). For Hill's writings, often in collaboration with poet-publisher George Quasha and poet Charles Stein, see Gary Hill, *An Art of Limina, Gary Hill: Works and Collected Writings*. Ed. Paul Emmanuel Odin (Barcelona: Ediciones Poligrafa, 2007).

Herbert Lust

Eshleman and Emerson

It is with an inspired reluctance that American writers should always return to the Emerson problem. Each generation should consider what we still owe him.

Emerson and Eshleman resemble each other in many ways. Both saluted so many fields and with such amazing taste that they deserve that cherished title "man of letters."

Both were very influenced by their times. Emerson was however blessed with a grass roots readership that has long ago slipped away due to the movies, television, and an ever-growing obsession with the visual arts. Eshleman has almost no readership. Yet he pursues his high solitary path despite the current indifference to serious reading which, for the most part, has been relegated to the universities, somewhat like the monasteries of the dark ages.

I was transformed by Emerson when a student. However several things about him now stick in my craw. The first is that celebrated eulogy for Thoreau. A great example of "damned with faint praise." It shows little insight into Thoreau. In effect it shouts that if Thoreau could have been like Emerson that he would have been a great man. Emerson no doubt resented the fact that Thoreau never bent and that he sometimes did. Then that almost comical Whitman affair. To his credit he recognized Walt right off and even encouraged Bronson Alcott and Thoreau to visit him. However as soon as he realized that Walt was his own man he backed off. He didn't even include Walt in his contemporary poetry anthology. When Emerson realized that Whitman and Thoreau could not be literary diplomats he demoted them, though with impeccable patrician manners.

As compared to Emerson, Eshleman has never compromised. His perpetual defiance against all odds, his endless curiosity, his steel rising, forces me to place him on a higher cloud than Emerson. A man of letters must be judged by his generosity toward his gifted contemporaries. Both our men were very generous but Eshleman has been far more steadfast as indicated by the various magazines each man sponsored. While Emerson's *Dial* is revered, the legendary Margaret Fuller being its first editor, it doesn't read so well today and as it began to gasp Emerson turned away from it to his growing fame, pocket book, huge house with spacious gardens and seven servants. By comparison Eshleman looks much nobler. His endurance and loyalty, against so many jabs for four decades, with *Caterpillar* and *Sulfur*, is the most amazing heroic and lonesome highway. These magazines opened so many doors, exposed us to so many new artists, that one cannot imagine the American avant-garde without them.

Still it is hard to compare the two men. As far as poetry, both are important. Just wonderful, Emerson's spirit and rough-hewn lines. Still, as a poet, I much prefer Eshleman, the ecstasy sometimes bordering on hysteria, his defiance, his scars peppered with a few sneers, the forever celebration around dark and light. While there is much to disagree with in his prose, it is always challenging in the best way. The same cannot be said of Emerson's prose: his violent urging of humans to follow their own stars for example. The famous "trust thyself" could lead to a Hitler as well as to a Whitman. Very naïve. This writer has never met or heard about any human who, when the gory chips were down, ever did anything other than "trust thyself." Humans need no encouragement to be stubborn. Eshleman in his odd way is also a rank romantic, though he casts a larger net than Emerson, who, for example, slights sexuality as he advised Whitman to do.

Both men cover huge geographies unique for their times. Both are grudging and wincing idealists. Both attempt to include everything piercing for a higher human. Both salute the supreme voices. Both are beacons. However Eshleman does embrace more, wondering about prehistoric caves, fine food and wines, mythic as well as earthy eroticism, Vallejo, sexual anxiety, narrative art, and much more.

What bothers me most about Emerson is his failure to confront the darkest springs in human nature. Had he not read Hobbes and Voltaire? His essay on Montaigne misses almost all the main points. In a word, he did not believe, deep inside his bones, that evil exists. After missing the call on evil, he went on to reject the "body electric." He accepted the vapid New England Puritanism. Sexuality, except in serpentine forms, was pushed under the despairing rug. He loved the company of attractive young women but didn't understand why.

Yet it's impossible to compare such high gladiators in the eternal arena. My seeing there a thumbs-up for Eshleman is perhaps because he is so modern; his concerns mine. Yet let's be clear, Emerson is a giant, a God, and he came along with high courage at just the right time. However now his optimism seems bleary, his Puritanism daunting, his contemporary literary enthusiasms blurred by patrician patronizing. Whereas Eshleman is a river, a wonderful prod, a wound, a fuse into the heart, brain and genitals.

Peter Cockelbergh

Ferrying Translation between
Clayton Eshleman and Pierre Joris

Fremd bin ich eingezogen, fremd zieh' ich wieder aus.
Schubert / Müller, *Winterreise*

I

Upon rereading Clayton Eshleman's major book of essays, *Companion Spider* (2001), I was struck by the many potential crossovers with Pierre Joris's slightly later, but equally capital collection *A Nomad Poetics* (2003) — both, by the way, published by Wesleyan University Press. I'd like to start off with a somewhat pedestrian observation, be it one that directly sets up the discussion at hand: translation and (translation) poetics. In his Poetics essay "Community of Translation & Translation of Community in Robin Blaser," Joris touches upon what he calls Eshleman's "comparative analytical approach"[1] exemplified in "The Lorca Working," the third essay in *Companion Spider*'s second section, in which Eshleman systematically and with great care compares Jack Spicer's "After Lorca" poems with their "originals." These Lorca translations subsequently bring to mind a much earlier, uncollected review of Joris's: "Blackburn's Lorca," which also refers to and ties in with Eshleman's review of Spicer's Lorca, as well as with the first essay of *Companion Spider*'s second section, "The Gull Wall." Dealing with a central image in Paul Blackburn's poetry, Eshleman's "The Gull Wall" was first published in a 1974 Blackburn issue of the London-based magazine that Joris edited with William Prescott, *Sixpack*. To come full circle, Eshleman's *Sulfur* did a special issue on the 1997 Vancouver Robin Blaser conference, at which Joris pronounced the essay I mentioned earlier, and at which Eshleman delivered the fourth and final text in *Companion Spider*'s second section, the homonymous "Companion Spider," which also deals with translation, Blaser, companions and community.

Why draw attention to such a dense node of links and crossovers? Not to show how Eshleman and Joris published in each other's journals, or refer to each other's essays, talks and reviews. Nor to show how deep their friendship goes. Possibly to signal the importance of Blackburn as a translator (and, of course, poet and companion) for both – Cid Corman being the second major figure here, for Eshleman. Watching this Blaser / Lorca / Spicer / Blackburn / … back and forth unfold from the 1970s to the early 2000s, one is essentially reminded of how deeply Eshleman and Joris are both committed to translation, and how much they are (grand) masters at this trade. And, in turn, also of how quickly this unique feat is glossed over in biographies, blurbs or introductions: Eshleman's award-winning (and often collaborative) translations of Vallejo, Césaire, Artaud, Neruda or Deguy, his brilliant anthology *Conductors of the Pit*, and, similarly, Joris's equally award-winning translations of Paul Celan, his work, with Jerry Rothenberg, on Picasso and Schwitters, or their "Poets for the Millennium" project, etc. This handful of lines taken together represents what amounts to well over 80 years of working on what are often considered "difficult oeuvres," ferrying them over into new, English poetry. Eshleman, for instance, started his work on Vallejo around 1962, and Joris, who is a bit younger, began translating Celan in 1967. Still, apart from the effect of these poetries on English and American literature, and the space their translations open, the impact of such an undertaking – choosing to spend so many hours, days, years, even decades with the work of major (other-language) poets – on one's own poetry and poetics can hardly be underestimated, and is, consequently, well worth noting and examination.

II

Hence, back to my somewhat pedestrian starting point: Joris's remark on Eshleman's "comparative analytical approach" of Spicer's Lorca workings, which somehow intrigued me. In his note, Joris examines the so-called "necessary fiction"[2] each serious translator has to start with: namely, that in a good translation, an author's "original" or source text can be accurately transferred into a target language, with as little "loss" or "noise" as possible. This "fiction" according to Joris, is, basically what allows Eshleman to compare and gauge Spicer's "translations" and Lorca's "originals." It is also what makes these two such exceptional translators, since both Eshleman and Joris never fail to stress the importance of accurate translations, i.e. translations that remain in all respects as close to the source text as possible.

Here is how Joris describes the accuracy of Blackburn's Lorca poems:

> PB's translations are extremely faithful, nearly literal renderings
> of the original. This of course is the translator's primary duty: ac-
> curacy to the text underhand. But such accuracy can mean awk-
> wardness, and the final greatness of a translator resides precisely
> in the extent to which he is able to build, beyond word-literalness,
> a rhythmic construct that not only echoes the original but also has
> a poetic coherency of its own.

Both poets have, in this sense, more than shown their ingenuity and
skills in accurately ferrying over their various loads from one linguistic shore to another. Still, apart from countless side remarks, they have
furthermore written at length on this process; think of Eshleman's detailed "A Translational Understanding of Trilce #1" in the third section
of *Companion Spider* (which, contrary to the second section, actually deals
with "translation" properly speaking), or Joris's comparable fourteen-page
essay on translating Celan's poem "Todtnauberg." Eshleman's preoccupation with accuracy and assuming responsibility for the many stakes of
translation certainly is longstanding, and comes through as early as the "A
Test of Translation" series he inaugurated in the second issue of *Caterpillar*
(January 1968) — a series in which various poets / translators compare different renderings of a single source text. That same sense of commitment
and responsibility has remained unchanged to date. Take, for instance,
Eshleman's recent co-translation, with A. James Arnold, of the unexpurgated 1948 edition of Aimé Césaire's *Soleil cou coupé*. In a note, Eshleman
explains why that title has been translated as *Solar Throat Slashed*:

> Concerning our translation of the book's title: based on all of the
> above information [namely the Apollinaire poem "Zone," from
> which Césaire's title is derived, Ron Padgett's translation of the
> Apollinaire line as "Sun throat cut," Césaire recontextualizing that
> line, and a possible reference to the cutthroat finch that turned
> out to be irrelevant, etc.], it is clear to us that "cou" should be ren-
> dered as "throat," as the action would appear to be that of slash-
> ing a throat and releasing a gush of blood that is related to the
> brightness and force of the sun. While Padgett's rendering of the
> Apollinaire line ("Sun throat cut") is not inaccurate, in our opinion

it feels ſtiff in English and lacks the sound play of the original, the five vowels making up "Soleil cou coupé." As there is no way to match these sounds in English, we have proposed "Solar Throat Slashed," with two open "o" vowels and a consonant repetition of "r" in the firſt two words and of "s" in the firſt and third words.[3]

"Solar throat slashed": uttering or reading these four syllables in turn teſtifies to a "necessary fiſtion" at its very beſt — involving a careful weighing of hiſtorical context, references and reference texts, nuances of source and target languages, and a tremendous (poetic) care of what Pound would call melo-, phano- and logopoeia. Four syllables that, in short, give us the full and very accurate sweep of Eshleman's (or, for that matter, Joris's) art of translating.

III

It is this kind of scrutiny that also underpins Eshleman's claim for translation as poetic apprenticeship, or Joris's claim that translating is the closeſt form of reading available to him. Much-needed and fundamental as it is, focusing on the "necessary fiſtion" all the same ſtill remains a rather traditional appreciation of translation and its potential impaſt on the poetic output of poet-translators like Eshleman or Joris. Needless to say, neither fully subscribe to this fiſtion. In the preface to the second edition of *Conduſtors of the Pit*, for inſtance, Eshleman put a different spin on what is "necessary" and what is "fiſtion," and why the two are fundamentally antagoniſtic:

> My translations or co-translations attempt to reconcile two often incompatible aspeſts of the art of translation: the need to respeſt all aspeſts of the original text, to work within the boundaries that it eſtablishes – while working out improvisational ſtrategies to regiſter such accuracy in language that is fresh, potent, and as captivating as poetry can be written in American English.[4]

In such a take on translation, accuracy and literalness no longer form a tight-knit pair, but inevitably tend to drift somewhat apart. The greatness of a translator and the accuracy of a translation thus relates direſtly to such drifting, as a source text is not seen as having one essential correlate in a target language, say, with minor variations, but can be taken anywhere the translator inclines to take it – accuracy never is the direct path of a literally "literal" translation but rather the zigzag that allows the boat to ferry over as much as possible: "Solar throat slashed."

And, similarly, in the previously mentioned Blackburn / Lorca essay, Joris also qualifies the possible "accuracy" of a translation, stating, for instance, it can never be more than an "accuracy of time": "language is a live and therefore changing thing, just as speech and the ear are." Thus the need to reinvent and retranslate poems, to regain an "accuracy of time" – or, in Eshleman's words, "freshness," "potency," and "captivating poetry in American English." Again, a strange and interesting rift is observed here by both poets: for an absolutely "accurate" translation in this sense is always also temporary, in time, and therefore literally displaces the "original text" (in a new linguistic, cultural, historical context, etc.). And as soon as there is a fissure, rift or fracture — e.g. between two terms – there is also movement and stasis that interlock (and, for Joris, "nomadism"[5] seeps in, like water through a leak). A "literal" translation is, therefore, clearly no longer at stake for either poet, is something only a novice struggles with: the difficulty is the slight deviation that gets the source text across, the angle or incline that get its right. This is the deviation or distance that sets in and upsets the "fiction"; a "gloss" is a most literal rendering, as close as possible to the original's sense, an accurate rendering, however, implies distance and a complex process of ferrying over one's boat, moving within certain boundaries, crossing others as one has to make choices in order to "get it right." The translation here moves away from the source text, to come closer to it elsewhere, necessitating detour and deviation, transformation, awaiting, at the same time, in time, new translations, and the reader's inclination. In short, the poem (or its translator) here is fully conscious of its (or her or his) buying into the "necessary fiction," whereby, however, the emphasis now firmly shifts from the first to the second word, and beyond.

IV

This, however, also is a point where Eshleman's and Joris's translational roads seemingly part. Whereas Eshleman has, for instance, never professed a real interest in translation theory and studies, Joris has, and very much so. Several issues that are being researched or theorized in translation Studies have explicitly found their way in Joris's (nomad) poetics (or vice versa), which does not seem to be the case for Eshleman, who, nearly as a rule of thumb, approaches such theoretical or conceptual notions against the backdrop of concrete translations and translation problems. Does that mean that for Eshleman poems and translations constitute two separate entities, linked only by the same hand holding the pen? Does that mean that, after all, there is only a limited impact of so many years of translation on his poetry and poetics beyond a strict translation poetics? And, if not, how do both activities correlate, then?

Let's, for a moment, take a detour and go back to the previously mentioned discussion of Eshleman's "comparative analytical approach" that opens Joris's Blaser essay. Curiously, this discussion also serves, be it in an edited form, to wrap up another text by Joris, "Toward a Nomadic Conception of Translation," in which he proposes different, very concrete ways of exploring –through translation – the rift implied in the "necessary fiction" (which, one should not forget, enables such an exploration in the first place – at least theoretically). The breadth of his argument ranges, for instance, from how translation is an integral part of literary criticism, scholarship and historiography, and how it is important for creative writing programs and the Humanities at large, to experimental, "nomadic" method of translation, found in the writings of bp nichol, Kateb Yacine or OuLiPo. A good example of a nomadic translation by Joris himself is his rendering of Ibn Tarafah's pre-Islamic ode at the end of the "nomad manifesto."

But let's turn back to Eshleman, whose situation seemed to be somewhat different from Joris's. Yet, and this is the crucial point, even if less visibly or less explicitly expounded in his writings on poetry, and even if translation theory doesn't particularly tickle Eshleman's take on poetics, that doesn't mean – as noted – that he hasn't worked out a full-fledged poetics (and theory) of translation, or that the impact of his translational work would be limited to "translation" *stricto sensu*. It would be wholly absurd to think that Eshleman maintains an absolute and clear-cut division between translation and poetry, or that he limits himself to a hands-on poetics of translation, completely devoid of theoretical considerations, or experiments. As a reader, one simply has to look a bit more attentively. Returning, for instance, to the preface of the first edition of *Conductors of the Pit* and to the penultimate text of *Companion Spider*, the engaging interview with Keith Tuma that refers to that preface, Eshleman gives us a very concrete sense of how and to what an extent translation impacts his work as a poet. In a first instance, he says: "Besides attempting to make accurate, readable versions, I was also involved in a secondary plot or a subtext, wanting to shovel some of their [Rimbaud, Vallejo, Césaire, Artaud, Holan…] psychic coal into my own furnaces."[6] This then is linked to an "assimilative space," which Eshleman describes as follows:

> "Assimilative space" is the continuum that exists between my first reading of a foreign poem and whatever I might do with it in a poem of my own. This space consists of notes, research, drafts, correspondence with scholars, etcetera, and I call it "assimilative" to contrast it with absorptive influence. Assimilation involves transformation, a translating of the translated, as it were, into materials whose identity is primarily not that of the precursor.[7]

"Assimilative space" in this sense signals the full extent translation can have, in that Vallejo and Césaire affect Eshleman's imagination in, let's say, a deeper sense – beyond looking for solutions for translational problems, or translating poetry into poetry. The "assimilative space" opened by the many aspects of the translation process leads to surprising results in Eshleman's own poetry; poems that, if approached from Joris's point of view, could easily be added as examples of "nomadic translation." Take, for instance, the experimental transformation of a Vallejo poem, "The Book of Nature," which Eshleman started to translate in the early 1960s, and which in the 1980s led to his own poem, "The Excavation of Artaud" – a poem that retains Vallejo's tripartite form, the apostrophe / response structure for each stanza, and even specific locutions of the poem, transformed into Eshleman's own idiom. This is not simply a "variation" or an "imitation" – which would more relate to "absorptive influence," something denounced by both Eshleman and Joris – but a "translation" in the most radical sense of the word.

By the time one gets to the Tuma interview in *Companion Spider*, the careful reader will be reminded of an earlier appearance of the "'assimilative space' opened in the process of translation" –if not, a footnote points back to page 142, and the essay "At the Locks of the Void" which discusses co-translating Aimé Césaire. Here, again, two examples of what the assimilative opening up of the translational space can lead to: a 1980s poem, "The Sprouting Skull," that is based on four lines from Césaire, but deals with the Brown and Goldman murders and the O.J. Simpson case. And yet, one is nonetheless struck by an interesting difference with Joris, because this "assimilative transformation" again appears in the midst of very concrete reflections on translation: differences between a scholar and a poet translating (the latter making an offering to him- or herself, that of the previously mentioned psychic coal in the furnace), questions of influence through translation, translations as emanations or spectres and so on.

The second example of Césaire's "assimilated companionship"[8] – note the appearance of the word "companionship," something both Eshleman and Joris talk to in their Blaser essays – is "Short Story," with respect to which Eshleman says "aspects of Césaire's solemnity, ferocity and tenderness, startling imaginal shifts, and word coinage have become mixed into the strata of my subconcious."[9]

V

Startling imaginal shifts, word coinage, solemnity, ferocity, tenderness – these are, in fact, qualifiers that one might readily associate with Eshleman's own poetry. Here, we've reached a point, I think, where translation – both the translation of specific poets, and translation as a radical writing activity at large – becomes an integral part of, or even punctuates Eshleman's poetics as such. For the act of translating, transferring, ferrying, in short, transforming is core to his poetry. It appears in the irruption of psyche or imagination that informs Eshleman's remarkable use of image – the importance of the unconscious and dreams in this respect can hardly be underestimated and furthermore allows for interesting parallels to be teased out between Eshleman's work on the one hand, and "Surrealism," Deep Image and, say, Alice Notley's work on the other. But, in this more radical sense, translation also appears in Eshleman's take on poetry as informational and investigational – does not a form of translating what happens around the poet lie at the base of *Under World Arrest*? And in the importance of witnessing, so marvelously analyzed in "Complexities of Witness" – for what, if not "translation," is the responsibility of witnessing, which, as Eshleman duly notes, is a political act par excellence, and one not limited to alleged "direct eye-witnessing"?

It should be clear by now that whereas at first one observes "translation" in the strict sense appear in the third section of *Companion Spider* (texts on Césaire, Vallejo, Artaud, where we see Eshleman, the major translator, at work) and in the second section (with essays on Blackburn, Spicer / Lorca, and Blaser, and in which "translation" appears in different dimensions already), one can actually discern translation's radically transformational mechanisms – its impacts – almost throughout *Companion Spider*, indeed, throughout Eshleman's poetry and poetics. Whether in a more narrow sense, or in that wider, more radical sense, and with an expansion of Joris's statement in his discussion of the "comparative analytical approach," one can say that Eshleman truly is the masterful translator-poet.

Notes

¹ Pierre Joris, *A Nomad Poetics* (Middletown: Wesleyan University Press, 2003) 103.
² Joris, *A Nomad Poetics* 104.
³ Aimé Césaire, *Solar Throat Slashed. The Unexpurgated 1948 Edition* (Middletown: Wesleyan University Press, 2011) 174.
⁴ *Conductors of the Pit* xviii.
⁵ Eshleman has, by the way, a very different take on rhizomes and the "nomadic" – see the fascinating discussion between Eshleman and Joris in "Organized Nomadistorms of Broken Oases" in *The Price of Experience* 398-409.
⁶ *Companion Spider* 300.
⁷ *Companion Spider* 301.
⁸ *Companion Spider* 145.
⁹ *Companion Spider* 144.

Rachel Blau DuPlessis

"The Sisters' secret [interfering] child": Some Reflections on Clayton Eshleman

The intense yearning, the desire for something else, of which we too have only a dark and doubt-ful presentiment, remains, but our arête, *our ideal of vital being, rises not in our identification in a hierarchy of higher forms but in our identification with the universe. To compose such a symposium of the whole, such a totality, all the old excluded orders must be included. The female, the proletariat, the foreign; the animal and the vegetative; the unconscious and the unknown; the criminal and the failure – all that has been outcast and vagabond must return to be admitted in the creative of what we consider we are.*

Robert Duncan, "Rites of Participation," *The H.D. Book*[1]

Odes are, as an 18th century critic said, hymns in honor of Dionysus, "a bold, free, enthusiastical kind of poetry, as of man inspired by Bacchus – half-drunk."[2] It is peculiar how definition verges on suspicion. The insulting, or squeamish "half-drunk" is a revelation of the rhetoric of revulsion toward this provocative ancient mode: this long poem, of "irregular stanzas" "in three units" "with abrupt transitions" "un-and even dis-unified" "obeying no particular norm." "For most men their own heart is the most / precious food. The man to become the wine / places his heart in the damp nest / of the Sisters' knotted towel."[3]

Ode is the genre which symbolizes poetry. When ordinary people resist poetry, it is ode-like qualities which they are resisting: the apparent over-valuing of transcendence; the ecstatic, inexplicable events; the poetic diction of apostrophe and abstraction: excessive, embarrassing, over-blown, portentous, mellifluous: "As they strum on his entrails, / he is blended, the harp of their reciprocal pit."[4] Odes entail the very notion of, not to speak about dangers of, the sublime; the likelihood, not to speak of the temptations and necessity, of dissolution; the febrile outcries; the feminine encodings implicit in this genre, of "hysteria," emotionalism, self-importance, exaggeration, double and irreducible messages, even duplicity, are all so contemptible from a tight-lipped prose / informational / direct word "no slither" norm.

And yet, a little like straight Pentheus not believing the seductive long-hair avatar of Dionysus – who is, as it falls out, Dionysus – such a respondent to the ode finds it is both a seductive genre and one that will tear the unbeliever to shreds: Pound (of the anti-slither statement), Williams, all would return to the ode-like expanses in their major works. (And *The Cantos*, that struggle, it could be said, did tear Pound to shreds.)

The ode is the genre in which your ecstatic, orgasmic mother tears you, the unbeliever, to shreds. (The comparative rarity of odes then limited first to whomever can imagine such a mother?). The gender narratives in such a formulation leave some striking questions of poetics at large, charged. The ode as the site of the acceptance of the ecstatic mother – the ode as site of the breaching of ultimate taboo, the celebration of the repressed, the dance conducted with taboo – bring to a head the oedipal / pre-oedipal transgressions (to pleasure, to incest, to the chora) which the ode ultimately entails.[5]

This Bacchic genre, variously deployed, is arguably, the genre of choice for such notable contemporary writers as Robert Duncan, Susan Howe, Gustaf Sobin, and Clayton Eshleman, among others, most of whom are, in Eshleman's words, "Expressionistic *and* Objective."[6] And among these, the work of Eshleman has a special resonance as investigating the necessary anti-sublimity of the sublime, as forging a chthonic apotheosis out of the materials of despisal, the "Hadean," darkness.[7]

Transcendence, in the best of these modern odes (or ode-like gestures), has been critically restated in antiauthoritarian ways: transcendence being no longer possible, although the dispersal into the sublime is. It is a difficult line; I myself remain suspicious of the stance of priest-shaman-poet (despite my defense of the ode into which this figure of the poet is often projected[8]), suspicious even when it is inflected with pariah, as in this stunning homage to one of Eshleman's masters, which I cite in part, and whose syntactic awkwardness and verbal impaction or impasto are for me sympathetic and redeeming:

> Pariah in silence, coprophilially
> squatting in the corner of your cell for years,
> sealed open, who only came when called by your
> mother's name –

3 dead men, licking your electroshock-induced Bardo,
      have found
your atomic glue, the Kundalini compost they must eat to speak.

O shaman, from having been so masterfully plundered!
O priest, from having been fixed in antithesis!
O pariah, from having been so desired by the dead![9]

Odes undertake thinking within the work. They are issue-oriented, sometimes even brilliantly expository in intent. Which might mean – an exploration of the laden multiplicity of our interactive situation: the way in "Junk Mail"[10] the ludicrous heterogeneity of an ersatz arts conference on "Creativity and Madness" gets treated with a bitter, loving hilarious negative respect as symptomatic not only of the "North American psyche" but of little boy "Me" of an innocence so total that Nothingness can colonize it.[11] Tonally or rhetorically, such interactive analysis can call forth all levels (such a word is jejune) and types of discourses, all ranges and combinations of allusions and images, such as might be summed up in the terse *"Everything material"* of a recent poem.[12] In "Junk Mail," Eshleman stands forth with the following essayistic lines, in context perfectly suited to the stress-shifting, the coming at this phenomenon analytically, imagistically, psychologically, politically:

What *can* we say
    to those who would season their Royal Waikoloa
        Singles Luncheon with
"George Orwell and Rudyard Kipling: Abandoning
        Parents and Abusing Children?"
There is a repression in North American psyche so
        tough, so uncontactable because of the depth, now,
of the suffering midden of humanity creating goods for us,
that it is no longer disturbable – it can *enjoy* ANYTHING!
    Can enjoin any grief and discuss it
over pineapple – but I cannot fully believe this or I
        too would be consumed. That the shirts of these people
are being made somewhere in the world where the workers
        live less well than our pets

can turn the vise of the creative mind into itself to
    the point that not madness
but a simpering, descriptive, situation comedy runs out,
a pseudo-art the equivalent of the lectures to be
    delivered there.[13]

At best, Eshleman releases us into a sense of thought's process and its teeming, a non-exclusionary sense of connection which is politically and personally enlivening, even aggressive. The swing from ironic, bitter, desirous, outraged, grieving, hysteric, restrained, the purposeful (and not decorative or only controlling), the appeal to a range and multiplicity of discourses – the heteroglossia which Mikhail Bakhtin has theorized, are (by virtue of the prevalent notions of the sublime) generally not available in more regular ode-gestures. Heteroglossia is the political possibility which Eshleman gives to the genre. Eshleman's ode-poems are politicized by virtue of their heteroglossia, and his shaman-priest guise is therefore realistically inflected with our collective Amer-poet dialectic of political power / powerlessness, and the shame of our late-capitalist engorgement, our drinking of others' blood.

The language of odes has traditionally been intense, and one favored rhetorical mode, the apostrophe (o wild West wind; o ma douleur; o Attic shape; o you solitary singer / o solitary me) is not so much (as Jonathan Culler has argued) a figure of address to the object but "the pure embodiment of poetic pretension, of the subject's [the writer's] claim that in his [Culler's word] verse he is not merely an empirical poet, a writer of verse, but the embodiment of poetic tradition and of the spirit of poetry."[14] In a memorable phrase: "Invocation is a figure of vocation." It would be typical of Eshleman that in poem after poem, the sublime reach ("O my white, white father, you were the / bell dong clapper and tower of a construction arisen...") would be rooted in "O yellow po-ca dicka-da of an owl yet to be conceived / even before the egg" and would end as an invocation to Donald Duck as a major symbol / symptom of our cultural deadness which lives on the torture of others, invocation a figure of vocation.[15] "And the howl of this wound is so wide that it is the sound of the very day itself, the solar day like an opened heart packed with siphons and drains, feast parked in the heart of an Indian mother whose breasts are no more than ripped lips..."

The paradigmatic apostrophe (says Culler) would then be Shelley's "Be Thou, Spirit Fierce, / My Spirit! Be thou me, impetuous one"; words that desire self-effacing, yet self-aggrandizing exchanges with ultimate forces, words that are proudly saturated with boundlessness. For the lack of boundary is the crucial element of the ode as genre. Eshleman, in *Sulfur* 13: "Apotheosis, in an autophagic sense, might be a state of writerly awareness in which there is nothing to repress."[16] (Hence odes are the poems of the end of the lyric, the end of the manageable epiphany, the end of book's unity (but not its form), and even of the Book as ideal, and the beginning of drastic apocalyptical continuous writing.) But because its dionysiac basis opens it to limitlessness, the ode enters intellectually into major debate between limitlessness and limit. If an ode evokes limitlessness as a dream of bliss, pleasure, totality of fullness or of emptiness, still that ode will be marked by a rocking between limitlessness and boundary. (Let me note here only that boundary is never barrier.) As in Whitman, "Out of the Cradle Endlessly Rocking" in which this rocking between limitlessness and boundary shows itself in the context of "so much / too much" and then the subsequent search for one word, one "clew" which can hold and contain the contradictions of boundary and ecstasy.

But limitlessness (as Mary Jacobus argues) gives rise to the "orphic fantasy" – threats of possession, of never coming back; fears of dismemberment and dispersal; it is here that the Virgilian female functions in Eshleman's work. The insistent acknowledgements of Caryl Eshleman in several of Eshleman's recent works are one sign of the necessity of a boundary mark, of an Isisian figure who remembers the scattered parts, of a figure who, just at the void, can offer a steadying, human dialogue.

The intrusive (and everyone is going to find at least some part of Clayton Eshleman's work immoderately intrusive, unpalatable) is a deliberate response to that cultural condition of late capitalism analyzed by Edward Said as (in Hal Foster's words) "a 'doctrine of noninterference'" in which it "is tacitly assumed" and then unconditionally maintained that the humanities and politics are aloof.[17] It is this assumption that Eshleman heatedly and repeatedly denies. Thus Eshleman may be said to embody the critical postmodern intrusion: "a counterpractice of interference" – defined by Said as at least including: a breaking of academic field boundaries (cf. "the symposium of the whole" in Robert Duncan's words); an insistence on the political meaning of all acts and choices within the humanities; a denial of the "subjective and powerless" role of literature; a "crossing of borders and obstacles, a determined attempt to generalize exactly at those points where generalizations seem impossible to make"; a use of representation to "tell other stories than the official sequential or ideological ones produced by institutions of power." The praxis of interference is, as Foster pinpoints, more than a subversive gesture; it is a "practice of resistance."

How to arrange oneself permanently into the arena of risk, without the lavish extremes of self-description and / or self-indulgence –

How to write in, at, by the edge, trace the long topographic contours of the extreme –

How to stay with and in the extreme with analytic powers intact, inside the Hadean sublime, and conduct oneself with dignity therein, given the extensive challenges to fabrication (of language, tone, structure) when the extreme is one's hope –

In such works as "The Name Encanyoned River," "Our Lady of the Three-Pronged Devil," "Notes on a Visit to Le Tuc d'Audoubert" – in fact many of the poems from *Hades in Manganese*, *Fracture*, and recent work, the reader has the sense of being caught inside of being, embodying at core a dangerous and enriching place, and being made aware, through the impastos of image laden language, of the vibrant contours of this site: the social geography of the psyche, the psychic geography of society.

How? What is this how – this is what is provocative and helpful in an ethical or moral way about Eshleman's work: he is the centaur of the extreme. I was going to say he rides the bronco of the extreme, but this is not right, for he does not seek to tame or to domesticate the forces and materials with which he is engaged. As otherness, as the man-who-rides-the horse-he-is, as the horse-who-is-the-man-it-gallops, he is more like the imagined monstrous fusions (monstrous functioning as tropes for necessary, unconscionable, paradigm-breaking combinations): the borderline between man / other, human and beast, personhood incorporating the rejected aspects of person. The plea, the tirade, the constant argument in Eshleman's work is born from the tracing of the fissure of fault line (fracture) that separates and joins the animal otherside (in its clarity and purity, in its inarticulate need) to humankind the destroyer and the maker of image and language. And in a thoroughly convincing analysis of the meaning of prehistoric cave art, Eshleman points to the crisis of human consciousness as the separation of human from the animal, and his activity as a writer to gain access to "prehistoric psychic activity."[18]

This oeuvre has over decades been devoted to the insight that the extreme is a necessary, complex, and manifold *place or site* (not a quick incident of access in time). This space is chthonic (not Olympian), and therefore can be intimate, homely, filled with the pebbles of gods, the dailiness of encounters with forces; but is also exacting, vengeful, devoted to a complex of rights and knowledge, steeped in blood, tribe, code, and allegiances, representing the law prior to *The Law* of city, Father, patriarchy, judge.

The evocation of Aeschylus' *Eumenides* (part of the trilogy, *The Oresteia*) is deliberate, for the *Oresteia* is a work which performs a cultural resolution regarding these chthonic / female powers, making a cultural compact of their subordination which is, apparently, at the end of its hegemony. The female god who was born from the head of her father (and one might allude to Athene as a class traitor) casts the deciding vote in this allegory of the establishment of state over tribe, Law over custom, light over darkness, reasons over incantation, Father over mother, rape over incest (as the allowable crime, cf. Greek mythology *passim* for the rapes), abstract, impersonal justice over forms of situational, personal punishment (called vengeance). The female furies (Erinyes, the chthonic forces) are not sited in their recuperated niche under the City. It is Eshleman's passion to pry open and re-examine this solidified Olympian compact, this alliance of reasonableness and repression against Otherness, and to release the Erinyes from the repressive tolerance and pacification which has been their cultural fate, and Orestes from the fate of being automaton of the law.

The renegotiation involves a denial of male-based initiation rites whose "implication is always of rebirth from the male" instead of first birth from the mother.[19] If many of Eshleman's poems are like rituals, it is the initiation ritual that is both overtly and covertly invoked, and, connected to its gender issues, there is a concomitant quest for ways that do not "anchor the initiate's mind to established and frozen imaginations."[20] Instead, a third birth as from the mother, the cave, the space of the extreme is readied and executed.

Since the order established in the *Oresteia* ends a cycle of blood with "purification," the counterpractice to this Western order recommences a cycle of blood (menstrual, fertile, wounding, murderous, the blood in Tiresias' Hadean fosse, the ochre of the cave wall) and re-examines, critically re-engages with so-called pollutions: the lower body ("The lower booty"), navel, genitals, materials fecal, menstrual, fetal, grotesque, delirious, monstrous — materials opening Eshleman to various personal allegations, based upon the importance to his world view of the challenging of all taboos.

The career of Eshleman may be loosely described as an anti-Oresteia (I mean by this no comment on his life, nor any scenic allegory made of the Aeschylus). That is, it is the undoing of years of liberal cultural hegemony by the dialectical engagement with the terms of exclusion, the control of others and of Otherness. "I have no desire, / to live in a world of nature conditioned by patriarchy. / I kick off my head and live in the light / bounding in from my mother."[21] What the culture has repressed ("the fresh vale,"[22]) is not only returned to but engaged with a space of struggle, in part to end Orestean acquiescence and complicity with the final dispositions of power commandingly sanctified in Aeschylus' trilogy. Like Orestes, Eshleman – and it is part of his fascination – accepts his Apollonian duty to engage with the Hadean, the Bacchic; unlike Orestes, he does so not to be judged and praised by Apollo and Athene, but to confront his peers and be consumed by them.

[1987]

This essay first appeared in Tremblor *6 (1987): 94-97.*

Notes

[1] I cite this epigram from Robert Duncan because of its intrinsic importance and as well because of Eshleman's attention to this argument. Duncan's "Rites of Participation" was originally published in two parts in *Caterpillar* 1 and 2. The paragraph I have cited was originally published in *Caterpillar* 2 (1968) and reprinted in *A Caterpillar Anthology* 24. Eshleman called attention to elements of "Rites of Participation" as the basis for a poetics in *Sulfur* 13 (1985) 155. Contemplating the Duncan statement for me now it is especially important to bracket the elegiac, the nostalgia for the whole or, as Duncan says, for "the coming of all men into one fate" and the unexamined "we." Bracket, I mean, not to deny, but to consider another time. [See Robert Duncan, *The H.D. Book* (Berkeley: University of California Press, 2011) 154, for the final, revised version of this passage. Ed.]

[2] Statement on the Pindaric cited from Mary Jacobus, "Apostrophe and Lyric Voce in *The Prelude*" in *Lyric Poetry – Beyond New Criticism*, ed. Hosek and Parker (Ithaca: Cornell University Press, 1985).

[3] This poem in *The Name Encanyoned River: Selected Poems, 1960-1985* is also the source for the title, see 288.

⁴ *The Name Encanyoned River: Selected Poems* 229.

⁵ Julia Kristeva, *Desire in Language: A Semiotic Approach to Literature and Art* (New York: Columbia University Press, 1980) and *Revolution in Poetic Language* (New York: Columbia University Press, 1984). Without any help from ancient examples (like Sappho?) which cannot be examined by virtue of their loss, one might tentatively posit the possibility of a difference in the female use of the ode in our historical time, which allows for a certain generic duplicity or indirection in examining the site of female ecstasy from the peculiar perspective of a female writer who could place herself (dangerously) both as the orgasmic mother and as the incestuous writer. Susan Howe's most ode-like work is a Shakespearean masque of lyric fragments and bursts (*The Liberties*); Beverly Dahlen's "ode" is in prose (*A Reading*).

⁶ In *Sulfur* 13 (1985) 155. This statement is a spirited defense of the Rhapsodic as the quintessential and vital mode of poetry. [The statement is reprinted in *Antiphonal Swing* 199-204. Ed.]

⁷ It hardly seems necessary to remind ourselves that odes are in every way resistant and inimical to both the well-made poem of New Critical fame (when Duncan and then later Eshleman faced their vocation) and to its flaccid epigone, the contemporary nice-guy exemplum of Dullness, whose moral and intellectual limitations have been more and more (in critical works of wit, force, and despair) called into question: by Geoff O'Brien, by Rae Armantrout, by Charles Bernstein, by Hank Lazer, by Marjorie Perloff, by Clayton Eshleman, by Michael Davidson.

⁸ Odes displace and recuperate the religious and spiritual fervor away from the hymns of institutionalized religion into numinous otherness. Paul Fry has noted "the priestly role [which the speaker of an ode assumed] is not pastoral but hermetic." But an authoritarian function is a possible concomitant. *The Poet's Calling in the English Ode* (New Haven: Yale University Press, 1980) 7.

⁹ *The Name Encanyoned River: Selected Poems* 216.

¹⁰ *The Name Encanyoned River: Selected Poems* 196-8.

¹¹ In "The Spider and the Caterpillar," his excellent introduction to Eshleman's *The Name Encanyoned River*, Eliot Weinberger points to the interactive political and social relations of our historical moment which have necessitated the tracing of networks of relations: "one can see the world in a grain of sand only if one simultaneously sees thousands of undressed oiled bodies baking on the beach, the web of their social interactions, the raw sewage pumped into the sea and the contaminated lives of the marine animals, the kiosks with their pink bunnies and rubber ducks..." [See Weinberger above in this volume. Ed.] This has called forth in Eshleman and others an interactive, multidimensional writing in no way the pretty monotone of institutional "Poetry."

¹² "Impotence Still-Life" *Tremblor* 5 (1987) 38. This remarkable poem continues with the argument, "But if everything is material, then everything (mentally) / is edible" and goes on to propose the opening at least, and the plausible consuming of secretly nurtured and hidden impotence: "the male secret of despair."

¹³ *The Name Encanyoned River: Selected Poems* 197.

[14] Jonathan Culler, *The Pursuit of Signs: Semiotics, Literature, Deconstruction* (Ithaca: Cornell University Press, 1981) 143.

[15] *The Name Encanyoned River: Selected Poems* 180-86.

[16] *Sulfur* 13 (1985) 156.

[17] Edward Said, "Opponents, Audiences, Constituencies and Community" in Hal Foster, ed., *The Anti-Aesthetic: Essays on Postmodern Culture* (Bay Press, 1983). Citations from pages xiv, 155, 157, xv-xvi.

[18] *Fracture* 12.

[19] For illuminating discussions of the social functions performed by *The Oresteia*, see Froma Zeitlin, "The Dynamics of Misogyny: Myth and Mythmaking in *The Oresteia* of Aeschylus".

[20] "Introduction" to *Antonin Artaud: Four Texts* 1; Reprinted in *Antiphonal Swing* 86.

[21] *The Name Encanyoned River: Selected Poems* 230.

[22] *The Name Encanyoned River: Selected Poems* 116.

David Maclagan

Painting, with words

Clayton Eshleman's work, spanning forty-five years and including major works of translation (Césaire, Vallejo) as well as editing (*Caterpillar, Sulfur*) is much less well-known than it deserves to be. Rather than try to give some kind of an overview of this substantial achievement, I have decided to focus on Eshleman's writing about painting, in the hope that this will encourage some readers to explore his work further.

Writing about paintings in such a way as to do them poetic justice, to do more than just make a descriptive inventory of a work or bounce associations off its subject, is hard. It involves a difficult level of creative reception, and the ability to articulate this, and at the same time to allow the writing to take off in its own directions whilst still remaining faithful to the spirit of the work one is writing about. "Poetic justice" means more than attending to the outward appearance of a painting: it means attending at the same time to its inward resonances, in much the same way that poetry does. A painting doesn't come alive until it is met by the spectator's imaginative response: some of this is of course a matter of fairly conscious reflection – figuring out what is going on, locating what is responsible for certain effects, situating the work in relation to one's previous experience of art, and so on – but a substantial portion is subliminal, flickering at the edge of our attention.

Aesthetic experience is far from being as detached as much of its theory would prescribe: it evokes profound and sometimes disturbing imaginative reactions. At first these seem like almost purely subjective feelings, so deeply do they push their roots into a realm which could be called, to borrow Anton Ehrenzweig's term, "inarticulate." This means, first of all, that engaging with the material texture and handling of a painting involves coming to grips with relations between forms that are often shifting and slippery, things that language cannot easily grasp. With the kinds of painters about whose work Eshleman writes, a description is already loaded even where there are identifiable "things" in the painting. Take this passage, about a Soutine still-life:

It is very murky here, fleeced of sunlight.
The potted flowers grapple with the chair back.
The lilacs in their jug look like spoiled meat,
like scrapings turning scarlet with desire?
jug acrawl with roses, looking Argus-eyed,
face swarming with eyes, roses as blowflies,
release these ravens, peacock entail them![1]

It's not that these images and metaphors are somehow bolted onto what could otherwise be a supposedly more objective account: it's that they are fundamental, inherent to Eshleman's take on the painting, as different images are to each of our own responses. At the same time they bring into focus a glimpse of something like Soutine's "world," which is at once the source of his paintings and something that could only have come into being through them.

These images that build up, collide and collude refer to the inside of the painting, to its feel, as much as to its outward look; and this is where another sense of "inarticulate" comes into play. The idea that looking at a painting involves much more than the eyes is not a new one – it is to be found in Merleau-Ponty for example – but few writers dare to take the full implications of this to heart. There are precedents; Rilke on Cezanne's portrait of his wife, Artaud on Van Gogh, John Berger on Bonnard are some well-known examples; but writers who are prepared to take such risks or go to the lengths or depths entailed are the exception. There is surely an added weight when it comes to poems, for the poem doesn't seek merely to evoke, but in its own texture and verbal facture to create a kind of parallel object to the painting it deals with. Where a painting is more or less figurative it's always possible to envelop its objects in fantasy or to spin narrative elaborations about its apparent themes; but where it is non-figurative this risks seeming like an imposition. I don't know if there is such a thing as an abstract imagination; but much of our response to such painting is inevitably couched in figurative terms. And poetry can blow these up – both magnify and explode them.

This is only partly because we tend to "see" things in terms of figures (so-called "physiognomic perception" is only the tip of this iceberg); it is also because, in using words we have to bend and stretch language to reach after what we are trying to articulate. In a sense, poetry is the logical accomplishment of this attempt to say what we feel and feel what we say, and, as paint works in the painting the poem addresses, much is suggested or invented by language itself. For example:

> In the art of Unica Zurn, the known is redearranged,
> the red-eared angel is crushed into a thousand eyes,
> as if in Tantrik diffraction, cranial shapes
> break into heads in telescopic profiles, with eye lozenge
> clusters of hanging pods. Abyss weevils
> percolate with seed energies.[2]

While the poem can be read in its own right, it also takes on another dimension when read alongside the image (reproduced or remembered) of the work that inspired it. So, in one of several poems about de Kooning paintings, Eshleman writes

> The observational,
> vanished, figures emerge,
> as if by chance, through
> a meeting of my projections and stroke
> configurations. A Luba jaw
> curve juts stops spurts up as if along a crossed-out
> upper face. Khakis, sages,
> swank with white. Flotsam from Soutine's Ceret
> assembled on a beach.
> Only some "rope" and "ain't" are left from
> *European Painting.*[3]

To get the full measure of this you have to have an image of the painting alongside.

An artist's name often acts as shorthand for a particular perspective, a beacon whose roving beam lights up an entire world (e.g. Kakfaesque, Beckmannesque). Eshleman conjures up the daemonic realms of many artists: Soutine, Bacon, de Kooning, Bellmer, Michaux and Artaud, for example, as well as of some so-called Outsiders such as Nedjar, Darger and Judith Scott. These evocations are extensive: like a terrier worrying after a trail, Eshleman casts about, seeking to penetrate the artist's lair, to get at its specifics, using every twist and turn that language can afford. Take these extracts from a text on Michaux, almost certainly referring to his mescaline drawings:

A line encounters a line, evades a line.
A line waits, hopes, a line rethinks a face.
Ant-high lines. Ant-visibles streaming through lines.
A melodic line crosses twenty stratigraphic fractures.
A line germinates. Martyr-laughable lines.
Lines gaslighting lines. Lines budding on a dune.
A dream of paradise: lines in conversation with their liminal selves.[4]

There is a correspondence here between the restless succession of metaphors and personifications and the endlessly suggestive texture of Michaux's drawing: the scatter of images conveys the sense of elements hovering on the brink of dissolution, of radiant structures rearing up only to evaporate again.

But Eshleman's work is far more than a kind of poetic mimesis: it also involves a process that begins with incorporating these artists' works into his own world. Here I can see artworks functioning as what the psychoanalyst Christopher Bollas calls "transformational objects": they enter into our inner worlds in a talismanic fashion; they act as nuclei around which an imaginative crystallisation can take place. But one can't just swallow the work whole: you have to get your teeth into it before it can be imaginatively digested. Hence what might sometimes look like a piecemeal regurgitation in Eshleman's poems is more like a multifaceted re-presentation: like a pelican, what he serves up to us may look messy or chaotic, but it has been subject to a complex psychic and linguistic recombination. The risk is always that parts of this spread may be unrecognisable, or seem too "subjective" and are therefore supposed to belong in the poet's inner world.

But this "inner world" is not exclusively internal, nor is it simply personal: like anyone's, Eshleman's imagination feeds off its own autobiographical midden-heap, but this is woven into his poetic mythology so that it becomes more than just his story. Other elements have an archetypal dimension, drawing on a global range of gods, daemons and spirits. But the primal deposit of his (and our) imagination is the Upper Paleolithic: here is where human beings first began to define themselves through their art and it is psychologically as well as geologically archaic. This is the ground or underworld in which painting is often rooted, the inner cave wall where we all start from scratch. Eshleman has published an extraordinary book about this, *Juniper Fuse*, which combines twenty-five years of hands-on research with the most daring poetic testimony.

In between these extremes lies a polymorphous and subversive realm: that of the hybrid and the grotesque. Images that have been repressed or banished often assume distorted forms, become carnivalesque or caricatural disguises of themselves, and they inhabit the no-man's-land at the edge of consciousness. This is also the domain that many of the artists Eshleman writes about dabble in: Soutine or Gorky, for example. Here he is writing about the latter's "Good Morning, Mrs. Lincoln":

> Gorky testicles wiggling out of crab traps.
> octopus pods dissolving into albino eels,
> a vulva grail held forth by fingerless hands
> to whom a penis-headed man, palm on hip,
> displays his giant gully-raker…[5]

It's important to realise that these are successive "takes" on passages of Gorky's imagery, rather than definitive interpretations; they function as a spray of images, each of which lights up a feature of the painting in its own way, building up into a fountain of poetic imagination that plays over the whole.

There is an extravagant generosity at work here, and Eshleman is prepared to give free rein to his fantasy in ways that sometimes push the reader's tolerance to the limit: like a bull in the china shop of conventional aesthetics, he can sound wild or vulgar. A later passage from the poem on de Kooning's *February* quoted above reads:

> The Luba jaw is also the front half of a grand piano,
> the rear half of a peacock-blue bison.
> This jaw-keyboard-rump is being played or
> buggered by a sketchy ape with a feline face.
> How curb a dog that's slowly exploding?
> Spurting up jaw standing swab
> tattered cloak swipe of grey-green mist
> topped by white helmet-shaped woman's hair.
> Is "she" holding out a mangled gold foetus?[6]

The lens through which de Kooning is seen is no different from that employed in the rest of Eshleman's poetry: its aperture is wide enough to include images that are usually ruled out by the umpire of conscious control, and in subsequent working over even typographical slips can throw up new amalgams.

In the end how far you are prepared to go with Eshleman – and indeed with the art he is responding to – depends on what taking them seriously entails. Like Artaud, whose *Van Gogh, the man suicided by society* is clearly an exemplary avatar in this context, his vision is one with no holds barred, and of course it often feels uncomfortable or disturbing. I leave you with a passage towards the end of "An Arsenal in Seattle" quote earlier:

> Yet the force in the face of god
> as a beltway of circulating thrashers
> in the bandsaw of a shark's eye
> stayed with me. It said:
> imaginal density is greater than you have conceived.
> What most take poetry to be
> is at best an ortolan hors d'ouvre.
> On the far side of the muse
> there are cometary knots
> in which a Tarantula Nebula is volatilizing
> with all its tarantella power
> spit like fire through facial
> groin-horned snake-pouched feelers.[7]

Notes

[1] *From Scratch* 85.
[2] *Reciprocal Distillations* 56.
[3] *From Scratch* 61.
[4] *Reciprocal Distillations* 17.
[5] *Reciprocal Distillations* 52.
[6] *From Scratch* 61.
[7] *Reciprocal Distillations* 53–54.

Roberto Tejada

Taking It Out, Painting It In

Image density is the salient feature that renders poetic space distinct in Clayton Eshleman's animation of a language allowing for thick terms of concentration and complex shadings. This is to speak of degrees that extend back and forth, from comic-strip plain form, in emphatic warps of surface effect, to the half-light and roundedness of things no more than partially disclosed as heretofore sealed inside a cave; and this should come as no surprise from a writer who for over forty years in a commitment to poetry and intellectual life has thought intensely about history and its various objects, counting those we differentiate as art. His poems on things made are a reminder, too, of how much critical potential there is in acts of admiration and the ability to honor the artistry of other makers, forebears and fellow travelers alike.

Eshleman achieves the foregoing in diverse rehearsals of a poetic sub-genre that bears his unmistakable signature, in writing that performs the mediations of both maker and viewer: the dialogic lyric of the beholder. The poems here restage the personal and social struggles materialized in objects whose present time is manifestly out of place with the historic moment of a prior making, and because discontinuous—in an imperative sense thereby largely unassailable—Eshleman's writing about them explodes into moments of proliferating aesthetic reflection, and into mineral layerings that are the wagers of language in relation to History: "What is broken advances, / pillowed by what will not yield: / a thought drinking its shadow."[1]

Forebears and fellow travelers alike: Clayton's history of the image has unearthed an enabling narrative in the Upper Paleolithic, insofar as the poet gives name to such a "construction of the underworld." But this telling is not an origin story, nor a starting point identical to itself; it is a strangely familiar place that accounts for the social and political night terrors that are the human species becoming other to animal organization by means of mimesis and image-making. In "Chauvet, Left Wall of End Chamber" Eshleman submits what follows as a note-to-self and challenge

220

to the archeologist: "Check this: / animal holocaust in the late Ice Age / corresponds with the rise of war."[2] The suggestive nature of Clayton's assertion does not end there; he interrogates the metaphors of art historical conviction with regard to the upper Paleolithic, not as evidence or trace of *Homo sapiens* being separate or distinct from our anterior selves. Instead, Eshleman telescopes prehistory into the present so as to make visible the structure of political life in the modern age by dint of our representations. ["Rhino with 8 oversized curving parallel horns / as if drawn by Marcel Duchamp. / *Rhino Descending a Lion Stare* "[3]] The art historian and theorist Donald Preziosi suggests a link between what is at stake in the conventional art historical account of prehistory with the modern theory of mind when he writes: "In some way, our picture of earlier humans has always been conflated with our observations of our own children— the notion that human ontogeny, or infant development, recapitulates or repeats stages of human phylogeny or evolution."[4] Eshleman tells that his attention to the visual derived from reading "funnies" in the Indiana newspapers of his childhood, from comic books and his own early efforts at cartoon-strip depiction.

The particularly modernist account that is psychoanalysis provides a foundational model for describing the development of the self and such objects of human exchange and expenditure as to give continued shape to individuation. As a system, it looks to practices that deviate from the sexual or social norm, to the baffling exceptions that are literature and art, to states of behavior altered by the social order or otherwise induced—by neurosis, through perversion, or under pharmaceutical influence. An evolutionary method for understanding cultural production, it can look to a maker's biography, to her historic moment, and to something defined loosely as the temperament colliding between the two. As Sarah Kofman reminds us, Freud suggested also a structural method for relating forces and phenomena to each other in such resonance as may be found in the otherwise unexamined detail. This circular interpretation makes it possible for a non-unified or absent historic identity to be structured as a breathing subject. It relies on certain assumptions: that truth is revealed in its distortions; that it is constructed from displacements or substitutions; and that there is no first-order artwork referring only to itself, but rather to the never-ending play of second-order effects. It's a technique Eshleman deploys in some of his most insightful readings of art in poetic form. He looks at the Biblical tableaux of Caravaggio, the monumental figures of Leon Golub, the psychic girl-legion battlefields of outsider artist Henry Darger, and the exhaustive drawings of visionary Unica Zürn. This last artist, still largely under-appreciated, was the companion of Hans Bellmer in Paris from 1953 to 1970, the year of Zürn's death by defenestration, and Eshleman affords her sometimes drug-induced work a primary place of its own.

Eshleman's poems in general, but those on artworks in particular, begin with a premise that for the knowable to be known it must undergo a necessary and always reiterated "de-arranging" at the moment we render it representable. At a recent live reading, Eshleman's framing device to the poem devoted here to Unica Zürn serves as paradigm for his own writerly practice—and as the primary contest for commentators of his own poetic singularity—when he claims that "[Zürn's] work is incredibly, richly interior, with lots of moves that are not describable; so it's an interesting challenge to try to articulate stuff like this that you're really […] having to invent phrasings and words for" [at the Kelly Writer's House, University of Pennsylvania, October 19, 2005]. The predominance of eye imagery that composes the tissues of Zürn's scrawled fields give way to a series of improvisations lending particular valence, for example, to the first line of the passage below—the word "tear" doubling over into lachrymal conduit precisely as it opens up into cleft or slash.

> To travel within Unica's tear, to view the celestial
> viper-vibrational
> xylophone of her mind, the cartwheel
> cocoliths of her insectile-thronging dark.
> Eyes as trowels.
> Raccoon nautiloids in millipedal waver.[5]

Eshleman's interrogations of the formal qualities that animate Zürn's brand of image-making are an invitation for the poet himself to turn comparable inflections of excess, dizzying gradations of sense and sound that produce both a readerly turbulence – "xylophone of her mind, the cartwheel / cocoliths of her insectile-thronging dark" – and the light-headed exhilaration of overload. In those moments of pleasure and stress, Eshleman's aesthetic – together with the choice and range of artists he engages – defies our conventional notions of decorum. The vocal axis of the poem unhinges, too, off the organizing cadence of the poet-speaker to assume the subject position of the artworks' producer—the "viper-vibrational" self of a projected "Zürn" thrashing back into the poem's transitory middle-voice again. [In live performances, Clayton inhabits to great effect a de-centered speech: a sort of cartoon gigantism attached to certain phrasings in order to perform the split that exists between the rationally argued and that which decomposes at the point of saturation.]

To turn to this poem a propos of Zürn is to acknowledge the peculiar brand of surrealism to which Eshleman is heir – a lineage that points simultaneously back to Europe (Artaud, Bataille), Latin America, and the Caribbean (Vallejo, Césaire). We can look to the very suggestive writings of Roger Caillois – a figure whose intellectual commitments as well joined Europe and Latin America – to illuminate the relationship between "personality" and "space," so crucial to Eshleman's poetics. Caillois claims that insofar as I can assimilate into my surroundings, there is a decline in my feelings of personal attributes. To the degree that I generalize space, the more distinct become my feelings of mental and somatic sovereignty. So, the fate of indulging with fantasy may lead to such mimetic incorporation of the animate in the inanimate, and vice versa, as to engender progenies disfigured by the imagination. Enabled by Caillois, art historian Rosalind Krauss has thus argued that surrealist doubling is, fittingly, an invasion of the body by space. In light of the art objects that compel his attention, Eshleman's practice constitutes a kind of invasion of the poet's imagined body – the "phantom anatomy" of psychoanalysis – by the idealized quantity projected into the historic nexus of interpretation between the beholder and beheld for which the poem is an analog. Consider the following lines occasioned by figures in the Dapper Museum of African Art, Paris:

> If, over my tall blue pearled neck, I stare in terror, it is because
> foxes have gotten inside me,
> foxes are tearing apart my death.
> Pitch-black head breaking out in red currants, in spikes, in
>   blisters,
> head a field sprouting buds, pebbles, studs,
> head issuing a living waving horn,
> head asleep, head replete, head whose dream matrix pustulates
> the prayer of all things: to emerge, at once.[6]

The space of writing together with the nascent shapes of the mediating objects forge the site of a dialogue: in a language by which the act of viewing itself is incited, interrogated, seductively teased, and argued with. Eshleman likewise discovers in each poem the form and word-tone commensurate with his subject. Reflexive phonic textures match the quietude of the painter's vision in "Corot, 1870."[7] Elsewhere, verbal designs are drafted in relation to the calligraphic paintings of contemporary Syrian artist Khaled Al-Saa'i so as to mimic a modulation that

> ... sees nature as intelligible word lore mortal scored rims
> or rhymes, a lingo ribbonesque with inner din
> (questers sounding themselves
> off stone in a darkness sparkling with
> ghoul-infested whirligigs ...[8]

This poem ends with a description not only of its subject but of its own emergence – as well "a lacework of letter flavor cometary clover!" Close examination of that particular last line, its prosodic stress (• | • • | • • • | • • • | •) and the range of what its references suggest, yields the "interlocking sway" of the "alpha radiant omega" linking galaxy to blade of grass, genesis to spiral terminus, and choice to complexity. With a resemblance now and then to Elias Canetti's *Agony of Flies*, Eshleman's poetry lends aphoristic care to the philosophical promise of fauna in chromatic scale: that is, of animals and colors as primary terms that can be interchangeable: "Once razed, the mind's hive releases mastodontal honey."[9]

In the end, however, it is this poetry's relevance to art history I want to argue. As Mikhail Bakhtin claimed of the novel, poetry too has the ability to enfold and incorporate other genres and media, but this has been much less the case for what classifies as art historical discourse. The degrees to which art histories claim a scientific detachment may serve as the alibi for disciplinary investments in "naturalizing and validating the very *idea* of art as 'universal' human phenomenon [... art history being] a powerful *instrument* for imagining and scripting the social, cognitive and ethical histories of all peoples."[10] Without forfeit of so-called art historical "accuracy," the limberness of poetic discourse considering the strict partitions of subject and object, of self and other, provides empirical agency for a palpable, wider-reaching knowledge; and the kind of intuitive leaps that only a poem can make available are in such excess of standard academic remarks as to offer sufficient counter-statement to so much lackluster scholarship. These moments of poetic elucidation cannot be generalized, nor are they easily earned, nor are they often possible to isolate without injury to the overarching argument or to such abundant phenomena specific to the lyric genre.

Joan Mitchell once claimed, "The word blank is what bothers me. It has no image to it. B L A N K. It's nothing, something on a typewriter; or a mind that's nowhere [...] To me figure/ground means the use of space. [...] Now if I have a blank space in there and it isn't working as a positive space, as well as an unpainted space then I'll take it out or paint it in."[11] It is art-historically coherent for Eshleman to inaugurate his poem "Joan Mitchell's Spinnerets" with a description of the painter's brushstrokes as "[w]hite flowers scissor-billowing the hemlock;" it is consistent not only within the logic of that metaphor but operates as a figure of speech proper to the cut and swell, the action of carving by way of enlargement, that constitutes a brush technique resistant to the negative dialectic of the blank painterly field. To a historic Mitchell's "blank is what bothers me," the poet's surrogate Mitchell proffers a "blob of vermillion and a swath of no." This attention to a subtractive mathematics coloring an otherwise value-added brushstroke—negative, positive: "take it out, paint it in" – is especially relevant given the sexual politics of post-war art production in the United States, largely masculine in its social formation and patriarchal in its tenor. Here and elsewhere, Eshleman shows scholarly interest in questions posed similarly by T. J. Clark with a view to Jackson Pollock: What makes one brushstroke successful, and another not? Of Mitchell's overarching critical implications the poet asks:

> Whose death mask is being molded with
> these rampant arctotheric clouds?
> How divine the state of the union in
> the entrails of
> Daisy Mae?[12]

This conclusion, its coloring applied in layered dashes, requires a brief annotation of terms: "arctotheric" being a reference to the short-faced bear common to North America; Daisy Mae Scragg, the voluptuously rendered heroine of *Li'l Abner,* Al Capp's popular U.S. comic strip of the early to mid twentieth century. The artwork is that holdout surviving the contact zone, Eshleman claims, of the material world in the face of demise; that this confluence should take place in the bowels of a mass-culture representation is nothing short of inspired; it's also release from a tragic masquerade, for in the comic strip Daisy Mae represents a prison house of femininity so long as her agency remains largely unrecognized and unrewarded. To view Mitchell's kind of nonfigurative practice at the slippage of what compels the lexis of *death mask, cloud, state of the union,* and *entrails,* is to analogize even as it is to insinuate the nuclear menace that determined what an entire generation of so-called New York School artists could make legible in paint. To this, Eshleman blows wide open the forceful work of Leon Golub with the political inquiry: " If abstract color fields are peeled away, / What terrors will show through?" This question is posed as an "or else" in the same poem regarding Golub's series of full-canvas fighting male nudes:

How much degradation can an image take
and still, scraped into and from the canvas itself, manifest
this world's lethal embrace? The age
demanded an image, right? ok? here it is:
man as ruined monumentality.[13]

The terrors for which the distortions of caricature serve as social compensation leads the poet to probe the visionary work of Henry Darger in an attempt to address the problem of pathology in art and mental life: "Why was Darger Darger?" Indeed, Eshleman sees the psychoanalytic struggle of a subject in excess of itself not as a fin-de-siécle parlor drama but once again as a peculiarly U.S. American cartoon or gazette motif. The cartoon's visual economy of perverse form and overstatement is the visual equivalent for a social temperature that necessitates asking, "Is paradise the absence of adults?" In the poem, a catalog of the titles comprising Darger's personal library remains unembellished, but its "order of disclosure" – George Oppen's celebrated words – provides an indelible version of the man who owned them and leads to the following first-person identification, a kind of knowledge that a scholarly account could not possibly contain:

I am Chicago Weather, Hendro Darger the Volcanologist,
author of a 15,000 page novel, Pepto-Bismol bottle collector,

I rescue crucifixes from trash cans,
my eyeglasses held together by tape,
wallet tied to shoestring attached to belt loop.
Jesus, are you a little girl? Jesus, am I in
your body? Nail-wracked Jesus,
      am I your daughter
         self?[14]

I cannot resist quoting the final couplet of this poem, not only because it is emblematic of Eshleman's style, but because its joyousness derives too from the fact that such effects are impossible in any other medium beyond that of embodied speech or the "vocal utopias" so dear to Michel de Certeau, not always pacific and describable perhaps likewise as a

Comic strip valley aswarm with cradle-shaped rangers
Radiant sweetness shot-gun emptied into dot-eyed zombies.[15]

About the life and work of Caravaggio, "The Beheading" is an art story in the stressed fabric of language, tightly woven and teeming with psychologically consistent kinks and snags. Crisscrossing between the biographical account, visual analysis, and psychoanalytic examination— and delving into the great homosexual themes to which the Biblical figures of David, Goliath, John the Baptist and Christ can correspond—the poem tenders a startling syllogism: the potential for buggery is to the fear of castration what the real political threat of decapitation was to the various Caravaggio renderings of "Salomé with the Baptist's Head" and "David with the Head of Goliath." Eshleman links the artist's obsession with beheadings to a formal strategy in as much as Caravaggio's survival was contingent upon repressing erections in his painting. It's a poem that shows Eshleman's range as a writer not only of wild lyric lines of flight but of relaxed phrasings confident also in argument and exposition.

I want to return now to the place where I began: to Clayton's demanding image-structure and thus to a poem that summarizes his particular poetics as a theory of art. To account for the rendering of the deity Ganesha, the short poem "Obstacle Breaker" alters the initial terms to make the figure's elephant trunk a living organism reproduced asexually, a birth requiring only one parent, generative method of the gods:

Parthenogenetic

uroboros. Take a self-subtracted
art from me. Feed your adder.

You are mist.[16]

The adder, or Northern viper, coils here at a two-fold remove: one that
permits the technologies of a self to withhold or abstract the substance
that it simultaneously adjoins and suspends in the act of image making.
For wordsmith and image-maker alike, what artworks and poetry in dialogue allow is that to devour one art form or series is, paradoxically, to
begin to give birth to the other. One of our founding art historians, Aby
Warburg, for whom the serpent was an image of agency and causality, at
least in his marvelously idiosyncratic reading of the Pueblo Indian practices, wrote in 1923 that: "Human culture evolves toward reason in the
same measure as the tangible fullness of life fades into a mathematical
symbol."[17] For Eshleman the sign of a self-devouring and self-generating
serpent, representative of the negative/positive space of exchange between
what we see and what we say, loom as though attainable for an instant
even as it fades likewise into mist. Warburg's writing is exemplary for art
history: it recognized that there can exist an "object" of art only insofar
as it is contingent and intertwined; self-proclaimed disinvestment in any
description will be reliant always on a first-person immediacy, inevitably
suppressed, but in whose encounter subject and object are for a moment
indistinguishable.

Caught in the stress point between a kind of materialism and ideal
constituted in the double acts of expenditure and conception, Eshleman
reveals the appetite of a realist. Writes the critic Keith Tuma: "It is as
if the poetry must be as complex and crowded – as agonized, hilarious,
confused, lucid, derivative, singular, as full of farts, food, and ecstasies – as
life itself."[18] But fueling this corporeal reality principle is a kind of uto-
pianism that sees community in art as an ethical archetype. Throughout
Reciprocal Distillations there is a touching sense, one of wonder before
the state of our present history, that art is even possible at all or that its
makers have in actuality lived among us. To the fact that they are often
friends Eshleman pays tribute in poems on work of contemporaries as far
and wide as Bill Paden, Nora Jaffe, Leon Golub, Nancy Spero, and Ana

Mendieta. Increasingly more symptomatic of our cultural climate is the reality that present-day agents of visual practice in the United States are aware almost not at all that poetry can be an equally critical rehearsal to assess the value of visual meaning. That poets likewise speak with scarce authority to the contemporary art world and its complex association with the market economy is hardly encouraging given a suggestion that "visual studies is helping, in its own modest, academic way, to produce subjects for the next stage of globalized capital."[19] Evidence points to a transnational capital that is inclined rather to make us more and more specialized so as to further solidify barriers in communication across technical and disciplinary boundaries.

Eshleman beckons the drive that uniformly animates the objects of art as well as the subjects of its history – at that "interlocking sway" of manufacture and reception, between a spectator's encounter and the broader social project of evaluating value. He deploys the visual object and the varieties of its potential meanings to galvanize the very specific effects of the poetic medium in works whose model is that of the dialogue – as much a song for two voices resembling the address of erotic love and discord, as it is an appeal for instruction: How next to speak? In an unremitting imperative that so turns the visual inside out as to make it a series of written figures possible only at the level of the spoken is built the ethics of an appetite whose multi-part arrangement refutes conventional distinctions of form and content, of the public and private. These lyric works endure at last to claim a case in point that poets might have something relevant to contribute to the cultural conversation writ large.

This essay first appeared in the online journal Fascicle. *It was subsequently reprinted as the foreword to* Reciprocal Distillations.

Notes

[1] *Reciprocal Distillations* 41.
[2] *Reciprocal Distillations* 28.
[3] *Reciprocal Distillations* 29.
[4] Donald Preziosi, *Rethinking Art History: Meditations on a Coy Science* (New Haven: Yale University Press, 1989) 143.
[5] *Reciprocal Distillations* 56.
[6] *Reciprocal Distillations* 1.

[7] *Reciprocal Distillations* 14.

[8] *Reciprocal Distillations* 39.

[9] *Reciprocal Distillations* 16.

[10] Donald Preziosi, *The Art of Art History: A Critical Anthology* (New York: Oxford University Press, Oxford History of Art, 1998) 18.

[11] Cora Cohen; Betsy Sussler, "Joan Mitchell (Interview)" *Bomb: A Quarterly on New Art, Writing, Theater and Film* (Fall 1986) 22.

[12] *Reciprocal Distillations* 44.

[13] *Reciprocal Distillations* 59.

[14] *Reciprocal Distillations* 22.

[15] *Reciprocal Distillations* 26.

[16] *Reciprocal Distillations* 27.

[17] Margaret Iversen, "Retrieving Warburg's Tradition" in *The Art of Art History* 221.

[18] *Companion Spider* 296.

[19] Svetlana Alpers; Emily Apter, Carol Armstrong, Susan Buck-Morss, et. al. "Visual Culture Questionnaire" *October* 77 (1996) 25.

Niall McDevitt

"The Outright Lie":
Clayton Eshleman and the Rules of Engagement

I acknowledge the American government's infiltration of my psyche
— Consternation I[1]

I imagine Clayton Eshleman standing on two giant shoulder-poems: William Blake's *America a Prophecy* and Robert Duncan's "Up Rising." Blake's poem has a special relationship with U.S. poets not only for its incendiary celebration of America's overthrow of the British Empire but in epitomizing how an engaged poet can write against his or her own nation's imperial interests. Though Eshleman has not commented on *America a Prophecy*, the Blake watermark of "archaic and symbolic reality" appears and reappears throughout his oeuvre as spirit-guidance; and that the Duncan poem is a gold standard is evident in the opening gambit of his important essay "Wind from All Compass Points":

> Not long ago in an issue of the politically liberal *New York Review of Books*, the poet/reviewer Charles Simic praised as a major achievement a poem by the then Poet Laureate Billy Collins which basically expressed Collins' "sensitive" surprise that cows actually moo. In a separate article, Simic dismissed Robert Duncan's in-spired confrontation of the American destruction of Vietnam in 1967 in his poem "Up Rising" as "worthless". This downgrading of Duncan's imaginative engagement with power, and the extol-ling of Collins' work, which is hardly even sophisticated enter-tainment, sadly exemplifies much of what is supported these days by editors, reviewers, and judges as endorsable American poetry.[2]

The first key phrase is "imaginative engagement with power." There are no rules of engagement for poets; it's more a case of privations, obstacles, punishments. Pound castigates the "botched civilisation" of WWI England, but later in the Mauberley cycle laments his "final exclusion from the world of letters." Unlike Pound, Eshleman will not be charged with treason. He is savvy enough to ask and answer: "Am I a traitor? Certainly not. I am not committed to the overthrow of anyone or anything."[3] Neither is he a patriot. There is a natural Protestant dissent coursing through his veins. He further follows Blake's example in that a visionary poet turns to berating the artistic bureaucracy in turbulent prose, as above. Like Blake, Eshleman has written in two centuries. In the latter half of the 20th century he joined a lineage of American poets, engineering an "innovative push", whose post-wwii luminaries included Louis Zukofsky, Charles Olson, Robert Duncan, Muriel Rukeyser, George Oppen, and Jackson MacLow. His profound immersion in the triumvirate of world-poetry outsiders he systematically translated— Artaud / Césaire / Vallejo—hurtled him ever further into the realms of free and "freed" verse.[4] Open forms were accompanied by political openness, not such that every poem was political, but such that not every poem was apolitical.

Eshleman has extended this postmodern—a term first applied to poetry by Charles Olson in a 1951 letter to Robert Creeley—American tradition into the 21st century. In another blast at the "official verse culture" from his 2006 essay "An Alchemist with One Eye on Fire", Eshleman deftly points to the paradox of literary politics:

> Not only has the laudable democratization of poetry been compromised by being brick-layered into the academy but with few exceptions there is a lack of strong "signature" and a tacit affirmation of the bourgeois status quo, the politics of no politics.[5]

This second key phrase— "the politics of no politics" —sums up the neutrality of what is purveyed in the media and the academy as "contemporary poetry". Eshleman is not guilty of the "self-sensitivity" that characterizes much modern poetry, and even less so of the self-censorship that is endemic in the art. After 2001, poetry could not be expected to carry on as usual but had to deal with the complete turning upside-down of reality caused by the American Troy of 9/11. Guy Debord's "Society of the Spectacle" took on a new meaning with its emphasis on the "the" i.e. *the* spectacle was no longer a plurality of cinemas, theatres, stadiums, billboards etc. but a single incident: the assault on the twin towers, a terrorist attack somehow watched live by a worldwide audience, and studied again and again in action replays. While most poets *did* carry on as if nothing had happened, Eshleman dealt with the new "all's changed, changed utterly" reality in poem after poem. "Consternation I", "Consternation II", "Torture I" and "Torture II" from 2010's *Anticline* are emblematic; their titles speak volumes. 9/11 itself is subjected to an in-depth poet's enquiry in the explosive poem "The Assault", a fusion of conspiracy theory prose and druidically eviscerating poetry. In his introduction, Eshleman encounters more problems with the literati:

> I sent my piece to *The Nation*, a weekly whose politics I respect. I sent it to the editor, Katrina Vanden Heuvel; she wrote back that *The Nation* had covered all the points my poem raised. Since I read *The Nation* weekly, I knew this was not true. In fact, *The Nation*, to my knowledge, had not published a single article disputing the official version of 9/11. So I wrote Vanden Heuvel back, asking her to point out to me where my information had been discussed. Her response was to ask me not to write to her anymore.[6]

For poets, there is a more fascinating disclosure:

> The lyric outrage in part two is all my own (other than when factual), and participates in the tradition of the sirventes; Robert Duncan's poem "Up Rising," which condemns President Johnson for the carpet-bombing of Vietnam, hovers over "The Assault," a predecessor ghost.[7]

The "sirventes" is a Troubadour format in which a poet imitates the outstanding poem of a predecessor for pastiche or satire. Here, Eshleman is not parodying Duncan but using Duncan's critique of the Johnson administration to critique the administration of George W. Bush. A stanza in "part two" erects a grotesque totem-pole of powermongers:

Bush, Jr. entangled with pa
crawling Nixon's raging animus,   Nobel Carter mottled with Khmer Rouge
      horror, Johnson cloaked in
"We seek no wider war," whipping out his big dick to reporters, declaring
      "This is why we're in Vietnam!"
Reagan as a goggle-wearing grub, chirping:
"Contras are the moral equivalent of our Founding Fathers."

Fest camps where baby Pinochets bud   (Nobel Kissinger
on his knees gripping the altar-bowl vomiting up a stomach hash of millions—
   suddenly his ghost stands up through him,
   called to lead the 9/11 investigation!)[8]

This is not only "free speech" but his deployment of the vulgar image of Lyndon Johnson flashing at a press conference—the demotic "big dick"— is an example of what Eshleman calls "freed speech." Perhaps one rule of engagement is that all language options are on the table. The investigative poem concludes:

Should 9/11 be seen as a 3000 body count down payment on a Turkmenistan-
   Afghanistan-Pakistani UNOCAL oil pipeline?

3000 dead? More like 8000 —
for this figure must include the Afghanistan dead bombed in retribution—for
   what? Nothing they did but inhabit land we
– and here "we" partitions my heart – seek to exploit.
The unutterable humiliation of 9/11!
Holocaust of firemen to make millionaires billionaires!
Workers, executives, of the capitalist epicenter –
but much more importantly, beloved citizens who went to work that day
(overhearing me, bored Bush turns aside:
"Adolf, let's go fishin.")

   In our hearts we know
   In our hearts we do not know

Baby Bush now spectre-entangled in the entrails of the nation.[9]

The common denominator of the various Eshleman quotes so far, whether from poems or prose, is their ringing sincerity, which also echoes Blake. His tone is always true-to-himself. It's gratifying that such an intelligent and erudite poet-essayist is unafraid to question the official 9/11 version of events, neither malcontent nor fruitcake, but a poet who believes in "weighing all affirmation against, in an American's case, our imperial obsessions and our own intrinsic dark." The body politic intrudes, impacts on the poet's consciousness, targeting it in such a malevolent and manipulative way, that it is then purgatively channelled into poetry. 2004's "From a Terrace" in a normal poet's hands might have been a fine Italianate travel poem; in Eshleman's hands, it celebrates the view of Lake Como, whilst meditating via television on fresh U.S.-inflicted carnage. The travel poem is invaded by a war poem. The reader "mental travels" to both Bellagio and Fallujah:

> Sunday lakeside serenity.
> People with their skin burned off, hospitals bombed by
> an us I bleed in
> psychically, my government
> completely corrupt…[10]

Eshleman has liberated himself. He doesn't have to choose between solipsism and agitprop. He takes what David Gascoyne calls a "third way." The two approaches first contrast, then coalesce:

> Across Lake Como
> mountains rest on the waterfold,
> slant shadowed rows. They are
> mammoth heads with verdant folded eyes,
> beautiful, meaningless
> > in
> an extinction-tinctured view.[11]

The '*us* I bleed in / psychically' is—paragrammatically—the U.S. and nothing is as antidotal to "politics of no politics" than the candid phrase "my government completely corrupt." This imitates human consciousness, representing it as poetry. As political a poet as Eliot Weinberger has praised Eshleman for his fearlessness. Both are poets profoundly engaged with their own Americanness and how to atone for it, not wishing to live as blinkered beneficiaries of the imperial project, especially in the so-called "New American Century." Note how the Blakean terminology of the "spectre" informs Eshleman's outlook, as well as his own definition of what it is:

> The American poet reaps and suffers the rewards of American
> terrorism, which are part of his spectre, his anti-imaginative

blockage, whether he acknowledges such or not. All of us are connected to the rubble of Fallujah by a poisoned umbilicus.[12]

It is, rightly, a recurring theme, a recurring daymare:

This asunder-written No to
the interventional might of America,
millions raked into invisible piles,
the 9/11 blowback a drop
in the bucket blood of
Guatemala
Nicaragua
Serbia
Iraq
     How terrible
     not to feel pure
     grief for the
     WTC dead, how
terrible to have to
contextualise to be honest.[13]

Some "no politics" poets might defend their own silence on these matters—the technical but ethically loaded term seems to be "quietude"—as
a statement of tacit disapproval, but unconvincingly. It could equally be
read as tacit approval. If popular American poets such as Bob Dylan in
"Masters of War," Michael Stipe in "Orange Crush" and Patti Smith in
"Radio Baghdad" can castigate U.S. militarism in incandescent song lyr-
ics, played to large audiences, there is no reason why a mainstream lyric
poet cannot do the same in verse to a small audience, unless poetry is
somehow a spineless artform, a castrato choir. A cartoonist can attack the
status quo with impunity in daily newspapers read by millions, but not a
poet in a journal read only by its contributors. What's wrong? Publically,
the apolitical poets claim to be above "polemic" but a merely polemical
poetry is merely a bad political poetry. Arguing against "polemical" poetry
per se is a sleight-of-hand, an excuse to snidely dismiss masterpieces like
"Up Rising" à la Charles Simic. Elsewhere, "didacticism" is tut-tutted by
the lyrical civil service; but it's not about telling readers what *to* think, it's
about telling them what *you* think. Ginsberg—a brilliant political poet,

clearly approved by Eshleman—claims "the difference between poets and politicians is that poets can tell you what they really think whereas politicians only tell you what they want you to *think* they think." This quote shows up the "politics of no politics." The apolitical poets are acting like politicians; they are being "politic"; they are being polite; they are being solid citizens of the polis, any polis... this pusillanimity is universal. Witness Eshleman's problems in Lima:

> I had been hired as editor of a new bilingual literary magazine, to be called *Quena* at the Peruvian North American Cultural Institute. Because I was working for the Institute (which turned out to be an annex of the American Embassy in Lima), most of the Peruvian writers and critics whom I met thought I was an American spy. Only when I turned in the three hundred page manuscript for the first issue of *Quena* did I realise what the Institute represented. My boss told me that translations I had included of Javier Heraud could not be published in the magazine because, although the poems themselves were not political, their author, after visiting Cuba, had joined a guerrilla movement in the Peruvian jungle and had been killed by the army. Since his name was linked with Cuba and revolution, my boss told me, the Institute did not want to be involved. I refused to take the translations out of the manuscript and was fired.[14]

Or witness his problems in pre-revolutionary Prague, in the poem "Master Hanus to His Blindness":

> Poets in Czechoslovakia are deprived of expressing
> their pain, are made to lie to publish.[15]

And in the poem "This Doktor Urbanova," Eshleman is criticised by a Czech academic for talking informally to some students about Allen Ginsberg:

> the Seminar is not endangered,
> the point is not political,
> the point is to keep everything a desert [...]
> she personally resents my having made real

contact with a few students,
that a little water got into the desert,
and such is not Communistic nor Capitalistic
nor Czech nor American—it is
all of them, and none, it
is a condition of character always always present,
keep the blood from flushing out,
hide warmth, channel all energy to officially
determined ends[16]

The South American and East European examples illustrate how a certain type of poet and/or poetry is feared by the authorities, excluded from official publications, but also that this is a human situation and can happen wherever poets and authorities co-exist.

Is Western poetry susceptible to state interference because it is so often a government-funded and charitably-statused art? Eshleman sums up the unofficial American censorship as follows:

It is as if we are now watching anything that is confrontational, up front about experience (meaning some of it is bound to be negative, or despairing, given the world we all live in) sink out of sight, with the outright lie that such poetry does not reward study [...] if one expects to be anthologized (and taught etc.) one's poetry [...] should not be emotionally confrontational, seriously critical of government and society, or imaginatively dense.[17]

I imagine "the outright lie" as a forcefield around official poetry designed to keep out those poets who would resurrect the prophetic modus operandi of "speaking truth to power." "The outright lie" is a myriad of excuses, strategies, log-rollings, stone-wallings. It is motivated by canonization and prizemoney, facilitated by mediocrity and clubbability. Its sophistication is its sophistry. Two mainstream English poets, Paul Farley and Michael Symmons Roberts, have co-written a typical opt-out clause: "As poets in the English lyric tradition, we are drawn to the idea of praise, of celebration." (Note the cerebral vacuity of "the idea of praise"). But poetry has always had a dual lyric/satiric function in which a poet-as-wise-fool figure, judiciously and eloquently, singles out what is praise-worthy *and* what is blame-worthy in life, allowing us to know both poet and life a little better. "The outright lie" highlights clauses about poetry as celebration but redacts clauses about poetry as criticism. For Eshleman, "affirmation is only viable when it survives repeated immersions in negation."

As for naming names, it's just not cricket. Neil Rollinson, another English mainstream poet, once stated that no contemporary "major poet" would do what Shelley did in "The Mask of Anarchy" and actually name-drop politicians. Where has Rollinson been? Unlike Simic, he hasn't even read Duncan's "Up Rising"; or—note the subterfuge—he would not dignify Duncan with the status of "*major* poet." Rollinson's assumption is a tissue in "the outright lie." His scruples are probably threefold. Firstly, it would not be the done thing for a mainstream poet with a mainstream publisher to risk libelling a public figure and possibly bankrupting the publisher if a case went to court. Secondly, it might jeopardize future Arts Council funding for poet and publisher. Thirdly, aesthetically, there is a worry that naming a leader fixes the poem to a specific time-period, dating and disempowering it as soon as a new leader succeeds. Eshleman has no such worries but laments the main problem with political poetry i.e. that it is not read by politicians:

> Politically, the contemporary poet is undermined because, unlike Yeats or Whitman, say, he is not intimately related to figures of power (he is mainly aware of them via the sensory deprivation tank of media filtration).[18]

Even in his imaginary encounter, George W. Bush snubs him to go fishing with Hitler. Eshleman's naming and shaming of leaders in the course of his oeuvre is gleefully unscrupulous and allows the reader to continually x-ray the poet's mind in relation to the history that is impinging on it. He psychogeographically and psychohistorically traces an America-in-progress, an Empire-in-progress. Poems about Gulf Wars waged by Bushes senior and junior allow for a striking continuity. The U.S. war leaders are public demons exorcised in the course of Eshleman's hexing, no-holds-barred, "Aurignacian-Apache" utterances.[19] The twisters of humanity, reality, language, mathematics are—in a magical act of public retribution—twisted in their turn; all whom in Blake's words "wish to lead others when they should be led."[20] Another of these figures,

Ronald Reagan, is savagely delineated in the astonishing satire "Reagan at Bitburg," which deserves to be quoted in full by way of illustrating everything that is at stake in this essay:

REAGAN AT BITBURG

Difficult and necessary to imagine the arsenal attached to his elderly
    frame.
Even Mahu Vishna's war bonnet of an oily orange blast won't do,
but it does connect Reagan to holocaustal fire as he walks by an SS
    tomb,
a match that could strike the air into a global roar.
Spiky flames seem to be growing from his back,
a bony fire, like stegosaurian plates—
he possesses unlimited fuel,
an old imprisoned king whose senility can only be relieved by the
    breast pushing through his bars,
the remaining breast of a 40 year old macheted Salvadoran
wearing a red welt from shoulder diagonal to waist,
the model upon which military decoration is based.
Reagan opens his public heart—
the spirit's hot flame is fed by the monstrous pain of unborn
    grandchildren,
the rack of vacuity upon which all are bound and pulled apart
wobbles like a perverse water wheel
through us, exposing the anguish in our pleasure,
the pleasure in our anguish, the boredom in our appetite,
our appetite for boredom—
one can almost smell (but never really smell)
the fumes from still hot German guilt drifting Bitburg,
substantial flames, bouquets of blackened garden eels waving from
    each tomb.
The souls of the innocent dead could not be here,
their wrath is cobra-like but gentle,
in serpentine flocks they roam each German acre, imprisoned in
that part of us that does not, in unison, effect an end to racial
    stratification.

240

Can any image grasp Reagan, amazingly still human, the depth of
   his numbness
within minutes of collapsing mind? He is a kind of prism
made of endless glass enclosures, in whose groundmass
is embedded our reality's decomposing kingdom.[21]

There is something timeless in this satirical poem from 1985; it could
be Celtic, Slavic, Latin. Far from being dated it serves to signpost history.
America a Prophecy looms in the background, dragon-flamed, a poem which
names historical characters such as the heroic "Washington, Franklin,
Paine & Warren, Gates, Hancock and Green" and, in the opposite corner,
the villainous: "The King of England looking westward trembles at the
vision." We are also reminded of Shelley's George III, perennially "old,
mad, blind, despised and dying…" as depicted in the revolutionary sonnet
"England in 1819." The poet satirizing a leader is an eternal recurrence.
The Mandelstam/Stalin manifestation is perhaps the most notorious and
tragic case. In contemporary Kazakhstan, the poet Aron Atabek is serving
an 18 year prison sentence for lyrically ridiculing President Nurabayev.
Eshleman warily revels in his own personal-political-poetic freedom:

Unlike poets in China, Iran, and Nigeria, I can still say anything I
want to say (for a while at least). This is not only suspect freedom
— it renders my situation absurd. I am like a maniac allowed to
wander about screaming "fire" in a theater of the deaf.[22]

At least he can write unflatteringly about Reagan *et al* without fear of
the electric chair. (Another predecessor ghost, Antonin Artaud, excori-
ates American militarism in the first section of "To Have Done with the
Judgement of God", post-Hiroshima, recorded after a period of incarcera-
tion and electroshock treatment, a poem which Eshleman has translated.)
Here the former B-movie actor-cum-U.S. President is vilified for blood-
shed in El Salvador whilst paying a ceremonial visit to Chancellor Kohl in
Germany, including a controversial trip to a graveyard at Bitburg that contained S.S. tombs. Eshleman writes from the margins of American poetry,
but other American artists to satirize this bungled exercise in diplomacy
include such talents as Frank Zappa, Michael Moore and The Ramones.[23]
It's a blackly comic history lesson. The concluding image of the "prism"

shines a co-incidental light on the U.S. government surveillance scandal of today, just as Ezra Pound's money-grubbing pen-pusher "Mr. Nixon" pointed to a later nadir in American history.

Question: what would the literary bureaucrats of William Blake's time have thought of *America a Prophecy*? Answer: they didn't. The vista of a British poet raging against the British Empire, in one of the most out-there poetic texts of the 18th century, going even further than Eshleman would in willing its overthrow, might have been adjudged insanely unpatriotic. True, the Conservative Edmund Burke also supported the American Revolution, and Blake was writing after the event; but had it and other texts been read by the authorities, Blake may have been tried for sedition ten years earlier than he eventually was. That this self-published book has, since 1793, gone through thousands of illustrated, annotated editions and been translated into scores of languages surely takes a demolition ball to "the outright lie that such poetry does not reward study." Like politics, literary politics is short-termist, especially in its failure to rig immortality. The torch is passed. The revolutionary hero Washington is now the capital of Empire, against which a few Elijah-like poets continue to waxeth hot. Eshleman has learnt from all his spirit-guides the art of breaching the forcefield: "Treating boundaries as stage scenery."

From 1966, the missing voice of Duncan plays us out:

> But the mania, the ravening eagle of America
>   as Lawrence saw him "bird of men that are masters,
>   lifting the rabbit-blood of the myriads up into…"
>   into something terrible, gone beyond bounds, or
> As Blake saw America in figures of fire and blood raging,
>   … in what image? the ominous roar in the air,
> the omnipotent wings, the all-American boy in the cockpit
>   loosing his flow of napalm, below in the jungles
>   "any life at all or sign of life" his target, drawing now
>   not with crayons in his secret room
> the burning of homes and the torture of mothers and fathers and
>   children,
>   their hair a-flame, screaming in agony, but

in the line of duty, for the might and enduring fame
    of Johnson, for the victory of American will over its victims,
    releasing his store of destruction over the enemy,
in terror and hatred of all communal things, of communion,
    of communism[24]

In the short-term, one thing is certain: the American government will continue to infiltrate Clayton Eshleman's psyche without Clayton Eshleman's poetry infiltrating the American government's psyche in return.

Notes

[1] *Anticline* 37.
[2] *Archaic Design* 322.
[3] *An Alchemist with One Eye On Fire* 5.
[4] *An Alchemist with One Eye On Fire* 4.
[5] *An Alchemist with One Eye On Fire* 3.
[6] *Archaic Design* 137.
[7] *Archaic Design* 137.
[8] *Archaic Design* 142.
[9] *Archaic Design* 143.
[10] *An Alchemist with One Eye On Fire* 56.
[11] *An Alchemist with One Eye On Fire* 57.
[12] *An Alchemist with One Eye On Fire* 5.
[13] *An Alchemist with One Eye On Fire* 57.
[14] *Archaic Design* 19.
[15] *Hades in Manganese* 58.
[16] *What She Means* 90.
[17] *Companion Spider* 238.
[18] *Companion Spider* 123.
[19] The phrase 'Aurignacian-Apache' is from a personal email of Eshleman's to me.
[20] William Blake, "The Voice of the Ancient Bard."
[21] *Hotel Cro-Magnon* 25-26.
[22] *An Alchemist with One Eye On Fire* 5.
[23] From the Wikipedia entry on Bitburg: "The Ramones recorded the song 'My Brain is Hanging Upside Down (Bonzo Goes to Bitburg)' which alludes to *Bedtime for Bonzo*, a movie from Reagan's film career that co-starred a chimpanzee, and Frank Zappa recorded 'Reagan At Bitburg'."
[24] Robert Duncan, "Up Rising" *Bending the Bow* (New York: New Directions, 1968) 81.

James Pate

The Politics of the Head: Eshleman's *Anticline*, or Poetry in the Age of Neo-Liberalism

As a portraitist, Bacon is a painter of heads, not faces, and there is a great difference between the two. For the face is a structured, spatial organization that conceals the head, whereas the head is dependent of the body, even if it is the point of the body, its culmination. It is not that the head lacks spirit; but it is the spirit in bodily form, a corporeal and vital breath, an animal spirit... Bacon thus pursues a very peculiar project as a portrait painter: to dismantle the face, to rediscover the head or make it emerge from beneath the face.
      Gilles Deleuze, *Francis Bacon: The Logic of Sensation*

Spirits of the head.
Brow of unpolished wood.
My left eye a rouge of blood and sperm.
Eyeball: a rabbit balled-up in a cage.
A Mohawk hairjolt stiffened with soot.
The inner head, beat-up version of somebody else.
      Clayton Eshleman, "Spirits of the Head," *Reciprocal Distillations*

The head instead of the face: both Eshleman and Deleuze suggest that there is an animalistic and spiritual quality about the head as opposed to the face. Deleuze writes about the head as "an animal spirit." In "Spirits of the Head," Eshleman's poem inspired by Francis Bacon's portraits, we're told the eye is like "a rabbit balled-up in a cage." If the face is human and quotidian, wearing the features of the knowable world (personal memories, personal epiphanies), the head is, according to Deleuze, "the spirit in bodily form, a corporeal and vital breath." In other words, the head is pre-human and post-human. It is the element in us that is animalistic in one direction (meat, bone, teeth) and spiritual in the other (the seat of dreams, logos, imagination). And Eshleman, in his career as a poet, much like Bacon in his career as a painter, has obsessively been the poet of the head.

But this focus on the head instead of the face can be seen as a political move too. It would be too simple to equate the face with neo-liberalism and its visions of *Homo Economicus* (the rational self, the self-coherent self, the sense of the "I" equaling the self to its fullest measure), and the head with a politics of liberation and fluidity and experimentation – after all, plenty of very good politically-inflected art has been an art of the face (the films of Costa-Gavras, for example). In Eshleman's hands, though, the attempt to write from the head, to create a poetry inspired by the spirits of the head, has clear political implications. In the opening lines of "Spirits of the Head," he writes, "You want to recover the original wholeness? / Re-enter chaos. / Kill your profane existence. / Become a chocolate skull wrapped in white silk, teeth sewn shut, sockets / shell-stoppered." To break away from the neo-liberal moment, become a head.

We can see this movement in one of Eshleman's most recent books: *Anticline*. Here, Clayton Eshleman takes on many of the themes that he has been dealing with through his prolific career –the underlying violence of the American empire, the border between the animal and human, the ways in which the visual arts and poetry attempt to express the "the human" in all of its often inhuman complexity (with Bosch being especially relevant in this particular book), and also how the imagination can both trap and liberate us. I have to admit, I think Eshleman has become a better and better poet over the years, and *Anticline* is one of my favorite books of his yet. His images have become both clearer and stranger, and his political instincts, while always being critical of those in power, were sharpened even further during the Bush years. And yet he has continually kept away from the self-congratulatory moralizing that has bogged down so much political poetry since 9/11. His more political poems tend to be too messy, too riddled with conflict, and, frankly, too horrific, to be self-congratulatory. If the image of war we find in some American poetry can seem as sanitized as the images we see on CNN, the imagery in Eshleman's political poems is like the more uncensored pictures of conflict we find on Al Jazeera. As Simon Critchley points out in his book *Infinitely Demanding: Ethics of Commitment, Politics of Resistance*, modern politics is now more than ever about "the control of the image."

The political framework in Eshleman's poetry begins with ugliness, with disgust, and he does so in a way that never allows us to keep a safe distance. For example, in "Consternation II" he writes about the "burnt black arm of an Iraqi 12 year old," a line that ends with the image of the boy instead of the burnt arms (in other words, not "a 12 year old Iraqi boy with burnt arms," the way it might be written in a news account). Such a move gives us not an inventory of horrors, an inventory that keeps us at a distance, but rather it places us among these sights: we see the arm first, and then look up to see the boy.

Ugliness, disgust: one of the most insidious aspects of neo-liberalism is its success at controlling images. All too often, the word "neo-liberalism" does not conjure up the image of Pinochet, or the disappearances in Argentina; all too often, "neo-liberalism" is seen as some sort of compromise between left and right, and not as a force, or set of ideas, that has wrecked the lives of millions. To his credit, Eshleman is often determined to show just how much blood is on the hands of neo-liberalism. In "Torture II" he describes the "American Abyss" as "a white 13 by 13 foot room with bash board / on one side / so bodies can be smashed but the damage remain unobservable." Eshleman is determined to recoup those damaged bodies, to remove them from the context of the small, hidden white room, from the "American abyss."

His political poetry also manages to be personal without being confessional or narcissistic. He doesn't feel a vague, troubling anxiety about the rise of free-market capitalism and the reach of the American empire, nor does he think he can extricate himself from it and offer himself up to the reader as a morally pure being; instead, Eshleman's poetry is full of rage and nightmares and confusion. "I acknowledge the American government's infiltration of my psyche," he writes in "Consternation I." "My mental atmosphere has become grainy, hyphenated, / cabbage-odored with seized distractions." Even his Blakean approach to religion is infused with the current political fevers. In "Muse Holes," he writes of seeing:

A five-armed Rumsfeld Vishnu:
one arm thrashing an Iraqi
one arm salivating
one arm a slot machine lever
one arm holding up a smashed Mesopotamian vase
one arm in buddhistic mudra.

Eshleman's *Anticline* suggests that a great deal of poetry written from the standpoint of "the face" is incapable of going far enough. Such poetry sees its face in the mirror it holds up to the world. But what if, as the Zen saying goes, we break the mirror? What if the clichés and oppressive visions of neo-liberalism (which has led to the torture chambers not only of Iraq, but of Chile, Bolivia, and many other countries) do not reflect a

246

face we would ever want to wear? What happens to the so-called reality principle at such moments?

*

For there is a community of the arts, a common problem. In art, and in painting as in music, it is not a matter of reproducing or inventing forms, but of capturing forces. Paul Klee's famous formula – "Not to render the visible, but to render visible" – means nothing less. The task of painting is defined as the attempt to render visible forces that are not themselves visible.

Gilles Deleuze, *Francis Bacon: The Logic of Sensation*

Eshleman is a poet of the 1960s, but he has never been a prisoner of it. To me, his work has often reflected the best of the adventurous spirit of the 1960s – he is invested in experimenting radically with form (without ever becoming a dry formalist), he has a strong inclination toward excess (a quality he shares with other poets who came into their own in the 1960s and 1970s, such as Alice Notley and John Ashbery), and he's attracted to the more turbulent, unsettling branches of unconscious (and sometimes even mystic) experience. The most interesting aspects of the 60s – even the kookier side that was interested in astrology, Tarot cards, etc. – were always about the head. We even see this in Jefferson Airplane's "White Rabbit": *Feed your head.*

And the art of the head does not tend to be elegant or tasteful. Bacon comes to mind again, with his meat creatures, his beasts, his screaming popes. The face wants to communicate human concerns in a human language: the head does not. In his poem "Abyssand" – one of the early poems in *Anticline* – Eshleman writes, "Without ugliness and horror at the base of a poetics, form and beauty / are a sham," and again and again in the collection he returns to the fundamental ontological theme of being and non-being, exploring the echo chamber between sex and death, consciousness and the unconscious. No wonder that in the same poem he calls upon Kali, wondering "But am I up to Kali? Will she deign to show me / life's full complement – / the worm strumming in my palm / Stigmata Sutra?" As that last line also demonstrates, Eshleman's spirituality is intensely physical, not so much a breath in the lungs as a worm in the stigmata.

This visceral quality in Eshleman's work is one reason why he has been able to explore the self in such a bold and original manner. If art that reflects the face is often bound by personal biography, by a journalistic belief in our ability to communicate experience in the terms already laid out for us, art that revolves around the head tends to be a step behind and a step ahead of the common language of the times. If art is about "capturing forces," as Deleuze contends, then the common language of the times is never enough, never up to the task. Along with his interest in Bacon, Eshleman has long been fascinated by Hieronymus Bosch, and that fascination finds a strong outlet in *Anticline*, in the section entitled "Tavern of the Scarlet Bagpipe." In the poem, Eshleman tries to locate the human within a world that is in a state of perpetual mutability. At one point Eshleman writes, "Might not the swarm of 'human' wraiths percolating Paradise / be the progeny of an exfoliating vision by which 'holy ghosts' / are brought into physical conversation – / conversion with birds, beasts, flowers, fruit?" The "physical conversation" with the "holy ghosts": here too Eshleman is tracing the contour whereby materiality and pulse and breath and sinew curve toward the spectral, the fantastic. But even his poetic immersion into the realm of Bosch doesn't take him from his time. (And why should it? Bosch was immersed in his own time too.) At one point, he writes:

> The furnaces of immortality are fed with the bodies of
> people who look a little different from us.
> How does this work, Donald Rumsfeld?
> Does your Reaper retreat an inch for each sixteen-year-
> old Iraqi boy snipered while out looking for food?
> Men with political power are living pyramids of slaugh-
> tered others.
> Bush is a Babelesque pyramid of blood-scummed steps.
> The discrepancy
> between the literal suit and psychic veracity is nasty to
> contemplate.

*

Of course, the question of self and subjectivity has been a contentious one in American poetry since the late 1960's. Some of the debates have been stunningly reductive, with one side arguing for a lyrical, coherent "I," and the other for a poetry devoid of the self, believing that to rid poetry (and thought in general) of the "I" would be a move toward permanently disabling the chief means of exploitation and domination. Yet many of the best poets in the past thirty or forty years have had a much more nuanced take on subjectivity. Alice Notley and Michael Palmer have both found ways of thinking about the first person that thoroughly complicates the above opposition. And Eshleman has too. In "A Transmigralation," Eshleman writes "There's a pouch of menstrual blood & semen / attached to the back wall of imagination." The image could be said to be a kind of origin story for the self: a self that is curiously impersonal (the "wall of imagination" seems to simply exist, unattached to any manifestation of personhood, while also echoing cave imagery) and yet absolutely material, visceral (the "pouch of menstrual blood & semen"). Like Artaud and Vallejo, Eshleman is fascinated by the elemental (blood, semen, rock, dust, shit, bones), by that aspect of life we try to fit into knowable categories – whether they be linguistic, aesthetic, political, or philosophical – in order to control. And the head is the elemental fundament of the self: that haunted, meaty, echoic, and anonymous "self" that gives rise to the social face. Few American poets have written "from the head" so courageously.

Earlier versions of this essay appeared on the blogs Exoskelton *and* Montevidayo.

Paul Stubbs

The Metaphysical Web: *Anticline*

Clayton Eshleman is one of America's moſt pivotal visionary poets writing today, a word-creator and a language inventor whose work has delved deeper than nearly anyone else into the ſtrata of the poetical core of this planet. An "anticline" is what, on a geological map, is recognized as a sequence of rock layers shown to progressively incline towards the surface of the Earth, and, as the title of a poetry colleƈtion, it fits perfeƈtly with Eshleman's life-long love of cave drawings and artwork, and of the multiple geological shelves of "thought" that conſtruƈt themselves within this poet's cranium. Eshleman seems to be a believer in and follower of the philosophical/theological diƈtum *"creatio continua"* — Heraclitus' theory that the world has no ſtable truths, but is in a ſtate of endless change and flux. Nietzsche argued againſt it and blamed the likes of Plato and Chriſtianity for believing the world to be conſtruƈted on theological re-alities only. Eshleman (and the majority of non-religious mankind) has created his own ideas of truth, throwing off the cobwebs of illusion to suggeſt, as the German philosopher and hiſtorian Max Weber did (while coining the phrase *"the disenchantment of the world"*), that secular thinking has maybe dissolved the myſteries of the cosmos.

To cobweb and make decrepit the universe is to *ſtop* thinking about it, for when subsequently free of the human mind, it can remain unfet-tered, in *askesis* and true; only the imagination has thus far prevented the cosmos from realizing the truth of its non-human goals. Simply put, it is only *man's hiſtory* that has ſtained the debris left over of the purity of its beginnings, and Eshleman, unsatisfied by any exclamations of salva-tion, continually attempts to re-birth the universe in the same way that, perhaps, a blind, deaf and dumb person attempts to '"re-birth" *appearance* by brushing the flesh of an alien hand. Everyone is an anceſtor of this poet's mind, even if someone is indifferent to his vaſt and complex word-syſtems; for while the universe continues to echo back "No!" to everything that Eshleman asks of it, he never ſtops trying to queſtion what, in his mind, remains unworthy of the conditioning of his own consciousness:

I greet what I cannot account for,
I depart to where I might become an unfiltered phantom facing
filtered war.
If the sound is the heart noise of being,
does it have a commonwealth, a gong modality
coursing our lives?

Cosmic lisp occurs most poignantly before falling asleep.
An oyster in shell-static, I hear a rapids spewing blood and gold —
I am again takes on flavor.

—"Hmmm"

By constraining poetry to probably the longest umbilical-cord in literature, Eshleman, through an almost insupportable use of "atavism", has
condemned his language to a most necessary death by a *hierarchy of law-
lessness;* his wisdom a reconciliation between flesh and bone which would,
like Baudelaire, undoubtedly allow him to be described as "*both wound
and knife*", a blood-jet as ruinous as the rage of time. In advancing his
word-armies, he lives inside of and in charge of a language *without* history, and so his "style" resembles a perpetual squabble with his own ideas;
a jarring, convulsing and epileptic *spirit* which pervades all of the most
terminal thought-crevices of his brain. All of his originality has the essential tendency to pulverize his own idioms, those which trouble him
with the automatism of only half-creations, half-successes, but that kind
of internal reasoning of course is scarcely conceivable for a poet who by
merely breathing *insinuates* words from his mouth; here is a poet who never mistakes his own mind for anyone else's, despite the fact that literature
rarely, if ever, has been able to match the concentration of the best minds
in poetry; it can only, in an off-handed way, stupefy and paralyze the terror of being long enough for a poem to be finished; and thus Eshleman,
whether demoniacal or mawkish, seems incapable of ever being *corrected*
by language alone; yet what is profound in his work is its ability to reason
with itself in polemics, defying as it does a personal censorship of either
good or evil, by creating an *ever afterwards* as a paradise locked inside of
the parenthesis of now, before, then.

There is no freedom.
There is only the intensification of
the sensing of forever as one lives *now*.

—"Octavio's Labyrinth"

In his pivotal and multifaceted poem *The Tjurunga,* one of two poems (the other being *The Book of Yorunomado*) which Eshleman describes as *"the soulend"* holding *"the rest of my poetry in place,"* he has constructed both a psychological and imaginative matrix in which poets and "names" most important to him have been mobilized and intertwined as if to form (in a poetical sense) a genealogical tree of the antecedents of his soul.

I had to create a totemic cluster in which imagination
could replace Indianapolis, to incorporate ancestor beings
who could give me the agility
—across the tjurunga spider's web—
to pick my way to her perilous centre.

—"The Tjurunga"

Keats wrote that *"Men of Genius are great as certain ethereal Chemicals operating on the Mass of neutral intellect,"* for just as the chemical (in this case "atavism") is spilt onto the ontological and still neutral force fields of his page, Eshleman's imagination begins to spit forth fire, sprouting up in supernatural clusters of word-growths on the horizon, beyond the eye-ridges that appear above the unexpected tectonic shifts of self. The figures in his poems microphone and mouth back the forms of the fitful interior monologues of his mind: a mind that reveals itself in an unyielding semi-otics of metaphysical signals. It is thus a poetry that struggles at the halter of the leash of its own limits, at its own shamanic and global will. From poem to poem he switches on and turns his image-dials until an atavistic transmission is reached, a high imaginative word-frequency in which the history of the living species begins once more to tune-in; and he writes himself into this frequency by admitting:

Never *is* oneself,
the aſtronomical amount of absence loaded into every conscious being.

—"A Transmigralation"

He is saying that to *be* a body is not juſt *having* a body, and his poetry is a theology of the body in which the mind, flesh *and* soul are equal
components in the conſtruction of total and absolute *self.* The same self
chalked up of course onto the cave-walls in the south of France that have
so engrossed this poet for over forty years. He asks for the impossible from
language, and treats his own human gait as a spirit-level to regulate the
unexpected physical shifts of his imagination.

We muſt ask the poem for the impossible, locate ourselves
within this asking, spot the Stone of Division,
then attaching ourselves to this Stone
articulate the amoebic split-off of the divine and the human.

—"Poem to Help Will Alexander Fight Cancer"

Religion is something that flares up but burns in a much more complex
way for this poet, and he beſt sums up his "position" when he asks, in
Placenta: "*is the function of religion to keep humankind from becoming fully
born?*" A queſtion that almoſt pre-empts a need *for* and practice *of* theod-
icy. In his introduction to *Anticline,* Kenneth Warren ſtates that throughout the book Eshleman "*generates fresh hang-time on the cross of a signifying
culture that crucifies human imagination*" — but Eshleman is *not* a religious
poet, rather he is that of the anthropological and psychic doctor unpeel-
ing the bandages of the flesh of human presence, to reveal to us only a
God's firſt teleological absence from the world, *before* the now centuries
old kenotic x-ray of the sun began to lampshade our living flesh. Jesus
Chriſt is evoked, but is not in any way a messiah or a saviour, for such
is the continually regenerating network of mental activity that functions
inside this poet's brain, you get the impression that he could never actually
see the nailed theological Chriſt up on biblical Golgotha: rather he would
see firſt those aboriginal peoples, shouldering branches out of a foreſt and

preparing the way for God to introduce the cross. Just as "Gaia theory" has re-established the link between humans and the rest of nature which was affirmed in mankind's first religion, animism, so too in Eshleman's poetics this "link" is constantly made between the earth and the still powerful anthropological forces that drive his mind forward. The work of many painters also drive this poet's imagination, such as Munch, Pollock, Rousseau and above all the eschatological works of Hieronymus Bosch where we find a solar coupling of souls and an atomic explosion of creative energy that enables Eshleman to ask of the reader:

> Imagine a flea with a howitzer shadow
> or a worm whose shade is a nuclear blaze.

> —"Tavern of the Scarlet Bagpipe"

The landscape of Bosch's garden aligns well, it seems, with the metaphorical animality of Eshleman's poems, both in the courageous artistic sense and in the shape-shifting polymorphous interaction of the discourse between his images. Madness is and can be the great chemical freedom of the imagination, the pulsing blood-river on which the most incredible and sometimes unlikely word-associations can be rafted, set sail, kept afloat:

> I give a functionality to the void, instilling it with a gear-work of irrational transmission.
> [...]
> Madness to be here, so let's slip back into the egg, or feed a cherry the size of our heads to a blood-red dolphin.

> —"Tavern of the Scarlet Bagpipe"

He goes on to ask *"through the foliage, whether Satan can be heard snickering?"* the "foliage" it seems of both the *"garden of earthly delights"* and the actual earthly living systems of the planet today. God then has become no more believable or sustainable than a celestial monstrosity that might want to deposit the eggs of the bodies of the saved onto the great burning dung heaps of hell. This poet wants to *"slit open"* sin as if it were a biological cell, as for him, man's wrong-doings and catastrophes on earth are too natural a disaster for any belief in theological sin.

The New Testament Greek verb "*harmartano*", translated as "to sin" literally means "to miss" (a target) and, by extension, "to fall short" of a moral standard. Yet the sin that Eshleman speaks of is not the *felix culpa* of the Bible, but the earliest atom (after a two-thousand-year-old drum roll) beginning to unsheathe itself of sin's original dark film. Certainly the poet applies himself with his pen in no less vigorous a manner than Bosch did with his paintbrush, and Eshleman's pen is continually akin to a pair of scissors, for he frequently snips the flowerhead of paradise and sends it back to hell, a hinge. The page is the lens in his primordial laboratory, and at times the writing in this powerful collection of poems resembles that of a hallucinated Darwin peeling back the bark from "*The Tree of Life*" to reveal only the earliest discovered bone on earth.

> I wonder:
> might this Fountain of Life,
> a mineral-plant-monstrance,
> liquids peeing through orbs and dishes,
> balanced on percolating muck
> —be the pumping heartwork of an androgynous matrix?

—"Tavern of the Scarlet Bagpipe"

The Romanian-French philosopher E.M. Cioran, in a section of his book *The Temptation to Exist*, wrote: "*if all peoples had reached the same degree of fossilization, or of cowardice, they would readily come to an understanding.*" Eshleman develops this idea and derives his potent poetical energy from the same principle extended to all living forms; he sees and reacts to the absurdity of any *human* glory as of course an "over-civilization" of kairic time, preferring in his poetry to time-lapse figures suspended between a perpetual state of life and death. He states this himself in the notes for his poem *Eternity at Domme,* when he stood overlooking the Dordogne River: "*a mass of contrasting ideas and feelings from my decades of cave research kaleidoscopically locked into focus. Suddenly I had realized my life.*" And he clarified the importance of this experience when he wrote in the same poem:

> I'm ancient as never before this afternoon

—"Eternity at Domme"

It is the moment when every historical figure since the beginning of time resumes the foetal position within the womb of his being, the moment when the mask of the first created human face tips from his chin and drops back into the mould, as the rib in the chest of every man is sandblasted clean again by this fresh new revelation. In *The New Revelations of Being*, Antonin Artaud described something similar in this way: *"I have struggled in my attempt to exist, in my attempt to consent to the forms (all the forms) with which the delirious illusion of being in the world has clothed reality."* "Being" is the botched gait of our still unresolved species, and like Blake, Eshleman is fully prepared and equipped to follow the worm back into the first pore of creation, to crawl into the still unanswerable holes of the head, to participate in any necessary or punitive ceremony, to chant and hold aloft his pen like a torch until locating his own face chalked up onto the wall of some still undiscovered Paleolithic cave.

E.M. Cioran once wrote of Rimbaud and Nietzsche that they were writers and thinkers *"straining at the extreme limits of themselves"* and this also could quite easily be applied to this writer who in *Anticline*, at seventy five years of age, is still writing at the height of his powers and locating the *"resurrectional spirit"* of poetry through the writing and translation of a poet like César Vallejo—one among pivotal visionary poets for Eshleman, that are still *"positioned"* deeply within his *"being,"* and who form a vital link within the complex web of his imagination; poets such as Blake, Artaud, Olson, figures keeping alive the still living systems of ideas, ancestral poets who aid both his genetic and unsuperstitious search for the revelation of truth, whatever "truth" that may be.

A final truth can be found in the poem *Descent*, in which Eshleman it seems has reached something of his own internal "incline" when now in later age and facing the ever steepening mind-ridges of his creativity, he witnesses finally what has gone before and what is still, yet, maybe to come:

> Below closure's boneyard,
> Absence:
> source of the next
> poem's being.

Paris, December 2010

256

Michael McClure

Smile of the Beast

for Clayton Eshleman

THE BEAST FACE IS MY FACE

IS THE CAT'S FACE

IS THE SURFACE   SCREEN

TOPOLOGY

thumb print
of universes of meat under meat
under   through   STARS

MATTER
being MIND BEING WHOLLY MATTER
as *PHYSIS*   hiding
but not hiding in the shown face
BUT EACH POINT WHICH IS ALL
OF THE CENTERS

Doing that as you
LET IN SIZELESSNESS
of Twombly's pansies

OUR HELLO AND GOODBYE TO THESE DIMENSIONS
OR A FREEZING GOPHER
in a puddle of water
and the deer who will barely walk
to let

the car pass
              showing dumb trust
          on their faces…

NUMB DUMB STUNNED BY THE BRIGHTNESS
        of it BEING ME   standing in this flesh
          forever backwards and forwards

          Our face like the snake's is on the wings
                  of a butterfly
            and hurled all directions making
                    galaxies
              of particles and imagination

                BLARING WITH STARK
            POWER OF FLESH IMAGINATION

              The boychild making universes
                of beings – all himself

          Steady except for the sizeless variations
            of emotions, beyond, and less than

          A HUGE SIMPLE FACE

                  NO DIFFERENT
              from a tunicate, owl, crystal,
            dimensions of star systems
                          POURING

          No such thing as power or weakness

                    BUT

                vast VASTER
            than power or weakness

JUST A BIG CARTOON DEMON FACE
PAINTED ON A SCREEN, SIMPLE AS POLLOCK PAINTING
HIS BELOVED OR TWOMBLY HIS PANSIES

PERCY BYSSHE SHELLEY CONFRONTS MONT BLANC
being himself in the caves,
the snowstorms, eagles, and glaciers,
with Shelley as the river
far below
the rickety bridge

ALL OF IT RIPPLING,
RIPPLING INFINITELY
back into

non-beginning.   Where it starts.
There was no ending long before that

and the BEAST FACE IS HERE
WITH BLACKNESS AND MUSCLES
AND raw delicate colors

and the deep solid blackness
OF RUBENS

But forget beauty — it is laughable

FORGET CONFRONTATION IT IS MUCH
HUGER THAN THAT
Nothing
NOT A THING BUT EYES
and a mouth in a grimace that is all emotions ever
known in their combinations
upon every cliff wall,

ſtellar barricade, and between whorls,
in thumb print rivers of kisses and bites
LOCKED
IN A FLOWING
RICTUS

with liberty of all

and any
Natures
and ten trillion white wings
as loving and hungry
as is ſtrength, beyond simple power,
with the face turned inward
moving in the white fat between muscle,
able to believe and move ſtrong fingers

Or a lovely toothed smile at some
tiny success

THIS LUMP THIS BULK GREW ITSELF
to touch velvet lips
and have blood
in the breathing passages   and the flexing
of ſtriations   MERELY THE PRELUDE…

THE SECRET WAS NOT MEANT TO BE KNOWN
in the absence of inspiration,
nor imagination to be
burdened with the
taſte and smell of apples
or a dead mouse whose soul has flown
from a flat rock in the May sun
— like a thumbprint and beaſt face smiling
with fulfillment —
THE HUNGER FOR GROWTH
JOY AND FULFILLMENT

surely is meant to add itself to itself.
ALL IS LIBERTY FOR THIS CHOICE
which is constant Spring smiling

and snarling and grinning   A cartoon

is a picture of it, FREED OF LOCATION

hanging hungry and feasting
bringing each no-place forward

to laugh with or without lips
and painted with a child's skill
in dusty smoke and lightning
AMONG MIGRATIONS

Always the deer, the vole,
the glorious goddess of the lovable
and loving assassins
JUST AS MOZART AND HAYDN
AND AN ORCA and the sheet of nebulae
have this thing scrimshawed
and carved in the missing
dimensions of an inner heart

— it is graffiti on a concrete wall in Beijing
and THE MEAT of your cheek

CERTAINLY IT IS NOT LIBERTY BUT
FAR MORE AND LESS THAN WHAT
MIGHT BE IN A SMILE
and not truth which matters less   than the
flow
of petals and laughs and death groans with the eyes
rolled upward into everywhere
lying like a cheetah

on
roses of sharon

and, if ANYTHING, LAUGHING GRINNING
at itself in simple being   less and more
than free and all ways more dead
than alive in the voluptuousness

of sinking freely through bright coldness
of a dewdrop or a kiss thrown from
a passing car
No touch of death just
liberty
of not and ever
in a squint of eyes
or the prehension
of a snowflake at sea bottom landing
on a gleaming furnace

Heady as the red lavender poppy
to the bee

OR THE FLOWS OF FLESH EVERYWHERE

HIDING WITH NO INTENTION

the beast smile always
As I know when I do not think
or see it as tenuous

as a thumb nail or tar pit

being silence and roarings

AND SURELY A VERY LARGE SMILE
but no SMILE as smiles are known

Books and Chapbooks

Mexico and North (Tokyo, Japan: privately published, 1962). Poetry, 54 pages.

Pablo Neruda, *Residence on Earth* (San Francisco: Amber House Press, 1962). Translation, 64 pages.

The Chavín Illumination (Lima, Peru: La Rama Florida, 1965). Revised edition reprinted in *On Mules Sent From Chavin: A Journal and Poems*. Poetry, 16 pages.

Aimé Césaire, *State of the Union* (New York: Caterpillar, Caterpillar Book 1, 1966). Co-translated with Denis Kelly. Translation, 42 pages.

Lachrymae Mateo: Three Poems for Christmas, 1966 (New York: Caterpillar, Caterpillar Book 3, 1966). Reprinted in *Indiana* (Black Sparrow Press, 1969). Poetry, 6 pages.

Walks (New York: Caterpillar, Caterpillar Book 10, 1967). Partially reprinted in *Indiana* (Los Angles: Black Sparrow Press, 1969). Poetry, 47 pages.

César Vallejo, *Poemas Humanos / Human Poems* (New York: Grove Press, 1968). Translation, 326 pages.

Cantaloups and Splendour (Los Angeles: Black Sparrow Press, 1968). Reprinted in *Indiana* (Los Angeles: Black Sparrow Press, 1969). Poetry, 18 pages.

Brother Stones (New York: Caterpillar, A Caterpillar Book, 1968). 19 Loose leaves with 6 woodcuts by William Paden. Partially reprinted in *Indiana* (Los Angeles: Black Sparrow Press, 1969). Poetry, 19 pages.

The House of Okumura (Toronto, Ontario, Canada: Weed/Flower, 1969). Partially reprinted in *Coils* (Los Angeles: Black Sparrow Press, 1973). Poetry, 37 pages.

Indiana (Los Angeles: Black Sparrow Press, 1969). Poetry, 178 pages.

T'ai (Cambridge, MA: Sans Souci Press, 1969). Reprinted in *Coils* (Los Angeles: Black Sparrow Press, 1973). Poetry, 35 pages.

A Pitch-blende (Berkeley, CA: Maya Quarto, 1969). Poetry, 11 pages.

The House of Ibuki (Freemont, MI: Sumac Press, 1969). Poetry, 49 pages.

The Yellow River Record (London, England: Big Venus Press, 1969). Poetry, 12 pages.

Altars (Los Angeles: Black Sparrow Press, 1971). Poetry, 120 pages.

Bearings (Santa Barbara: Capricorn Press, 1971). Prose, 22 pages.

The Sanjo Bridge (Los Angeles: Black Sparrow Press, Sparrow 2, 1972). Prose, 15 pages.

Coils (Los Angeles: Black Sparrow Press, 1973). Poetry, 147 pages.

Human Wedding (Los Angeles: Black Sparrow Press, 1973). Poetry, 8 pages.

Aux Morts (Los Angeles: Black Sparrow Press, Sparrow 18, 1974). Partially reprinted in *The Gull Wall* (Los Angeles: Black Sparrow Press, 1975). Poetry, 15 pages.

Realignment (Kingston, NY: Treacle Press, 1974). Illustrated by Nora Jaffe. Partially reprinted in *The Gull Wall* (Los Angeles: Black Sparrow Press, 1975). Poetry, 50 pages.

Antonin Artaud, *Letter to André Breton* (Los Angeles: Black Sparrow Press, Sparrow 23, 1974). Reprinted in *Conductors of the Pit* (Brooklyn: Soft Skull Press, 2005). Translation, 15 pages.

César Vallejo, *Spain, Take This Cup From Me* (New York: Grove Press, 1974). Co-translated with José Rubia Barcia. Translation, 77 pages.

Portrait of Francis Bacon (Sheffield, England: Rivelin Press, 1975). Reprinted in *The Gull Wall* (Los Angeles: Black Sparrow Press, 1975). Poetry, 11 pages.

The Gull Wall (Los Angeles: Black Sparrow Press, 1975). Poetry, 111 pages.

Antonin Artaud, *To Have Done With the Judgment of God* (Los Angeles: Black Sparrow Press, Sparrow 23, 1975). Co-translated with Norman Glass. Reprinted in Antonin Artaud, *Four Texts* (Los Angeles: Panjandrum Books, 1982). Translation, 23 pages.

The Woman Who Saw through Paradise (Lawrence, KS: Tansy, Tansy 2, 1976). Reprinted in *What She Means* (Los Angeles: Black Sparrow Press, 1978). Poetry, 8 pages.

Antonin Artaud, *Artaud the Momo* (Los Angeles: Black Sparrow Press, Sparrow 47, 1976). Co-translated with Norman Glass. Reprinted in Antonin Artaud, *Four Texts* (Los Angeles: Panjandrum Books, 1982). Translation, 23 pages.

Cogollo (Newton, MA: Roxbury Poetry Enterprises, 1976). Partially reprinted in *What She Means* (Los Angeles: Black Sparrow Press, 1978). Withdrawn from publication at Eshleman's request. Poetry, 27 pages.

Core Meander (Santa Barbara: Black Sparrow Press, Sparrow 57, 1977). Partially reprinted in *What She Means* (Los Angeles: Black Sparrow Press, 1978). Poetry, 15 pages.

Grotesca (London, England: New London Pride, 1977). Partially reprinted in *The Gull Wall* (Los Angeles: Black Widow Press, 1975) and in *What She Means* (Los Angeles: Black Sparrow Press, 1978). Poetry, 38 pages.

Oasis 19: New Poems and Translations by Clayton Eshleman (London, England: Oasis Books, 1977). Poetry and translation, 39 pages.

The Gospel of Celine Arnauld (Berkeley, CA: Tuumba Press, 1977). Poetry, 19 pages.

The Name Encanyoned River (Riverside, RI: The Woodbine Press, 1977). Reprinted in *What She Means* (Los Angeles: Black Sparrow Press, 1978). Poetry, 30 pages.

On Mules Sent from Chavin: A Journal and Poems (Swanea, UK: Galloping Dog Press, 1977). Poetry and prose, 70 pages.

César Vallejo, *Battles in Spain: Five Unpublished Poems* (Santa Barbara: Black Sparrow Press, Sparrow 65, 1978). Co-translated with José Rubia Barcia. Reprinted in César Vallejo, *The Complete Posthumous Poetry* (Berkeley: University of California Press, 1978). Translation, 15 pages.

What She Means (Los Angeles: Black Sparrow Press, 1978). Poetry, 194 pages.

César Vallejo, *The Complete Posthumous Poetry* (Berkeley: University of California Press, 1978). Co-translated with José Rubia Barcia. Translation, 339 pages.

A Note on Apprenticeship (Chicago: Two Hands Press, 1979). Prose, 6 pages.

Nights We Put the Rock Together (Santa Barbara: Cadmus Editions, 1980). Partially reprinted in *Hades in Manganese* (Santa Barbara: Black Sparrow Press, 1981). Poetry, 46 pages.

The Lich Gate (Barrytown, NY: Station Hill Press, 1980). Partially reprinted in *Hades in Manganese* (Santa Barbara: Black Sparrow Press, 1981). Poetry, 16 pages.

Our Lady of the Three-Pronged Devil (New York: Red Ozier Press, 1981). Partially reprinted in *Hades in Manganese* (Santa Barbara: Black Sparrow Press, 1981). Poetry, 32 pages.

Foetus Graffiti (New Haven: Pharos Books, 1981). Reprinted in *Fracture* (Santa Barbara: Black Sparrow Press, 1983). Poetry, 4 pages.

Hades in Manganese (Santa Barbara: Black Sparrow Press, 1981). Poetry, 114 pages.

Aimé Césaire, *Some African Poems in English* (Pasadena, CA: Munger Africana Library, California Institute of Technology, 1981). Co-translated with Annette Smith. Reprinted in Aimé Césaire, *The Collected Poetry* (Berkeley: University of California Press, 1983). Translation, 15 pages.

Antonin Artaud, *Four Texts* (Los Angeles: Panjandrum Books, 1982). Co-translated with Norman Glass. Translation, 99 pages.

Visions of the Fathers of Lascaux (Los Angeles: Panjandrum Books, 1983). Poetry, 27 pages.

Fracture (Santa Barbara: Black Sparrow Press, 1983). Poetry, 145 pages.

Aimé Césaire, *The Collected Poetry* (Berkeley: University of California Press, 1983). Co-translated with Annette Smith. Translation, 408 pages.

Michel Deguy, *Given Giving: Selected Poems* (Berkeley: University of California Press, 1984). Translation, 189 pages.

Antonin Artaud, *Chanson* (New York: Red Ozier Press, 1985). Drawings by Nancy Spero. Reprinted in *Watch Fiends and Rack Screams* (Cambridge, MA: Exact Change, 1995). Translation, 17 pages.

The Name Encanyoned River: Selected Poems 1960-1985 (Santa Barbara: Black Sparrow Press, 1986). Introduction by Eliot Weinberger. Poetry, 245 pages.

Bernard Bador, *Sea Urchin Harakiri* (Los Angeles: Panjandrum Press, 1986). Translation, 128 pages.

Aimé Césaire, *Lost Body* (New York: Braziller, 1986). Co-translated with Annette Smith. Reprinted from Aimé Césaire, *The Collected Poetry* (Berkeley: University of California Press, 1983). Translation, 131 pages.

Conductors of the Pit: Major Works by Rimbaud, Vallejo, Césaire, Artaud, Holan (New York: Paragon House, 1988). Reprinted in revised second edition *Conductors of the Pit* (Brooklyn: Soft Skull Press, 2005). Translation, 242 pages.

Mistress Spirit (Los Angeles: Arundel Press, 1989). Reprinted in *Hotel Cro-Magnon* (Santa Rosa: Black Sparrow Press, 1989). Poetry, 38 pages.

Hotel Cro-Magnon (Santa Rosa: Black Sparrow Press, 1989). Poetry, 161 pages.

Antiphonal Swing: Selected Prose 1962-1987 (Kingston, NY: McPherson, 1989). Edited by Caryl Eshleman, Introduction by Paul Christensen. Prose, 256 pages.

Novices: A Study of Poetic Apprenticeship (Los Angeles: Mercer & Aitchison, 1989). Prose, 79 pages.

Aimé Césaire, *Lyric & Narrative Poetry, 1946-1982* (Richmond: University of Virginia Press, 1990). Co-translated with Annette Smith. Translation, 235 pages.

César Vallejo, *Trilce* (New York: Marsilio Publishers, 1992). Translation, 304 pages.

Under World Arrest (Santa Rosa: Black Sparrow Press, 1994). Poetry, 197 pages.

Antonin Artaud, *Watchfiends and Rack Screams: Works from the Final Period* (Boston: Exact Change, 1995). Co-translated with Bernard Bador. Translation, 342 pages.

Nora's Roar (Boulder, CO: Rodent Press, 1996). Reprinted in *From Scratch* (Santa Rosa: Black Sparrow Press, 1998). Poetry, 32 pages.

The Aranea Constellation (Minneapolis: Rain Taxi, Brainstorm Series 1, 1998). Reprinted in *Juniper Fuse* (Middleton, CT: Wesleyan University Press, 2003). Prose, 17 pages.

From Scratch (Santa Rosa: Black Sparrow Press, 1998). Poetry, 190 pages.

Hades en manganese. (Paris: Belin, 1998). Translated by Jean-Paul Auxemery.

César Vallejo, *Trilce* (Middleton, CT: Wesleyan University Press, 2000).

Erratics (Rosendale, NY: Hunger Press, 2000). Reprinted in *My Devotion* (Boston: Black Sparrow Books, 2004). Poetry, 85 pages.

A Cosmogonic Collage: Sections I, II, & V (Ypsilanti, MI: Canopic Press, 2000). Reprinted in *Juniper Fuse*. Poetry, prose, 38 pages.

Aimé Césaire, *Notebook of a Return to the Native Land* (Middletown, CT: Wesleyan University Press, 2001). Co-translated with Annette Smith. Revised second edition. Translation, 63 pages.

Companion Spider (Middletown, CT: Wesleyan University Press, 2002). Foreword by Adrienne Rich. Prose, 333 pages.

Sweetheart (Ypsilanti, MI: Canopic Press, 2002). Reprinted in *My Devotion* (Boston: Black Sparrow Books, 2004). Poetry, 10 pages.

Bands of Blackness (Coulimer, France: Estepa Editions, 2002). Japanese translation by Eda Takaomi, French translation by Auxemery, with an engraving by Matsutani. Poetry, boxed, 24 pages.

Juniper Fuse: Upper Paleolithic Imagination & the Construction of the Underworld (Wesleyan University Press), 2003. Poetry, prose, 291 pages.

Everwhat (Canary Islands: Zaŝterle Press, 2003). Partially reprinted in *Reciprocal Diŝtillations* (Boulder, CO: Hot Whiskey Press, 2007**)**, *An Alchemiŝt with One Eye on Fire* (Boŝton: Black Widow Press, 2006), and *Archaic Design* (Boŝton: Black Widow Press, 2007). Poetry, 58 pages.

My Devotion (Boŝton: Black Sparrow Books, 2004). Poetry, 123 pages.

Conductors of the Pit: Poetry Written in Extremis in Translation (Brooklyn, NY: Soft Skull Press, 2005). Second edition, subŝtantially revised of *Conductors of the Pit* (New York: Paragon House, 1988). Translation, 242 pages.

An Alchemiŝt with One Eye on Fire (Boŝton: Black Widow Press, 2006). Poetry, 107 pages.

Reciprocal Diŝtillations (Boulder, CO: Hot Whiskey Press, 2007). Foreword by Roberto Tejada. Poetry, 73 pages.

Deep Thermal (Santa Barbara: Simplemente Maria Press, 2007). With digital prints by Mary Heebner. A 17" x 13" portfolio of six pigment prints and six letterpress poems printed in an edition 26 copies. Poetry, 6 pages.

A Shade of Paden (Hopewell, NJ: Piedoxen Printers, 2007). With a wood-cut by Bill Paden. Poetry, 10 pages.

Archaic Design (Boŝton: Black Widow Press, 2007). Prose, 342 pages.

César Vallejo, *The Complete Poetry: A Bilingual Edition* (Berkeley: University of California Press, 2007). Translation, 717 pages.

The Grindŝtone of Rapport: A Clayton Eshleman Reader (Boŝton: Black Widow Press, 2008). Selected poetry, prose, and translations, 619 pages.

Hashigakari (Belgium: Tandem / Eŝtepa, 2010). Translated by Jean-Paul Auxeméry and Takaomi Eda. Sign limited edition, 30 English / French, 30 English / Japanese, signed and numbered in a case with an etching by Matsutani. Reprinted in *Anticline*.

Eternity at Domme / The French Notebooks (Paris: Eŝtepa Editions, 2010). Translated by Jean-Paul Auxeméry, with monotypes by Kate van Houten, hand-bound, hard-bound edition of 200 signed and numbered on verge paper. Reprinted in *Anticline* (Boŝton: Black Widow Press, 2010). Poetry, 26 pages.

Anticline (Boŝton: Black Widow Press, 2010). Poetry, 181 pages.

Bernard Bador, *Curdled Skulls: Selected Poems* (Boston: Black Widow Press, 2010). Some of these translations originally appeared in Sea Urchin Harakiri (Los Angeles: Panjandrum Press, 1986). Translation, 117 pages.

Bei Dao, *Daydream* (Minneapolis, MN: OHM Editions, 2010). Co-translated with Lucas Klein. Reprinted in Bei Dao, *Endure*. Translation, 23 pages.

Bei Dao, *Endure* (Boston: Black Widow Press, 2011). Co-translated with Lucas Klein. Translation, 131 pages.

An Anatomy of the Night (Buffalo: BlazeVox Books, 2011). Poetry, 65 pages.

Aimé Césaire, *Solar Throat Slashed: The Unexpurgated 1948 Edition.* (Middleton, CT: Wesleyan University Press, 2011). Co-translated with A. James Arnold. Translation, 183 pages.

The Jointure (Buffalo: BlazeVox Books, 2012). Poetry, 38 pages.

The Price of Experience (Boston: Black Widow Press, 2013). Prose, 483 pages.

Aimé Césaire, *The Original 1939 Notebook of a Return to a Native Land: Bilingual edition* (Middleton, CT: Wesleyan University Press, 2013). Co-translated with A. James Arnold. Translation, 120 pages.

Penetralia (Boston: Black Widow Press, 2014). Poetry.

Broadsides

The Crocus Bud (Reno, NV: Camels Coming, 1965). Poetry, 4 mimeographed pages.

The Wand (Santa Barbara: Capricorn, 1971).

The Bridge at the Mayan Pass (Valencia, CA: Peace Press, The Box, 1971). Reprinted in *Coils* (Los Angeles: Black Sparrow Press, 1973).

One of the Oldest Dreams (Detroit: The Alternative Press, 1971).

The Last Judgment: For Caryl Her Thirty-first Birthday, for the End of Her Pain (Los Angeles: Privately printed through Plantin Press, 1973).

Still-Life, with Fraternity (Lawrence, KS: Cottonwood Review, 1976).

For Mark Kritzer (Northridge, CA: Herb Yellin, 1977).

Rancid Moonlight Hotel (Storrs, CT: University of Connecticut Library, 1977). Reprinted in *What She Means* (Santa Barbara: Black Sparrow Press, 1978).

For Cheryl Lynn Wallach (Northridge, CA: Herb Yellin, 1978).

Eternity (Los Angeles: Jazz Press, 1977). Reprinted in *What She Means* (Santa Barbara: Black Sparrow Press, 1978).

Chrysanthemum Lane (Binghampton, NY: The Bellevue Press, 1978). Reprinted in *What She Means* (Santa Barbara: Black Sparrow Press, 1978).

César Vallejo, *Paris, October 1936* (Binghampton, NY: The Bellevue Press, 1978).

Dot (Binghampton, NY: The Bellevue Press, 1978). Reprinted in *Hades in Manganese* (Santa Barbara: Black Sparrow Press, 1981).

The American Sublime (Barrytown, NY: Station Hill Press, 1980). Reprinted in *Hades in Manganese* (Santa Barbara: Black Sparrow Press, 1981) and as "Un Poco Loco" in *The Name Encanyoned River: Selected Poems* (Santa Barbara: Black Sparrow Press, 1986).

Aimé Césaire, *The Woman and the Knife* (New York: Red Ozier Press, 1981). Reprinted in Aimé Césaire, *The Collected Poetry* (Berkeley: University of California Press, 1983).

Antonin Artaud, (from:) *Suppôts et Suppliciations*. (New York: Red Ozier Press, 1984). Co-translated with A. James Arnold. Reprinted in Antonin Artaud, *Watch Fiends and Rack Screams* (Cambridge, MA: Exact Change, 1995).

Reagan at Bitberg (Santa Barbara: Table Talk Press, 1985). Reprinted in *Hotel Cro-Magnon* (Santa Barbara: Black Sparrow Press, 1989).

Brown Thrasher (Ann Arbor, MI: Shaman Drum Bookshop, 1986). Reprinted in *Hotel Cro-Magnon* (Santa Barbara: Black Sparrow Press, 1989).

Antonin Artaud, *Indian Culture*. (Ann Arbor: Other Wind Press, 1987). Co-translated with Bernard Bador. Artwork by Nancy Spero. Reprinted in Antonin Artaud, *Watch Fiends and Rack Screams* (Cambridge, MA: Exact Change, 1995).

Picked up the Rotted Doormat (Encinitas, CA: Ta'Wil Broadside, 1993). Reprinted in *Under World Arrest* (Santa Rosa: Black Sparrow Press, 1994).

El Mozote (Ashland, KY: Bullhead Broadside Series #1, 1995). Reprinted in *From Scratch* (Santa Rosa: Black Sparrow Press, 1998).

Jisei (Ellsworth, ME: Backwoods Broadsides, 55, 2000).

César Vallejo, *Wedding March* (Ellsworth, ME: Backwoods Broadsides, 99, 2006).

Editor

Folio (Bloomington, IN) 3 issues, 1959-1960.
Quena (Lima, Peru) 1 issue, suppressed by North American Peruvian Cultural Institute, 1966.
Caterpillar (New York City – Los Angeles) 20 issues, 1967-1973.
A Caterpillar Anthology (New York: Doubleday, 1971).
Sulfur (Pasadena – Los Angeles – Ypsilanti) 46 issues, 1981-2000.
Paul Blackburn, *The Parallel Voyages* (Tucson, AZ: SUN/Gemini Press 1987). Co-edited with Edith Jarolim.
A Sulfur Anthology (Middleton, CT: Wesleyan University Press, 2015).

Archival Materials

Lilly Library, Indiana University
Fales Library, New York University
The Archive for New Poetry, University of California, San Diego
Beinecke Rare Book and Manuscript Library, Yale University

Bibliography

Martha J. Sattler, *Clayton Eshleman: A Descriptive Bibliography* (Jefferson, NC: McFarland & Company, American Poetry Contemporary Bibliography Series no. 4, 1988).

Rachel Blau DuPlessis is internationally known as both a feminist critic and scholar and for her poetry and essays. Her many creative and critical works include the classic study, *The Pink Guitar: Writing as Feminist Practice* and the multi-volume long poem, *Drafts*. She is Professor of English at Temple University. Among other awards and honors, DuPlessis received Temple University's Creative Achievement Award in 1999 and, in 2002, she was awarded the third Roy Harvey Pearce / Archive for New Poetry Prize, given biennially to an American poet/scholar who has made a significant lifetime contribution to American poetry and literary scholarship.

Peter Cockelbergh is a Belgian poet, scholar and translator living in Lille, France. He studied at the universities of Antwerp and Leuven (Belgium), at the EHESS in Paris, and was a doctoral research fellow at the Technische Universität Darmstadt (Germany). Editor of *Pierre Joris—Cartographies of the In-between* (Litteraria Pragensia, 2011), his current projects include the French translation of Joris's *A Nomad Poetics*, the poetry and prose of Robert Kelly, and an online anthology of Deep Image(-related) magazines and writings.

James Hillman (1926–2011) studied at the Sorbonne in Paris, Trinity College in Dublin, and the University of Zurich as well as earning an analyst's diploma from the C. G. Jung Institute. He served as Director of Studies at the Institute until 1969. Author of more than twenty books, including *The Soul's Code*, and known as the founder of archetypal psychology, Hillman was considered to be the world's foremost post-Jungian thinker.

Pierre Joris is a poet, translator, essayist & anthologist who has published more than 50 books, most recently, *Meditations on the Stations of Mansur al-Hallaj* (poems) from Chax Press and *The University of California Book of North African Literature* (volume 4 in the *Poems for the Millennium* series), coedited with Habib Tengour. *Exile is My Trade: A Habib Tengour Reader* and *Pierre Joris: Cartographies of the In-between*, edited by Peter Cockelbergh, came out in 2012. Forthcoming are *Barzakh — Poems 2000–2012* (Black Widow Press) & *Breathturn into Timestead: The Collected Later Poetry of Paul Celan*. (FSG).

Andrew Joron is the author of *Trance Archive: New and Selected Poems* (City Lights, 2010). Joron's previous poetry collections include *The Removes* (Hard Press, 1999), *Fathom* (Black Square Editions, 2003), and *The Sound Mirror* (Flood Editions, 2008). *The Cry at Zero*, a selection of his prose poems and critical essays, was published by Counterpath Press in 2007. From the German, he has translated the *Literary Essays* of Marxist-Utopian philosopher Ernst Bloch (Stanford University Press, 1998) and *The Perpetual Motion Machine* by the proto-Dada fantasist Paul Scheerbart (Wakefield Press, 2011). Joron lives in Berkeley, California, where he theorizes using the theremin.

Robert Kelly is author of more than fifty books of poetry as well as essays, manifestoes, short fiction, and a novel. His work as an editor and contributing editor includes *A Controversy of Poets* (with Paris Leary), *Trobar*, *Chelsea Review, Matter, Caterpillar*, and *Sulfur*, among other journals. Honors include an Award for Distinction from the American Academy and Institute of Arts and Letters and a fellowship from the National Endowment for the Arts. He has taught and lectured at many colleges and universities, including Bard College, with which he has been affiliated since 1961.

Stuart Kendall is the author of *Georges Bataille* and *The Ends of Art and Design*. He has edited and translated books by Bataille, Maurice Blanchot, Paul Eluard, Jean Baudrillard, René Char, and Guy Debord. Other works include an edited volume, *Terrence Malick: Film and Philosophy*, and *Gilgamesh*, a new version of the eponymous Mesopotamian poems.

Herbert Lust graduated from the University of Chicago in 1948. Soon after, he was awarded a Fulbright scholarship for study in France. After returning to America in 1951 he taught literature for a few years at the University of Chicago and then became an investment banker. He is the author of a novel, *Violence and Defiance*, as well as *A Dozen Principles for Art Investment, Giacometti: The Complete Graphics and 15 Drawings*, and *Enrico Baj: Dada Impressionist–A Catalogue Raisonne for the Paintings*. He divides his time between Connecticut and New York City.

David Maclagan is a writer, artist and retired art therapist and university lecturer. He has published many articles on art, imagination & psychoanalysis, and his book about the imaginative reception of paintings, *Psychological Aesthetics* (J Kingsley, 2001) engaged with some of Eshleman's poetic responses to visual art. He lives in West Yorkshire, UK.

Michael McClure is an internationally known American poet, playwright, songwriter, and novelist. He has collaborated with prominent artists, poets, and musicians, including Allen Ginsberg, Jim Morrison, Terry Riley, and Ray Manzarek. McClure's journalism has been featured in *Rolling Stone, Vanity Fair, The Los Angeles Times,* and *The San Francisco Chronicle.* He has received numerous awards, including a Guggenheim Fellowship and an Obie Award. His books of poetry include *Mysteriosos and Other Poems, Huge Dreams, Rain Mirror,* and many others. He lives in Oakland, California.

Niall McDevitt is an Irish poet living in London. He is the author of two collections of poems, *b/w* (Waterloo Press, 2010) and *Porterloo* (International Times, 2012). He is poetry editor of http://www.internationaltimes.it/ and a psychogeographical explorer of the city and beyond who follows the trails of revolutionary poets such as Coppe, Blake, Rimbaud and Gascoyne. As an activist he has campaigned to secure the future of the Rimbaud/Verlaine House at 8 Royal College Street; to get Burmese and Kazakh poets Saw Wei and Aran Atabek released from prison; to oppose riverside development in London by staging the world premiere of Shelley's verse play *Swellfoot the Tyrant* on the site of Queen Caroline's death in Hammersmith; and for the purchase of 'the Jerusalem Room' in which William Blake lived for 18 years and where he wrote and engraved *Jerusalem: the Emanation of the Giant Albion.* By refusing to write designer Irish poems and by mucking in with the nonconformist natives, McDevitt's work has created a new political frisson which he describes as 'Judeo-Apache, urban sha-manic, avant-folk'.

Eric Mottram was a poet, critic, editor, and educator. As a poet and as editor of *The Poetry Review,* he was a major figure in the British Poetry Revival. His critical writings include influential books on William S. Burroughs, Allen Ginsberg, and Paul Bowles among many other works.

Jay Murphy is a writer and independent curator currently based in Glasgow. His work has appeared in *Parkett, Contemporary, Art in America, Metropolis, Afterimage, Third Text*, among other publications; he edited the alternative journal *Red Bass* and the book anthology *For Palestine* (1993). He was twice a finalist for the Sundance Screenwriting Labs and his collaborative Internet projects have been shown at the Sundance Online Film Festival. In 2013, 2011 and 2009 he organized exhibitions and programs of film and moving image work from the Middle East and North Africa for venues in Aberdeen, Dundee, Edinburgh, and Glasgow, and in 2008 gallery exhibitions in New York and Edinburgh.

John Olson is the author of *Backscatter: New And Selected Poems*, from Black Widow Press; *Souls Of Wind*, a novel about the notorious French poet Arthur Rimbaud in the American West, from Quale Press; and *The Nothing That Is*, an autobiographical novel from Ravenna Press. *Larynx Galaxy*, a collection of essays and prose poetry, appeared in June, 2012, from Black Widow Press. *The Seeing Machine*, a novel about French painter Georges Braque, appeared from Quale Press in fall 2012.

James Pate graduated from the University of Iowa Writers' Workshop and has a Ph.D. in English and Creative Writing from the University of Illinois at Chicago. His work has appeared in *The Black Warrior Review, StorySouth, The Cream City Review*, and *Blue Mesa*, among other places. He is the author of a book of poems entitled *The Fassbinder Diaries* (Civil Coping Mechanisms, 2013). He currently teaches poetry and philosophy at Shepherd University.

Jed Rasula's critical writings include *The American Poetry Wax Museum* (1996), *Imagining Language* (with Steve McCaffery, 1998), *This Compost: Ecological Imperatives in American Poetry* (2002), *Syncopations: Contemporary American Poetry and the Stress of Innovation* (2004) and *Modernism and Poetic Inspiration: The Shadow Mouth* (2009). His books of poetry include *Tabula Rasula* (1986) and *Hot Wax, or Psyche's Drip* (2007). He is the editor of the anthology *Burning City: Poems of Metropolitan Modernity* (2012). He is Helen S. Lanier Distinguished Professor of English at the University of Georgia.

Jerome Rothenberg is an internationally renowned poet, performance artist, critic and scholar. He has published over eighty books, booklets and pamphlets of poetry, several of which have been translated widely. He has assembled, edited, and annotated ten enormously germinal anthologies of experimental and traditional poetry and performance, beginning with *Technicians of the Sacred* in 1968, and has been a leading voice in the approach to creative work and mind that he named "ethnopoetics." Black Widow Press published his collection of recent poems, *Concealments and Caprichos*, in 2010 and *Eyes of Witness: A Jerome Rothenberg Reader* in 2012.

Paul Stubbs is the author of two poetry collections, *The Theological Museum* (Flambard, 2005) and *The Icon Maker* (Arc Publications, 2008), a long poem, *Ex Nihilo* (Black Herald Press, 2010) and various plays. The tutelary spirit of Francis Bacon hovers above each poem of his forthcoming third collection, *The End of the Trial of Man* (Arc Publications, 2013). His poems and reviews have appeared in a variety of anthologies and magazines (*The Wolf, Poetry Review, The Bitter Oleander, The Shop, etc.*). He co-edits *The Black Herald*, a Paris-based bi-lingual literary journal.

Roberto Tejada is the author of many books including *National Camera: Photography and Mexico's Image Environment* (University of Minnesota Press, 2009) and *Celia Alvarez Muñoz* (UCLA/CSRC; University of Minnesota Press, 2009). From 1987 to 1997 he lived and worked in Mexico City where he founded the journal *Mandorla: New Writing From the Americas*, a forum for advanced poetry and translation and worked as an editor of *Vuelta* magazine. Tejada is also the author of several poetry collections, including *Mirrors for Gold* (Krupskaya, 2006) and *Exposition Park* (Wesleyan University Press, 2010).

Kenneth Warren is the editor of *House Organ*, a quarterly letter of poetry and prose. His two collections of poetry are *Rock/the Boat: Book One* (Oasis Press, 1998) and *The Wandering Boy* (Flo Press, 1979). BlazeVox recently published his selective history of contemporary American poetry: *Captain Poetry's Sucker Punch A Guide to the Homeric Punkhole, 1980–2012.*

Eliot Weinberger is an essayist, political commentator, translator, and editor. His books of literary essays include *Karmic Traces*, *An Elemental Thing* and *Oranges & Peanuts for Sale*. His political articles are collected in *What I Heard About Iraq* and *What Happened Here: Bush Chronicles*. He is author of a study of Chinese poetry translation, *19 Ways of Looking at Wang Wei*, translator of the poetry of Bei Dao, and editor of *The New Directions Anthology of Classical Chinese Poetry*. His other anthologies include *World Beat: International Poetry Now* from New Directions and *American Poetry Since 1950: Innovators & Outsiders*. Among his translations of Latin American poetry and prose are the *Collected Poems 1957–1987* of Octavio Paz, Vicente Huidbro's *Altazor*, and Jorge Luis Borges' *Selected Non-Fictions*, which received the National Book Critics Circle award for criticism. He lives in New York City.

BLACK WIDOW PRESS

TRANSLATION SERIES

A Life of Poems, Poems of a Life
by Anna de Noailles. Trans: Norman R.
Shapiro. Introduction: Catherine Perry.

Approximate Man and Other Writings
by Tristan Tzara. Trans: Mary Ann Caws.

Art Poétique by Guillevic.
Trans: Maureen Smith.

The Big Game by Benjamin Péret.
Trans. / introduction: Marilyn Kallet.

Capital of Pain by Paul Eluard.
Trans: Mary Ann Caws, Patricia Terry,
and Nancy Kline.

Chanson Dada: Selected Poems
by Tristan Tzara. Trans./introduction/
essay: Lee Harwood.

*Essential Poems and Writings of
Joyce Mansour: A Bilingual Anthology*
Trans. / introduction: Serge Gavronsky.

Essential Poems and Prose of Jules Laforgue
Trans. / Ed.: Patricia Terry.

*Essential Poems and Writings of
Robert Desnos: A Bilingual Anthology*
Ed./introduction/essay: Mary Ann Caws.

EyeSeas (Les Ziaux) by Raymond Queneau.
Trans. / introduction: Daniela Hurezanu
and Stephen Kessler.

Furor and Mystery & Other Writings
by René Char. Trans. / eds:
Mary Ann Caws and Nancy Kline.

*Guarding the Air:
Selected Poems of Gunnar Harding*
Ed. / trans: Roger Greenwald.

The Inventor of Love & Other Writings
by Gherasim Luca. Trans: Julian & Laura
Semilian. Introduction: Andrei Codrescu.
Essay: Petre Răileanu.

Selected Prose and Poetry of Jules Supervielle
Edited / introduction by Nancy Kline.
Trans. Nancy Kline, Patricia Terry, and
Kathleen Micklow.

La Fontaine's Bawdy
by Jean de La Fontaine.
Trans: Norman R. Shapiro.

Last Love Poems of Paul Eluard
Trans. / introduction: Marilyn Kallet.

Love, Poetry (L'amour la poésie)
by Paul Eluard.
Trans. / essay: Stuart Kendall.

*Poems of André Breton:
A Bilingual Anthology*
Trans. / essays: Jean-Pierre Cauvin and
Mary Ann Caws.

Poems of A.O. Barnabooth
by Valéry Larbaud.
Trans: Ron Padgett and Bill Zavatsky.

Poems of Consummation
by Vicente Aleixandre.
Trans: Stephen Kessler.

Préversities: A Jacques Prévert Sampler
Trans. / editor: Norman R. Shapiro.

The Sea and Other Poems by Guillevic.
Trans: Patricia Terry. Introduction:
Monique Chefdor.

*To Speak, to Tell You?
Poems by Sabine Sicaud.*
Trans: Norman R. Shapiro. Introduction /
notes: Odile Ayral-Clause.

FORTHCOMING TRANSLATIONS

*Boris Vian Invents Boris Vian:
A Boris Vian Reader*
Ed. / trans: Julia Older.

Earthlight (Claire de Terre) by André Breton.
Trans: Bill Zavatsky and Zack Rogrow
(new and revised edition)

Fables for the Modern Age by Pierre Coran.
Ed. / trans: Norman R. Shapiro. Illustrated
by Olga Pastuchiv.

Pierre Reverdy: Poems Early to Late
Trans. by Mary Ann Caws and
Patricia Terry.